The Inclusive Corporation

D1557257

The Inclusive Corporation

A Disability Handbook for Business Professionals

Griff Hogan

Swallow Press / Ohio University Press
Athens

Swallow Press/Ohio University Press, Athens, Ohio 45701
© 2003 by Griff Hogan
Printed in the United States of America
All rights reserved

11 10 09 08 07 06 05 04 03   5 4 3 2 1

Library of Congress Cataloging-in-Publication Data

Hogan, Griff.
  The inclusive corporation : a disability handbook for business professionals / Griff
Hogan.
    p. cm.
  Includes bibliographical references and index.
  ISBN 0-8040-1055-2 (alk. paper) — ISBN 0-8040-1056-0 (pbk. : alk. paper)
1. People with disabilities—Employment—United States—Handbooks, manuals, etc.
2. Consumers with disabilities—United States—Handbooks, manuals, etc. 3. United
States. Americans with Disabilities Act of 1990—Handbooks, manuals, etc. I. Title.

HD7256.U5 147 2003
658.3'0087—dc21

                                                                              2002030961

For Kathy

Contents

Preface

During the middle decades of the last century, a man named Greeley sold newspapers on a downtown street corner in South Bend, Indiana. At that time, Greeley was a young man of medium height and powerful build. He had immense shoulders and a muscular right arm. Greeley had cerebral palsy, a condition that caused his left hand and arm to be almost totally paralyzed, bent at the elbow and wrist. He walked with a distinct limp, dragging his left foot. These characteristics could be noticed by most observers from afar; however, on closer inspection Greeley's most prominent attributes were his enormous smile and friendly, upbeat personality. His speech was slightly strained, but easy to understand, and his years of experience in serving his newspaper customers had provided him with excellent social skills.

I met Greeley at a time when my life was very unsettled. I was a student at Notre Dame University, taking difficult classes, studying endlessly and not having much fun. In addition, like many others at the time I was preoccupied by the war in Viet Nam, which was rapidly escalating. I found Greeley's happy and engaging nature a welcome antidote to my frustrations, anxieties, and loneliness. I always looked forward to seeing him at the Saturday recreation program in which we were both involved, he as a "participant" and I as a "volunteer," and at bowling and music activities held during the week.

On one occasion that year I spoke to a staff member at the community program that coordinated student volunteer activities, and mentioned to him how much I enjoyed Greeley.

"He always *seems* happy; I wish he always was," he said. I asked what he meant, and he replied: "He's attempted suicide more than once."

I was astounded. I said I found it hard to believe that anyone who always appeared to be so happy could have tried to take his own life.

The staff member replied: "The next time you're with him take a look at his wrists. The scars are there."

The following Saturday I made it my business to check out Greeley's wrists. Sure enough, there were two large, smooth scars running parallel across Greeley's otherwise dry, ebony skin.

Like most college students, I had taken an introductory psychology course, and I thought I knew something about the kind of severe depression that can prompt a suicide attempt. I found it hard to see any signs of depression in Greeley. I began to wonder if his attempts to take his life could have been caused by something else, and if so, what that "something else" might be.

Because of my friendships with many people with disabilities in South Bend, I soon found myself learning a great deal about them, and I became more deeply aware of the problems they faced. During that time I also visited two state institutions in northern Indiana, and saw for myself the abysmal conditions that prevailed for both adults and children who were mentally retarded. Through my friendship with Greeley, especially, I began to appreciate the social context of disabilities—the fact that many people's problems stemmed not from their own limitations, but from how others treated them, or, more often, ignored them. Like Ralph Ellison's *Invisible Man,* most of the people I came to know were of no concern to most of the rest of society. It was almost as if they didn't exist.

The subtle exclusion of disabled people from society fascinated me. Greeley —the disabled person I knew best—had a few acquaintances but no friends. One of the reasons he came to our recreation programs was simply to interact with people who wouldn't walk away from him. The relationships he developed at these simple volunteer activities were valuable to him. On one occasion, with a few other students, I helped Greeley host a small party at his apartment. He had no idea what to do, but beamed all evening at the delightful experience of having friends visit. That evening Greeley told me that not only was this the first party he had ever hosted, it was the first he had ever attended.

One incident that occurred during this time has particular relevance to this book. Early in the school year, I had recruited a friend of mine, Joe Daly, to give music lessons to Greeley, who wanted to learn how to play the trumpet. Joe found a used instrument, and the two of them went at their lessons in earnest. Greeley made gradual progress—his choice of instrument was a good one for someone with only one functional arm—but both he and his teacher got frustrated at times.

Midway through the year I issued a challenge: If Greeley could learn to play "The Notre Dame Victory March" by the end of April, I would take both student and teacher to dinner at a hotel located on the campus. Greeley and Joe accepted the challenge, and began to practice harder than ever.

By late April Greeley had learned to play the song passably well, and I was delighted to pay up. One evening we dressed in coat and tie and headed over to the Inn, where Joe and I met Greeley at the hotel entrance. In the dining room, we were greeted warmly by the hostess and given a lovely table by a picture window looking out on the golf course. When the menu arrived, we discussed the various possibilities—it made for good conversation and we knew that Greeley wasn't a reader—and all three of us ordered soup, salad, and roast beef. After the waitress had taken our orders, it occurred to me that Greeley wouldn't be able to cut his roast beef, and I resolved to offer to help him when the meals arrived.

We devoured the soup and salad, delighting in the great company and good food. When the main course finally arrived, the waitress leaned over and whispered to Greeley, "I thought this might make it a little easier for you." On his plate the roast beef had been carefully cut into bite-sized pieces. "Thanks!" he replied, rewarding her thoughtfulness with one of his incomparable smiles.

The simple kindness of that waitress made a profound impression on me. Her concern that her customer have what he wanted just the way he would enjoy it most was service at its best. Because of that waitress, our meal was a delightful experience that none of us would ever forget. That dinner was my introduction to the idea that a business could be welcoming to those whose needs were a bit out of the ordinary, my first encounter with an "inclusive corporation."

Treating the atypical customer or employee as a fellow human being ought to be more common than it is, and can easily be much more so. That is the lesson I learned many years ago in a hotel dining room, the one I continue to consider in this book.

Acknowledgments

I am indebted to many people who helped make this book possible. Most of all I want to thank my wife Kathy for her encouragement, assistance, and advice. She is my first and most prized editor. My children—Mame, Tom, and Ellie—reviewed my work, relished the reversal of roles, and made many helpful suggestions. They never cease to provide the encouragement that any writer would envy. My mother's support is and has always been a great blessing.

Ben Bonanno, my good friend and associate, reviewed the entire manuscript, caught innumerable errors, and made countless suggestions. I greatly value his wisdom, experience, and friendship. Don Beringer, Michael De-Francesco, Margaret Drain, Peg Gutsell, John Harris, Ann Lazarus, Margaret Roffee, and Ellen Young kindly shared their expertise by reviewing portions of the manuscript and suggesting many improvements. Gillian Berchowitz, my editor at Ohio University Press, was a great help and a delightful collaborator. Nancy Basmajian, my manuscript editor, contributed immensely to this book. I appreciate her great expertise and patience.

Every community should have a resource like the Public Library of Cincinnati and Hamilton County. The staff of the Main, Blue Ash, and Madeira branches helped me immeasurably in doing my research.

The Daniel and Susan Pfau Foundation and the Manuel D. and Rhoda Mayerson Foundation provided generous support during the early stages of my work with corporations.

For many years I have been privileged to learn from some of the best teachers in this country—experts in literature, education, special education and rehabilitation, law, medicine, communication, nutrition, and business. I have worked in service organizations both large and small, and have consulted with many corporations, small businesses, and nonprofit organizations. My debt to all from whom I have learned is immense.

Most of all, however, I have learned from the many people with disabilities I have come to know. This book, more than anything else, reflects what I have learned from them, and for all of that I am very grateful.

In a few cases, I have made minor alterations in descriptive material in order to protect confidences and confidentiality. Although I have taken pains to make all of the material in this book as accurate as possible, all mistakes and omissions are solely my responsibility. The opinions contained herein are my own, and no endorsement by anyone else should be inferred.

1

A Trillion-Dollar Market

It is the largest minority group in the United States and the only one that you could join today—if you are not already a member.

People with disabilities constitute 20 percent of the American population. They are members of every economic, cultural, ethnic, racial, and religious subgroup. They are found throughout our society, in every occupation, role, and age category. Approximately 29 percent of American households include one or more persons with a disability, and more than half the population has a close personal relationship with someone who is disabled. Little though we may want to think about it, we are all just one accident or one medical "incident" away from a disability. That fact is driven home by the term that some in the disability community have for those without disabilities: "TAB," for "temporarily able-bodied."

Yet for all its prominence, the subject of disability is little understood by most of us—what it is, what it is not, what we can and ought to do about it.

For businesses, the implications are enormous. First of all, any business hoping to compete in the modern marketplace knows that it must understand its customers, their needs and interests. The economic clout of this market sub-population is enormous and little understood. The preferences of its members for products and services are extensive and specific, and their loyalties to those who understand them are fierce. Reach them successfully and the benefits are enormous; ignore them, or worse yet offend them, and you do so at your peril.

Second, any employer of any size knows that the issue of employing people with disabilities is inescapable. Even an employer that successfully flouts anti-discrimination laws and never hires an individual with a disability will inevitably find itself dealing with disability issues, as employees experience accidents and illnesses and join the nation's largest minority, even on a temporary basis. Those who doubt this should consider the number of people who come to work each day sporting casts and slings, or using crutches and wheelchairs.

Third, employers desperate to utilize all available employee talent cannot afford to ignore those who have often been called the greatest untapped pool of talent currently available. Not only is the number of potential workers with disabilities enormous, their employability and job readiness is dramatically improved from what it was only a generation ago.

Finally, those with disabilities are the one minority group each of us is likely to join at some time in our lives, business executives not excluded. Seven out of ten workers between the ages of thirty-five and sixty-five will experience a disability lasting three months or longer during their careers. One in seven will be disabled for five years or more (Dietsch 2001). With aging, the likelihood of disability grows each year. Though disability might not be "our" issue today, sooner or later it will be. As one advocate has said: "Even if you're lucky enough to end your life by just keeling over, on your way down to the floor you will be disabled."

Definitions

To those with limited familiarity, the subject of disability can seem complex and convoluted. With the exception of a few conditions—for example, amputation—disability is a matter of degree, culture, and, to some extent, opinion. A person who needs eyeglasses only to read or drive will not be termed "visually impaired"; a person who has some difficulty hearing conversations only in noisy situations will not be considered "hearing impaired"; but if their abilities continue to diminish, at some point they can properly be said to have a disability.

Someone who has a moderate physical or mental disability and lives on a farm in Bird-in-Hand, Pennsylvania, could easily be regarded by neighbors as typical, although that person might be considered disabled if he or she lived in Los Angeles. A supervisor might think that one of her employees has a disabling condition, but the employee might strongly disagree.

Standards not only are generally indistinct but can evolve over time or be formally modified. When the customary mode of transportation changed from walking and horseback riding, the cognitive and motor skills required to drive an automobile became almost essential for normal daily functioning. Some people who had the skills required to utilize horse-drawn transportation found they were unable to handle the demands of the automotive age. Up until the 1960s, psychologists applied the status of mental retardation to those with IQs below 90. As demands for special education programming for children with mental retardation increased, psychologists came under great pressure to modify their definition and reduce the size of the qualifying group. So after much discussion, they took a vote and lowered the IQ cutoff from 90 to 70. Following the decisive meeting, a wag is said to have commented: "In one day we have cured more people of mental retardation than in all previous human history."

Since disability definitions often influence eligibility for services, protection, or other societal provisions, the government is usually involved in setting and modifying standards. With its enormous economic clout, the government's definition usually carries the day, although this by no means eliminates definitional disputes, and sometimes even adds to the confusion. In fact, the federal government has at least a dozen different definitions of disability. An eighteen-year-old might meet federal criteria for having a disability under special education law, but not be disabled according to the criteria of the Selective Services Administration or Social Security.

One federal agency, the U.S. Bureau of the Census, is the source of most of the available statistics on the subject. It defines disability as follows:

> A person is considered to have a disability if he or she has difficulty performing certain functions (seeing, hearing, talking, walking, climbing stairs and lifting and carrying), or has difficulty performing activities of daily living, or has difficulty with certain social roles (doing school work for children, working at a job or around the house for adults).

> A person who is unable to perform one or more activities, or who uses an assistive device to get around, or who needs assistance from another person to perform basic activities is considered to have a severe disability. (1997)

Note that this definition establishes some important parameters. It is *functional,* determining the status of having a disability by its practical implications, not by arbitrary standards of measurement. By specifying functional "difficulty," the Census Bureau definition excludes those who, although not perfect, can easily get through the challenges of daily life using ordinary aids, such as eyeglasses, automobiles, and volume controls. Also, it distinguishes those who need assistance to perform critical activities from people who simply have difficulty doing so. Those requiring assistance are said to have a "severe disability." This is an important distinction. Of the approximately 54 million Americans who meet the definition of having a disability, only about one-third to one-half have a severe disability. Finally, note that an individual could qualify as having a disability and still be in good health—as most people with disabilities in fact are. Conversely, an individual could be very ill—with, for example, a digestive disorder or blood disease—but unless that individual was functionally impaired, he or she would not be said to have a disability.

Of course a functional definition of disability is not the only type possible, nor is it always the most important from a business perspective. Many other definitions have been criteria- or test-based—such as the IQ cutoff for mental retardation. For the purposes of protecting people from discrimination because of disability, the Americans with Disabilities Act (ADA) extended its protections not only to people who meet the functional criteria referred to above, but also to those "who have a record of such a disability or are regarded as having a disability." The implications of this important difference will be explored in the next chapter.

Types of Disabilities

The various types of disabilities are frequently divided into major categories. Some systems simply differentiate between physical and mental impairments;

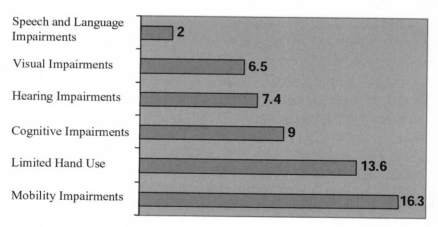

Fig. 1.1. Number of people with disabilities by type (in millions)
Source: Prager (1999)

Table 1.1. Estimates of fifteen disabling conditions
(prevalence for 100,000 population)

Hearing Impairment	8,300
Visual Impairment	3,100
Mental Illness	3,000
Diabetes	2,900
Mental Retardation	1,500
Arthritis	1,200
Stroke	500
Epilepsy	500
Parkinson's Disease	200
Cerebral Palsy	200
Brain Injury	100
Multiple Sclerosis	80
Spinal Injury	45
Muscular Dystrophy	20
Huntington's Chorea	10

Source: Disability Statistics Center (1992) and
U.S. Census Bureau (1994)

others create dozens of different categories. The number of groups identified is often determined by the complexity of the discussion involved, and the various types of categories, like the differing definitions, can make data comparisons difficult.

Figure 1.1 shows the overall incidence of several types of significant disabilities using six different categories. In this chart the term "cognitive impairments" includes those with mental illness, mental retardation, and learning disabilities, while five separate categories denote what might otherwise be referred to as "physical impairments." Other categories could easily be substituted.

According to this chart, people with mobility impairments constitute the largest group, followed by those with limited hand use. The smallest group is made up of those with speech and language impairments—*only* about 2 million people.

When category definitions change, the results can look very different. Table 1.1 indicates the wide variation in incidence among selected conditions in a typical population of 100,000, from the most common (hearing impairment) to the exceedingly rare (Huntington's Chorea). Note that hearing impairment placed a

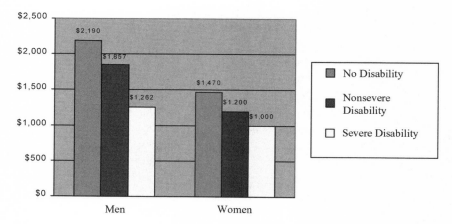

Fig. 1.2. Median monthly earnings, by disability status and sex (1994 dollars)
Source: McNeil (1997)

distant third in incidence according to figure 1.1, but appears far and away the most common in table 1.1. That is because the figure combines several conditions into the categories *cognitive impairments, limited hand use,* and *mobility impairments.* Clearly, disability statistics can change dramatically according to the definitions and criteria used.

It is also important to remember that such statistics convey only a "snapshot" in time. People go into and out of most of these categories all the time. They have accidents and are rehabilitated; they incur curable mental or physical illnesses and receive treatment.

Economic Impact of the Disability Market

Given the extremely large population of those experiencing a disability at any given time, it is obvious that their economic impact must be great. How great?

According to estimates based on the latest census figures, the total financial clout of the 20 percent of Americans who have disabilities reached approximately one *trillion* dollars in the year 2001 (Frost 1998), with discretionary spending approaching 200 billion dollars—more than twice that of teenagers. As an employee training video produced by Northwest Mortgage Inc., a division of Wells Fargo & Co., proclaimed: "Fact: People with disabilities have money!" (Prager 1999).

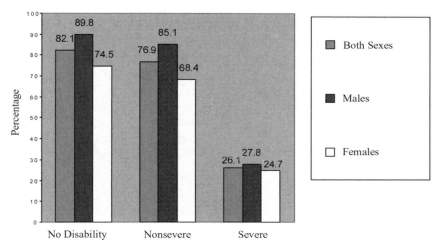

Fig. 1.3. Employment rate, by disability severity
Source: U.S. Census Bureau (1997), 1

The combined wealth of those with disabilities is not due simply to their enormous numbers. Among adults with disabilities between the ages of twenty-two and sixty-four, more than three-quarters receive no public assistance. In most disability categories, about 8 percent of those employed hold managerial, executive, or professional positions—slightly higher than the percentage in the general population. Disabled students entering college today are as likely to graduate as their typical peers (McNeil 1997).

Although unemployment among people with severe disabilities approaches 67 percent, a vast majority of all disabled people between the ages of twenty-one and sixty-five are employed. In general, affluence decreases and unemployment increases with the severity of disability (see figs. 1.2, 1.3, and 1.4).

Considered as a group, however, disabled people are unquestionably economically disadvantaged. The 1998 National Organization on Disability (NOD)/Louis Harris Survey summarized their situation as follows:

> Fully a third (34%) of adults with disabilities lived in a household with an annual income of less than $15,000 in 1997, compared to only about one in eight (12%) of those without disabilities. This twenty-two percentage point gap between the percentage of disabled and non-disabled persons living in very low-income households has remained virtually constant since 1986 (40% of persons with disabilities vs. 18% of the non-disabled in 1994; 51% and 29%, respectively in 1986).[1]

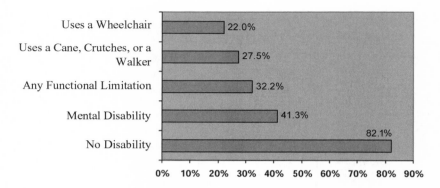

Fig. 1.4. Percent employed, by disability status
Source: U.S. Census Bureau (1997), 2

Transformation of the Disability Market

The economic status of those with disabilities has always lagged behind that of the rest of society. Though their numbers are enormous and their economic impact immense, in the past they have never been regarded by business as an "affluent" group. That perception is beginning to change, and for good reason.

During the past few decades, several major changes in American society have begun to transform the status of those with disabilities. Their lives are changing rapidly and dramatically for the better. It would be impossible to list all the factors that have brought about this improvement, but four stand out: education, transportation, architecture, and technology.

Education

Through the 1960s, children with severe disabilities were routinely turned away from public schools as "uneducable," or confined to segregated educational programs that offered little more than custodial care and parental relief. In 1975 the passage of the Education for All Handicapped Children Act outlawed discrimination on the basis of disability for all students, regardless of the severity of their impairment. Furthermore, the law required local school districts to provide each disabled child with a "free and appropriate public education" provided in "the least restrictive environment."

In practice, this law virtually eliminated the practice of educational exclusion for students with severe disabilities and led to their being educated in more "integrated" settings—putting children with disabilities alongside their typical peers, with additional supports and services provided as needed. The law eventually covered every child with a disability from preschool through the age of twenty-two.

More than twenty-five years later, we now have the first generation of individuals with significant disabilities who have received a public education. Many have been educated alongside typical classmates, gaining critical social skills in addition to academic knowledge. Special education services have also grown to be increasingly employment-oriented, often even more so than for nondisabled students. Today it is not unusual for a student with a severe disability to have his or her first employment experience at the age of fourteen, and to have had seven or eight jobs by the time he or she graduates from high school.

For all these reasons, educational progress for students with disabilities has been astounding. Nothing like this generation of well-educated, work-experienced, and employment-ready high school graduates with disabilities has ever been seen before.

Transportation

With education mandated for each disabled child, school districts were quickly forced to modify their transportation systems to accommodate students with special needs, especially those with mobility impairments, but also those with behavioral problems and even unusual medical conditions. School buses were equipped with lifts and wheelchair tie-downs. Transportation staff received additional training, and transporting students with disabilities of all sorts became commonplace.

The concept of accessible transportation spread rapidly from schools to the larger society. Even before they were required to do so legally, some public transportation authorities bowed to consumer pressure and began providing accessible services on a limited basis. When the Americans with Disabilities Act was passed in 1990, one of its key provisions mandated accessible transportation throughout the public sector. And this requirement covered all areas of transportation—trains, planes, and subways as well as buses.

The impact of this change has been enormous. Previously, the term "shut-in" had been synonymous with having a disability. Now, at least in urban areas where transportation is available to all, "all" now includes those with impairments of all sorts. Passenger-loading wheelchairs, flush subway entrances, airline transfer seats, and kneeling buses are becoming so commonplace that they are taken for granted. For people who only a few years ago would have been forced to stay at home, it is a new world.

Architecture

When people with disabilities get out and into the world, they find many more places accessible to them now than they would have only a decade ago. Prior to the Americans with Disabilities Act, accessible architecture had been mandated only for government buildings and major government contractors, but the new law required similar provisions in all public buildings and influenced virtually all subsequent public construction. Major renovations to existing structures were compelled to meet the new accessibility requirements of the law.

The ADA's impact on American architecture has been as revolutionary as any innovation since the advent of electricity and central heating. Reserved accessible parking spaces, entrance ramps, Braille signage, and a host of other access provisions are now ubiquitous. This architectural revolution has been so widespread that inaccessible buildings have become the exception rather than the rule. Although most business owners make their businesses physically ac-

Fig. 1.5. Accessibility features, such as ramps, benefit many people who do not have disabilities. *(Photo by Edgar Strook)*

cessible only when required to do so, many have found that such changes provide unexpected benefits. For example, a recent report from the General Accounting Office documented that implementing the access provisions of the ADA increased revenues in the hotel and hospitality industry by 12 percent (Coelho 1997).

Even in the area of private residential construction, to which the ADA does not apply, a growing market of consumers are requesting features of "universal design" intended to make residences livable by all family members throughout their lives. On average, incorporating accessibility features—such as wider doors and hallways, stepless entries, and handrails—adds only about 2 percent to the cost of construction, and can avert the need for costly remodeling later on.

For those with disabilities, the ADA's mandate of architectural accessibility has meant not only that they can get out of their homes, but that they can get to and around almost anywhere they want to go, including work—a vital component of independent living that most people without disabilities take for granted.

Technology

No law mandated the development of the dialysis machine, motorized wheelchair, or Internet; yet the blossoming of all sorts of technology has provided incalculable benefits for people with disabilities. Tiny in-ear hearing aids are becoming as commonplace, and as inconspicuous, as contact lenses. People with emphysema, who once would have been hospitalized, can now travel throughout the community with a portable oxygen dispenser. Those requiring constant medication can carry their own miniaturized pump with them. Motorized wheelchairs and scooters, once rarities, are now seen everywhere.

Even generic items, such as cellular telephones, have often proved to be a boon for disabled people and have created enormous opportunities for business. No industry has responded to the disability market more effectively than the computer industry. Bill Gates, chairman of the Microsoft Corporation, has summarized this phenomenon:

> [S]ome innovations meant for society at large have had disproportionate value to the disabled. The PC and the Internet are great examples. They are, in effect, accessibility aids for many people.
>
> People with speech impediments can "chat" via text on the Internet or other computer networks. Many older individuals and others who may not be able to get out much participate in social groups that communicate over the

Internet. They keep up with friends and the doings of their grandkids and other relatives.

A lawyer can sit in front of a computer and call up every brief her law firm has ever filed and every deposition. She doesn't have to run to somebody's office, or shuffle a lot of paper, or go to and from a file cabinet. She may even be able to work from home.

Anybody with limited mobility—or even just limited time—can appreciate how the Internet and electronic databases have opened vast amounts of information to easy access. (1997)

As a consumer group, people with disabilities are quick to respond to the liberating potential of new technology. According to the NOD/Louis Harris Survey (1998), 28 percent of people with disabilities own special equipment or technology to assist them because of their disability. Almost half (49 percent) of those who work full- or part-time use computers at work—a higher rate than for the general population. Disabled adults who use the Internet spend almost twice as much time online as typical consumers (Taylor 2000).

In these and many other ways, technology has contributed greatly to revolutionary improvements in the lives of people with disabilities.

How Disabilities Influence Everyone

While factors such as education, transportation, architecture, and technology have been transforming their lives, those with disabilities have in turn exerted a strong influence on American society. Three factors are most important here: demographics, the "curb-cut effect," and the "electronic curb-cut effect."

Demographics: The Aging of America

The increasing influence of disabled people is related to the increasing proportion of elderly citizens in America. The average age of the population is increasing rapidly, primarily due to "baby boomers"—those 79 million Americans born between 1945 and 1965. Figure 1.6 shows Census Bureau projections that indicate the proportion of the U.S. population over the age of 65, 12 percent in 2000, will increase to 20 percent by the year 2030—almost doubling in only thirty years—and level off thereafter. Some have called this the "Floridazation" or the "graying" of America.

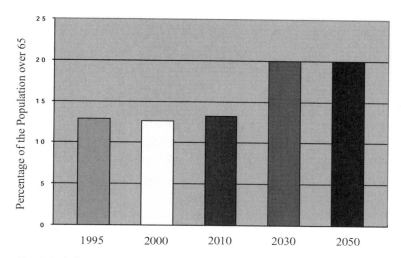

Fig. 1.6. Aging of the American population
Source: Day (1996)

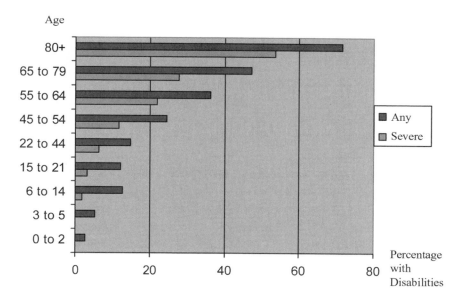

Fig. 1.7. Disability prevalence, by age
Source: U.S. Census Bureau (1997), 4

The aging of the population is of crucial importance because, although disabilities can occur at any time and at any age, they are more common among elderly people. As the average age of the population increases, the incidence of disabilities therefore also increases. As figure 1.7 indicates, among those over the age of 65, nearly half have some sort of disability; more than half of these disabilities are severe.

Put the incidence of disabilities among the elderly together with population projections and the conclusion is inescapable: in the next few decades the proportion of Americans with disabilities will increase dramatically. This will in turn influence nearly every aspect of our lives; indeed the changes are already well underway.

When we think about the increasing influence of disabled people in American culture, factors like voting patterns, retirement communities, and health care requirements come quickly to mind. These, however, are *effects* of that influence, not *causes*. Causes are fewer, but crucial to understand. We have already listed one—changing demographics—and now we present two more. They may be less obvious, but they are no less important.

The Curb-Cut Effect

The term "curb-cut effect" refers to the reality that when an accommodation is provided for people with disabilities, many others tend to benefit. The term was coined when architects and engineers began to realize that sidewalk curb cuts mandated for the benefit of those with wheelchairs and walkers were also being used by bikers, parents with strollers, skateboarders, delivery personnel, and pedestrians in general.

The curb-cut effect is so common that most of us no longer realize it is occurring. In commercial settings, we now expect to see signs in large letters and contrasting colors. As we enter a building, we appreciate the automatic doors, especially if we are carrying something, and we become slightly annoyed if a store hasn't provided them for us. Elevators that announce the floors provide us with a gentle reminder that we have arrived at our destination, and oversized restrooms are helpful if we are accompanying a child, toting a portfolio, or simply in need of additional space.

We enjoy all of these relatively new modifications to our environment because they make it more "people friendly," and we can appreciate all of them whether or not we realize they were initially created for the benefit of people with disabilities. Time and again such accommodations have achieved much wider acceptance—and use—than originally intended. Several studies have shown that over 80 percent of those who use accessibility provisions have no disability; they simply *prefer* to use them.

Electronic Curb Cuts

Technological innovations and modifications originally intended for people with disabilities, but that end up benefiting many more, are often called "electronic curb cuts."

Examples of these are almost endless:

- The most famous is the telephone. Alexander Graham Bell, as many know, was a teacher of deaf students (his wife also had a severe hearing impairment), and the research that led to the invention of the telephone was directly related to his concern for them.
- Less well known is that the typewriter was originally developed as a "writing machine" for a woman who was blind. The keyboards that we all use today are direct descendents of that "writing machine."
- During the 1930s the American Foundation for the Blind recorded the first "talking books," direct ancestors of today's universally popular books on tape.
- "Closed captioning" became commonly available on television broadcasts, and on televisions themselves, during the 1990s. Originally developed for those with hearing impairments, today captioning is commonly

Fig. 1.8. A "talking watch," an example of an electronic curb cut from a recent Hammacher Schlemmer catalog. Such watches were previously marketed only to individuals with severe visual impairments.[2] *(Photo courtesy of Hammacher Schlemmer)*

made available in sports bars, hospitals, airports, and hotel rooms. For good or ill, captioning has enabled many a viewer to watch television well into the night without having the sound disturb his or her slumbering mate.

• "Volume controls" were first installed on telephones to assist people with slight hearing deficiencies. However, consumers soon discovered that these controls could assist anyone dealing with a poor connection or attempting to converse in a high-noise environment.

Other examples of electronic curb cuts are innumerable, and new ones are appearing all the time.

Thus, while people with disabilities have benefited disproportionately from technological advances, the curb-cut and electronic curb-cut effects have meant that society in general also has benefited greatly from technology originally intended only for those who are disabled. (A more detailed examination of the curb-cut and electronic curb-cut effects is contained in chapter 6.)

The Family and Friends Multiplier

Although the economic influence of people with disabilities is usually estimated to be about one trillion dollars, this figure undoubtedly understates the real impact. That is because people with disabilities also have families and friends, and the needs, concerns, and priorities of the person who is disabled often influence the economic decisions made by those close to them.

Speaking with a group of restaurateurs, disability advocate Marcia Cassidy brought that point home:

> You might be willing to lose my business at your restaurant because you believe that the accessibility modifications you would have to make would be too expensive. But remember this: if I can't patronize your restaurant, my family won't go there either, at least when I'm with them. You stand to lose their business because you won't accommodate me. (1998)

The 29 percent of American households that include one or more members with a disability represent an enormous slice of the overall market. Add to this group those who are simply related to, or close friends of, someone with a disability, and those who feel strongly about the issue for whatever reason, and the full impact of the disability market becomes obvious.

Business Responds

One of the outstanding characteristics of the disability market is its diversity. This is "diversity" in the classical sense, meaning different and varying, not in the "politically correct" sense with connotations of preferences and protections. All businesses must remember that there is no such thing as *the* disabled consumer. People with disabilities may tend to share various needs, sensitivities, and preferences, but they are as varied and complex as any other consumer group. Consequently, there is no unique or ideal way to reach, attract, or satisfy them. This doesn't just mean that a marketing campaign intended to reach those with mobility impairments would be inappropriate for those with visual disabilities; it also means that no particular approach would be ideal for all potential customers, even if they shared a similar disabling condition.

Responding to the needs of disabled consumers, then, is not a simple matter. But many businesses have begun to rise to this challenge despite its complexities, probably most of all because they recognize the rewards that will accrue to them if they do so effectively.

Businesses have responded to the disability market in three ways: by developing products specially designed for it, by transforming generic products and services to appeal to the widest possible array of consumers, and by designing marketing messages that appeal to people with accessibility requirements.

Disability-Related Products and Services

The disability market obviously includes an enormous number of educational, medical, personal support, and rehabilitation services, health care products, orthopedic equipment, accessibility devices and modifications, adaptive technologies, and so on. The total value of these goods and services represents a sizable portion of the $1 trillion in annual spending power exercised by people who are disabled.

So enormous is this market that a small slice of it can be extremely profitable. Bob Montgomery, president of Cannondale Bicycles in Bethel, Connecticut, has a son with cerebral palsy. Although his son was athletic and involved in swimming, skiing, and karate, Montgomery was concerned that the only wheelchairs available were, in his words, "technological dinosaurs." Montgomery realized his company's bicycle technology could be applied to the development of lightweight racing wheelchairs, and set his company in that direction. Company spokesperson Bill Teel explains: "The market for lightweight wheelchairs is roughly $400 million per year. We're hoping to grab 10 percent of that in the next few years. . . . We've been getting calls nonstop since we made the first announcement" (Frost 1998, 3).

Like Cannondale Bicycles, many companies have discovered they can easily and profitably supply products to the disability market with just a little bit of creativity.

Consider the following examples:

- A travel industry survey indicates that about 10 percent of all vacation groups include an individual with either a physical or a mental impairment that limits mobility or activity. Almost 60 percent of those groups say they carefully consider the needs of the individual or individuals with a disability when planning their vacations (Robson 1998). Travel agencies, resorts, and cruise lines have realized that their products and services could be tailored to travelers with accessibility needs. Most cruise ships are now at least partially accessible, and many destination resorts, such as Flamingo Beach on the Caribbean island of Bonaire, have made accessibility modifications despite the fact that they are not legally obligated to do so (Frost 1998, 1).
- In 1964 *Reader's Digest* published its first large-type edition, and was surprised to attract more than 6,000 subscribers with almost no promotion. Circulation grew to 159,000 in 1980 (Frost 1998, 4), and reached almost 500,000 in 2000, despite the conversion from nonprofit to for-profit status during this time.[3] Says Philip Cara, publisher of the *Reader's Digest Large Edition for Easier Reading*: "The entire large-print marketplace is growing. Go into Barnes & Noble, and there's a whole section. It's the fastest growing area in the library" (Frost 1998, 4).
- Hallmark Cards has recently begun to offer product lines specifically designed for those with accessibility needs. It sold 37,000 cards in Braille shortly after they were made available, and over one million cards with large print in 1995, the year they were introduced (Hartman and Fry 1999). The company has also recently developed a "Forget Me Not" series featuring artwork that depicts characters with disabilities.

• Even children's toys have gotten into the act. Toys "R" Us now offers a catalog entitled "Toy Guide for Differently Abled Kids." In 1997, Mattel introduced Barbie's friend Becky, who is a wheelchair user. The doll sold out in two weeks, requiring the company to go back into production. In what will certainly be regarded as a watershed event in disability history, the company has since widened the elevator in Barbie's Dream House— in order to accommodate Becky's wheelchair!

Universal Design

With the aging of baby boomers and the growing realization that disability-friendly products and services are generally "people friendly" as well, there has been an enormous growth in what is known as "universal design." The universal design philosophy is that a product or service should be made in such a way that it can be used by the greatest number of people possible.

Universal design first became popular in residential construction. Homes were designed with stepless entries, wider doorways, door levers instead of knobs, grab bars in bathrooms, and so on. When done properly, such modifications simply make possible home access for the largest number of people regardless of age or ability, and without making the home appear contrived or institutional.

Universal design has since been applied to many other products. Some examples:

• Small appliances with easy-to-read graphics and easy-to-grab handles and knobs.
• Internet websites that are accessible to computers equipped with voice synthesizers that "read" the text to individuals with severe visual impairments.
• Car dashboard controls that use symbols instead of words.
• Restaurant menus that contain pictures along with written information.
• Easy-to-grip kitchen tools, like those manufactured by OXO International (fig. 1.9).
• Large-image picture playing cards.

The beauty of universal design is that by enabling people with disabilities, it generally provides ease-of-use benefits to many. It takes the curb-cut effect and applies it to an endless variety of products, services, environments, and experiences.

Fig. 1.9. OXO International specializes in products that feature universal design, such as the "Good Grips" pizza wheel and the one-handed salad spinner. *(Photos courtesy of OXO International)*

Marketing

In recognition of the value of the potential market, many companies have begun narrowcasting to disability consumer subgroups by sponsoring disability-related events like the Special Olympics and Paralympics Games. Businesses have placed ads in national organization publications such as *Arthritis Today, Modern Maturity,* and a growing number of independent publications and other media entities that reach such consumers.

In 1999, *WE* magazine, a disability-targeted publication, launched its own Internet website, *WEmedia.com,* with full-page ads in several national newspapers. It was soon followed by a competitor, HalfthePlanet.com, which took a similar high-profile approach. HalfthePlanet.com's full-page ad in the *Wall Street Journal* introduced its Internet portal service by proclaiming:

> Nearly half of the people on the planet either have a disability or have close ties to a person with a disability. HalfthePlanet.com is the premier web site for us to share our experiences, discover the latest resources, and explore the

planet. Our community is nearly 150 million strong in the U.S. alone and close to 3 billion worldwide. Sound big? You don't know the half of it.

Despite the hype, such niche marketing represents a small, though growing, portion of all disability-related initiatives. Much more common are approaches that target disabled consumers and their families and friends through more traditional venues.

Middle-aged consumers might not realize it, but companies are rapidly changing their products to deal with a "maturing" market. As an article in the *New York Times* noted tongue-in-cheek, "You're not getting older. Products are getting better." The article noted numerous examples of businesses catering to the waning abilities of the postwar generation. It cited examples like the Honeywell thermostat shown in figure 1.10, which has numerals much larger than before, pitched to consumers who might otherwise have to squint or put on glasses to adjust their room temperature.

The advantages of targeting elderly consumers are obvious, and the practice is now commonplace. This is "breakthrough" disability marketing: low-key, subtle, and progressive, using euphemisms like "mature" to refer to the reality of limited capabilities.

But a growing number of corporations are much more overtly targeting the disability market. These companies feature individuals with disabilities—consumers with obvious and significant impairments—not in narrowcast messages, but in their mainstream advertising.

Companies that have used individuals with disabilities in their national advertising include McDonald's, IBM, Charles Schwab, General Mills, Target, AT&T, Bell Atlantic, Pacific Bell, Sears, Bank of America, Pepsi, Coca-Cola, General Mills, VISA, Disney, Hallmark, DuPont, The Gap, Starbucks, Wal-Mart, NationsBank, and many others. Such advertising varies widely in its approach to the subject of disability, some featuring disability-friendly aspects of products or services, some, like the Nordstrom ad (fig. 1.11), simply depicting customers with disabilities among others without calling

Easy to See™ Thermostats Keep you in control of your comf

Fig. 1.10. Honeywell thermostat ad aimed at the mature market. *(Photo courtesy of Honeywell)*

Fig. 1.11. Nordstrom ad featuring a model with a disability. *(Photo courtesy of Nordstrom)*

attention to the issue. (See chapters 10 and 11 for a more detailed discussion of disability-related marketing.)

Featuring people with disabilities in advertising allows companies to appeal to a vastly expanded market while positioning themselves as "inclusive" corporations. Only a few years ago the concept of using those with disabilities in pictorial advertising would have been rejected by most marketing professionals as counterproductive and possibly offensive; today it is seen as an almost effortless way to achieve "cause-related marketing."

Comprehensive Responses

A small number of companies have begun to address the disability market through an integrated approach that involves all aspects of the company—management, human resources, marketing, product design, customer service, and so on. Among the leaders are McDonald's, Marriott International, Microsoft, UnumProvident Insurance, and Wal-Mart.

Visit a Wal-Mart store and you are likely to be greeted by a senior citizen or an individual with a disability. That receptionist can guide you to a complimentary motorized cart if you have difficulty walking. In the store you will notice that aisles are wide enough to allow easy navigation for those in wheelchairs, and in most stores resting benches are provided for the fatigued. You might also notice a certain professionalism in customer service, since sales associates have received training in meeting the unique needs of each shopper.

Marriott International has implemented a similar inclusion initiative in the hospitality industry. Mark Donovan, executive director of the Marriott Foundation, explains the company's rationale:

> Inevitably, belief in the importance of a world-class work-force led to the recognition that inclusion must be a guiding principle of the human resource discipline; that embracing the talents, gifts, and unique characteristics of every individual, including people with disabilities, is central to building the kind of work team that ensures business success. Employing people with disabilities is not the goal. The goal is attracting and developing the strongest, most diverse group of associates possible. Hiring people with disabilities (and, more to the point, capabilities) is just one of many important avenues to that goal. . . .
>
> Marriott is in the business of meeting the needs of guests; assuring their satisfaction, encouraging their return. Obviously, this demands that they be responsive to the individual requirements of each of these guests, including people with disabilities. With tens of millions of potential customers with disabilities in the United States, it would be foolish not to work hard to consistently and effectively meet their needs. And so the company strives to offer properties and products which are fully accessible, responsive and welcoming to this customer group.[4]

Companies like Wal-Mart, Microsoft, and Marriott not only implement a wide range of inclusive practices, but also make their commitment to inclusion obvious. In the end, their motivation boils down to one reason above all: it's simply good business.

Before business leaders can take advantage of the opportunities represented by the disability market, they must first digest a great deal of information related to this issue. The next chapter continues that process through a discussion of one of business's greatest concerns: the Americans with Disabilities Act.

Resources

Business Leadership Network (BLN)
www.usbln.com/
1331 F St. N.W.
Washington, D.C. 20004-1107
(202) 376-6200, extension 35 Voice
(202) 376-6868 Fax
(202) 376-6205 TTY
dunlap-carol@dol.gov

The Center for Universal Design
http://www.design.ncsu.edu/cud/
School of Design
North Carolina State University
Box 8613
Raleigh, N.C. 27695-8613
(919) 515-3082 Voice and TTY
(800) 647-6777 Info. requests
(919) 515-3023 Fax
cud@ncsu.edu

Disability and Business Technical Assistance Centers (DBTACs)
http://www.adata.org/dbtac.html/
(800) 949-4232 Voice/TTY
This number will automatically route your call to the DBTAC in your region.

Disability Statistics Center
http://www.dsc.ucsf.edu/
3333 California St., Suite 340
Campus Mail Box 0646
San Francisco, Calif. 94118
(415) 502-5210 Voice
(415) 502-5205 TTY
(415) 502-5208 Fax

National Business & Disability Council (NBDC)
http://www.business-disability.com
201 I.U. Willets Rd.
Albertson, N.Y. 11507
(516) 465-1515 Voice
(516) 465-3730 Fax

The National Organization on Disability (NOD)
http//www.nod.org/
910 Sixteenth St. N.W.
Suite 600
Washington, D.C. 20006
(202) 293-5960 Voice
(202) 293-5968 TTY
(202) 293-7999 Fax

Office of Disability Employment Policy (ODEP)
(formerly The President's Committee on Employment of People with Disabilities)
http://www.dol.gov/odep/
1331 F St. N.W., Suite 300
Washington, D.C. 20004
(202) 376-6200 Voice
(202) 376-6205 TTY
(202) 376-6219 Fax

2

Understanding the Americans with Disabilities Act

Fig. 2.1. July 26, 1990: President George H. Bush signs the ADA into law. *(Photo courtesy of the George H. Bush Presidential Library and Museum)*

The ADA has been a rousing success.
    —John M. Williams, *Business Week Online*

People . . . have used the ADA to trigger an avalanche of frivolous suits clogging federal courts.
    —Trevor Armbrister, *Reader's Digest*

I don't see how to get this statute to work.
    —Supreme Court Justice Stephen Breyer

This chapter presents summary information on the ADA and an analysis of its strengths and weaknesses from the point of view of business. A step-by-step guide to complying with the employment provisions of the law is contained in chapters 8 and 9.

On July 26, 1990, when President George Bush signed the Americans with Disabilities Act, it was immediately hailed as a milestone in the history of the disability rights movement. Although legal scholars could trace the origins of the ADA back to *Brown v. Board of Education* ("Separate but equal is inherently unequal"), the Civil Rights Act of 1964, and the Rehabilitation Act of 1973, it clearly broke new ground in federal policy.

The Act, in five sections (Employment, Public Services, Public Accommodations, Telecommunications, and Miscellaneous), not only extended civil rights protections to those with disabilities in ways previously afforded only to individuals on the basis of race, sex, religion, and national origin; it also created *affirmative* responsibilities in each area in order to promote the inclusion of individuals with disabilities throughout society.

At the White House signing ceremony, President Bush commented: "And now I sign legislation which takes a sledgehammer to another wall, one which has, for too many generations, separated Americans with disabilities from the freedom they could glimpse, but not grasp. Once again, we rejoice as this barrier falls, proclaiming together we will not accept, we will not excuse, we will not tolerate discrimination in America. . . . Let the shameful wall of exclusion finally come tumbling down." Years later, when asked to name the greatest accomplishments of his administration, former President Bush cited the allied victory in the Gulf War and the Americans with Disabilities Act.

From its earliest drafting, the ADA was a model of political consensus and bipartisan cooperation. Distinguished disability advocates worked with members of Congress, both Democrats and Republicans, to draft the language of the law. The final version sailed through both houses of Congress, and both political parties were well represented on the White House lawn on the bright July day of the law's signing.

Yet from the inception of this legislation, there were some dissenting voices, and many of them came from the business community. Businesses looked at the proposed legislation and predicted not only enormous problems in determining what the law required, but also enormous potential for litigation, and seemingly unlimited liability.

Before the law went into effect, economist Robert P. O'Quinn (1991) warned that "legislation enacted with the least partisan dispute often turns out to be the worst law because its provisions were never tested in any serious public debate. . . . Congress drafted the ADA broadly, using imprecise and undefined terms, and consequently left the task of fleshing out the meaning of its provisions to the federal judiciary. . . . Contrary to the claims of its proponents, the ADA imposes significant costs on American business firms and governmental entities."

Few critics noted the leap of logic made by President Bush and the bipartisan supporters of the law. That logic can be summarized as follows: The status, especially the economic status, of many adults with disabilities is deplorable. It is similar to the status of other minority groups involved in earlier civil rights struggles. Those groups were primarily victims of discrimination. Therefore, people with disabilities are primarily victims of discrimination, and disability antidiscrimination legislation, like earlier civil rights laws, is the primary answer to their problems. The "wall" separating people with disabilities from full inclusion in American life was, according to President Bush, "discrimination in America." Accordingly, prohibiting and remedying such discrimination would bring down that infamous wall.

The popularity of the ADA led to great expectations on the part of its advocates. They predicted it would provide profound benefits for America's largest minority, not the least of them being a reduction in the high rate of unemployment among severely disabled people, which stood at about 67 percent the day the law was signed.

Enough time has now passed and sufficient data have been gathered to evaluate whether or not the ADA has lived up to its promises, and to test the original assumptions on which it was based. Before doing so, however, it's necessary to review the major provisions of the law.[1]

ADA Terms and Definitions

(Person with a) disability	A person has a disability if he or she has a physical or mental impairment that substantially limits a major life activity. The ADA also protects individuals who have a record of a substantially limiting impairment, and people who are regarded as having a substantially limiting impairment.
Major life activities	Include walking, breathing, eating, talking, seeing, hearing, working, caring for self.

Substantially limited	Unable to perform major life activity, or significantly limited as to the condition, manner, or duration under which major life activity can be performed in comparison to most people.
Qualified person with a disability	A person who satisfies job requirements for educational background, employment experience, skills, licenses, and any other qualification standards that are job related; and is able to perform those tasks that are essential to the job, with or without reasonable accommodation.
Essential job tasks determining factors	• The position exists to perform the function. • There are a limited number of employees among whom the job can be distributed. • The function is highly specialized.
Reasonable accommodations	• Modification to the job application process. • Modification to the work environment or the manner under which the position held is customarily performed. • Modification that enables an employee with a disability to enjoy equal benefits and privileges of employment
Undue hardship	An accommodation would be unduly costly, extensive, substantial, or disruptive, or would fundamentally alter the nature or operation of the business. An action requiring significant difficulty or expense.
Undue hardship determining factors	• Nature and cost of the accommodation. • Overall financial site resources involved. • The number of persons employed • Effect on expenses and resources • Impact upon the operation of the site. • Geographic separateness and the administrative or fiscal relationship of the site or sites to any parent corporation or entity.
Direct threat	A significant risk of substantial harm to the health or safety of the individual or others that cannot be eliminated by reasonable accommodation.

Provisions of the ADA

The five sections of the ADA require the following:

Employment

- Employers with 15 or more employees may not discriminate against qualified individuals with disabilities, those who have a history of having a disability, or those who are regarded as having a disability.
- Equal opportunity must be provided in selection, testing, and hiring of qualified applicants with disabilities.
- Employers must provide "reasonable accommodations" to qualified job applicants or employees, unless doing so would impose an "undue hardship" or if doing so would pose a direct threat to the safety or health of those in the workplace.
- Employers may not discriminate against an applicant or employee because of a known disability of a person with whom they are known to have a relationship.

Public Accommodations Operated by Private Entities

- Public accommodations such as stores, restaurants, offices, museums, libraries, parks, private schools, and day care centers may not discriminate on the basis of disability.
- Reasonable alterations must be made to policies, practices, and procedures to eliminate or avoid discrimination.
- Auxiliary aids and services must be made available to those with disabilities so that they can have an equal opportunity to participate or benefit, unless to do so would impose an "undue burden."
- Physical barriers to access in existing facilities must be removed, unless doing so would impose an undue burden. All new construction of public accommodations must meet ADA accessibility standards established by the Architectural Standards Compliance Board.
- Alterations and major renovations must be accessible and meet ADA standards.
- Entities that routinely provide transportation must do so for those with disabilities.

- Individuals may initiate legal actions, including lawsuits, to stop discrimination. They can also file complaints through the Department of Justice seeking monetary damages and penalties.

Transportation

- New buses and rail vehicles must be accessible to those with disabilities.
- Other new vehicles, such as vans, must be accessible, unless the transportation company provides equivalent alternative service to those with disabilities.
- Transit authorities must provide paratransit services to people with disabilities who cannot use fixed route bus or rail services, unless doing so would impose an undue burden.
- New bus and rail stations must be accessible, and existing stations must be made accessible to the extent that the added costs are not disproportionate to the overall costs of all alterations.
- Existing Amtrak stations must be made accessible by 2010.
- Qualified individuals may file complaints with the Department of Transportation. In the case of privately operated transportation companies, complaints can be filed with the Department of Justice or bring legal action under the public accommodations procedures.

State and Local Governments

- State or local governments may not discriminate against qualified individuals with disabilities. All buildings, services, and communications must be accessible consistent with requirements of Section 504 of the Rehabilitation Act of 1973.
- Qualified individuals may file complaints through the Department of Justice or bring private legal action.

Telecommunications

- Companies offering telecommunications services to the general public must offer telephone relay services to those with hearing impairments who use teletypewriters (TTYs) or similar devices.
- Qualified individuals can file complaints with the Federal Communications Commission.

Impact of the ADA

Most of the provisions of the ADA took effect in 1992—two years after the law was signed. The implementation of the legislation was intentionally postponed to give business, state, and local governments time to comply. More than a decade later, sufficient time has passed to begin to measure the impact of the law.

Unfortunately, the results are decidedly mixed. To some, the ADA has been liberating. In one decade, American society has become much more generous in providing for the needs of disabled people, and accommodations are now widespread. The lives of many disabled individuals have been transformed by greater societal access, and many consider the changes wrought by the legislation to be their "dream come true."

Despite such benefits, others express great concern about the weaknesses of the law. They maintain that the ADA is critically flawed—offering protection to hordes of people with "questionable" disabilities and incompetent workers Congress never intended to shield under the legislation, and requiring dubious policies and accommodations: drug and alcohol abusers defined as "disabled" whose employers must provide them with rehabilitation treatment; seizure-prone large-equipment operators who must be employed despite the threat they pose to the public; and drive-up automatic teller machines required to have Braille signage. Above all, critics point out that the "revolutionary" impact on unemployment that the ADA proponents foresaw simply has not occurred.

A law intended to promote integration has done its share of polarizing.

Strengths of the Law

Providing Access

The most successful aspects of the ADA—and the most difficult to quantify—are those sections dealing with access. Few Americans fail to notice the radical transformation of American society during the past decade as public places, services, and amenities have been created or modified in order to provide access to disabled people. Ramps, wider doors, Braille signage, and a host of other physical accessibility measures are now everywhere. People with disabilities can access public transportation, enter public buildings, and use virtually all public and commercial services.

If the cost of such measures has been very close to the amount predicted by business, the benefits have also been much greater than anticipated. Few advocates for people with disabilities, much less members of the business community, understood the generalized benefits of the curb-cut effect discussed in chapter 1. Now, however, the concept that disability-friendly buildings are people-friendly buildings is so widely understood that accessibility-related expenses, once viewed exclusively as a cost of legal compliance, are increasingly seen as investments, and objections to them are rare. Today it is not unusual to find businesses eager to make disability-related provisions that go beyond the requirements of the law, simply because they have found such practices to be profitable. For example, many hotels now provide lighting remote controls and portable telecommunications devices for guests who are deaf, neither of which is required by the ADA.

Although the benefits of the access provisions of the ADA are obvious, one point needs to be stressed: they are the result of revised public policy, not the transformation of "shameful" attitudes. The theory that discrimination was responsible for most of the disadvantages experienced by disabled people is belied by the great improvements provided by the access provisions of the law. The employment provisions, which targeted presumed "shameful" attitudes and discrimination, have been much less effective.

Application to State and Local Governments and Public Accommodations

Prior to the ADA, federal legislation had targeted policies of the federal government itself and companies that were its contractors. The new legislation greatly expanded the government's reach. Title II of the ADA applied antidiscrimination and accommodation provisions to state and local governments;[2] Title III required disability-related accommodations in public venues such as hotels, restaurants, and theaters; and Title IV created specific access requirements for the telecommunications industry.[3]

These requirements were seen by many as an unwarranted expansion of the role of the federal government and as "unfunded mandates," the cost of which would have to be borne by business and local governments. While these sentiments are understandable, the many improvements provided thus far by the law are due largely to its immediate national impact. Whatever its other faults, the ADA reflected a consensus that rapid and comprehensive improvements were needed to improve the status of the nation's largest minority. More than any other group, those with disabilities require commonly accepted community access standards. It does disabled persons little good to know that they can board an accessible bus in one state unless they can be confident of accessibility when they arrive in another state. Solutions to such fundamental needs could not be left to local authorities for their own remedies. Comprehensive improvements required the leadership of the federal government, and the ADA provided it.

Reasonably Inexpensive Reasonable Accommodations

Prior to the enactment of the ADA, critics charged that providing job accommodations to disabled workers would present businesses with an enormous expense. This has not proved to be the case.

According to information provided by the Federal Government's Job Accommodations Network (JAN), the recent mean cost of job accommodations suggested by JAN was $1,242. In many cases, accommodations involve little direct expense or none at all. In addition, employers who implemented accommodations reported achieving savings of over $18 for each dollar spent in areas such as employee retention, training, disability insurance compensation costs, and productivity (JAN 2000).

Today, even anecdotal evidence to support the original fears of employers simply is not available, and most businesses seem much less concerned about the cost of accommodations. When all the benefits of having this large new pool of qualified and capable workers are considered, job accommodations are a bargain for employers.

Weaknesses of the Law

Lack of Clarity

Even during the drafting of the law, representatives of business argued that the proposed legislation was unclear, creating enormous uncertainties concerning the obligations of employers, and making compliance difficult to impossible. In particular, businesses asked what "reasonable" and "unreasonable" meant within the law, or "readily achievable" and "undue hardship." Many problems were predicted to arise from the law's definition of disability. Exactly who, critics wondered, would be covered under the law?

Critic Walter Olson argues that the drafters of the ADA "were disdainful of definition. It used to be, back in the old days in America, that the No. 1 rule was that a law should tell people what to do. This law says, 'Do what is reasonable, but it's $50,000 per penalty if we decide that you haven't done that'" (Elvin 2000).

Despite these concerns, during legislative hearings doubts about the soundness of the law generally were dismissed. By and large, the ADA's proponents viewed such objections as, at best, misguided, and, at worst, mean spirited. When the law came up for a vote, there were only 28 dissenting votes in the House of Representatives, and only 6 in the Senate. The overwhelming support for the law may have been due, in part, to the tactics used by its supporters. These included demonizing critics and occupying the Capitol rotunda, a demonstration that received great media attention. Few legislators or business representatives wanted to appear to be against remedies that were so manifestly popular, or to oppose advocates who were so energetically righteous.

In such a politically charged atmosphere, legislators were unwilling to improve the clarity of the law's definitions and requirements. Good politics does not always ensure good laws. Tony Coelho, one of the drafters of the legislation who would later chair the President's Committee on Employment of Persons with Disabilities, admitted, "We wrote it rather loosely" (Elvin 2000).

Many businesses claim that one of the most troubling weaknesses of the law is the uncertainty it creates about conflicts with other laws and related requirements. Problem areas include apparent conflicts with the Family and Medical Leave Act (FMLA), workers' compensation, state and local legislation, and collective bargaining agreements. Several court cases are making their way through the legal system, and their eventual resolution may provide clarity for this currently murky area of the law.

Presumptions about the Importance of Discrimination

As mentioned earlier, the drafters of the ADA were confident that they understood what caused disabled people to be disadvantaged: discrimination. The law's language, its design, and some of its key provisions all reflect that premise.

The ADA made sweeping assumptions about, and prescribed equally sweeping remedies for, the private sector, and state and local governments. Its approach to federal policy and responsibility was more circumscribed. Notably absent in the assumptions underlying the law, and the remedies it called for, was recognition that the plight of disabled people might be due in part to the failure of the federal government. Issues for which the federal government is largely responsible, such as inadequate public special educational services and public welfare provisions that create economic disincentives to employment, were ignored.

In the ADA, the federal government, like the gendarmes in *Casablanca,* rounded up "the usual suspects"—state and local governments and the nameless members of the private sector whose discriminatory practices had presumably caused the problem in the first place. By ignoring other contributing factors, legislators were able to enact a piece of legislation quickly and almost unanimously; but it would be a while before the cost of doing so became apparent.

Impact on Employment

No other objective of the ADA meant more to advocates than promoting the employment of those with disabilities, and no other outcome has been a greater disappointment. As advocates had long pointed out, people with disabilities had a high rate of unemployment prior to the ADA—67 percent among adults with significant disabilities. As a group, all people with disabilities had a labor participation rate of only 33 percent, much lower than the population in general. In addition, those who were employed tended to work much fewer hours and earn much less. It was these economic circumstances, more than any other factor, which led to the adoption of the legislation.

According to a landmark study published by the National Bureau of Economic Research in 1998, the ADA not only failed to promote the employment of adults with disabilities, in some ways it actually hurt the situation. The researchers summarize their findings as follows:

> Empirical results using [census data] suggest that the ADA had a negative effect on the employment of disabled men of all working ages and disabled women under age 40. The effects appear to be larger in medium sized firms, possibly because small firms were exempt from the ADA. The effects are also larger in states where there have been more ADA-related charges. (Acemoghi and Angrist 1998)

A few other studies, including a 1998 National Organization on Disability/ Louis Harris poll, have corroborated these findings:

> Only 29% of disabled persons of working age (18–64) work full or part-time, compared to 79% of the non-disabled population, a gap of 50 percentage points. Of those with disabilities of working age who are not working, 72% say that they would prefer to work.

Such research represents a devastating indictment of the employment provisions of the ADA. These findings are rarely cited by disability advocates, despite the fact that people with disabilities are the big losers. Walter Olson has summarized the situation as follows: "Hardly anyone has been rude enough to mention, for example, that the rate of workforce participation among the disabled, which everyone expected would rise under the new law, has instead plunged to 29% from 33% in 1986" (Olson 1999).

All of this has further deteriorated the economic status of disabled people. In 2000, the *Los Angeles Times* reported: "Historically, the work experience of disabled people rose and fell with the rest of the work force during economic swings. But between 1989 and 1998, average inflation-adjusted incomes for disabled workers dropped 4 percent, even though real incomes for workers overall rose 5 percent, according to a new study by Cornell University and the Federal Reserve Bank of San Francisco" (Reckard 2000).

The *Times* concluded: "Experts say some disabled workers have been held back by federal rules that until only recently cut off public medical assistance if their earnings exceeded a certain amount. The Americans with Disabilities Act may also be partly to blame. While requiring companies to make reasonable accommodations for disabled workers, some think the law has raised employers' fears of additional costs and lawsuits if they hire the disabled."

Widespread recognition of the failure of the ADA in promoting the employment of disabled Americans is having an impact. In 1999 the federal government finally began to attack the unemployment problem of disabled people by beginning to remove economic disincentives to work. Previously, many people with disablilities had not sought or had refused jobs because they were reluctant to forfeit their federally provided medical insurance coverage. The Ticket to Work and Work Incentives Improvement Act, passed in December 1999, now allows disabled people to retain Medicaid coverage for as long as ten years after they find employment.[4]

Another factor—education—is gaining greater recognition for its role in remedying the economic disadvantages experienced by disabled people. Unemployment statistics are beginning to indicate that young workers with disabilities—the first generation to benefit from mandated comprehensive educational services—are employed at a higher rate than their older counterparts.

Taken together, the impact of removing economically based employment disincentives and improving educational services has challenged the conventional wisdom that unemployment among disabled people is due primarily to discrimination.

Heavy Litigation and Significant Penalties

Prior to the passage of the ADA, business representatives warned that the result-
ant legislation would lead to excessive litigation costs, much of them borne by
business. To a great extent they were correct.

Figure 2.2 indicates the number of ADA-related charges recorded by the
Equal Employment Opportunity Commission between 1995 and 1999. At first
glance the numbers appear to be reassuring: from nearly 20,000 complaints filed
in 1995 the numbers decline to just over 17,000 in 1999—a 15 percent reduction.

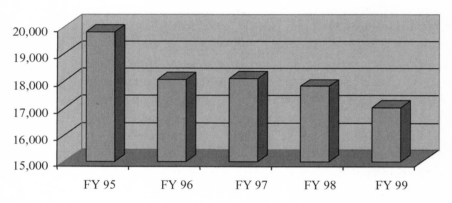

Fig. 2.2. ADA EEOC charges
Source: EEOC (1999A)

However, when the costs associated with litigation are examined, the story
is quite different. As figure 2.3 indicates, ADA-related monetary benefits
awarded through the EEOC have increased significantly, from just under $38
million in 1995 to almost $50 million in 1999. Thus, although the number of
cases has decreased, settlement costs have increased.

In addition, every employer knows that these numbers do not begin to convey the total costs of litigation, since they do not include the benefits obtained
through private settlements or, more importantly, legal costs and other expenses associated with administration and compliance.

Such costs are anathema to most business people. Through the EEOC, an
aggrieved worker or job applicant can file a complaint against businesses—alleging disability-, race-, ethnicity-, age-, or sex-related discrimination—with
virtually no cost (or liability) imposed on the filer, but the significant cost of a
legal defense immediately imposed upon the defendant. In other words, any

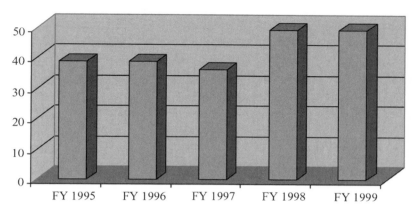

Fig. 2.3. ADA monetary benefits awarded through EEOC
Source: EEOC (1999A)

business can be easily "punished" by any disgruntled employee, even without any justification in fact.

Unsupported allegations are common. The EEOC's own statistics indicate that most of the ADA charges it receives are eventually determined to be groundless. In 1999 almost 60 percent of the ADA-related charges resolved by the EEOC (fig. 2.4) were dismissed because of "no reasonable cause" (1999a). What's more, ADA complaints represent almost one-quarter of all charges handled by the EEOC (1999b). This is no small problem for business.

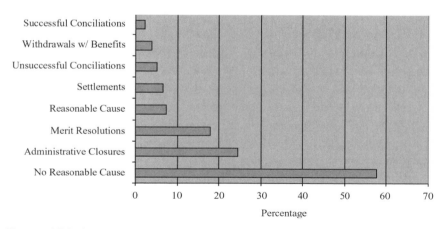

Fig. 2.4. ADA charges resolved in 1999
Note: Some cases have multiple outcomes, so percentages total more than 100 percent.
Source: EEOC (1999A)

Frivolous Litigation

Employers argue that oftentimes litigation represents not only groundless accusations by people with disabilities, but also complaints filed by those who should never have been protected under the ADA in the first place. As one critic has put it: "The confusion over what is—and is not—a protected disability has prompted lawsuits on the basis of such afflictions as myopia, body odor, morning sickness, chronic fatigue syndrome, infertility, obesity, multiple chemical sensitivity, attention deficit disorder and anxiety brought on by a supervisor's reprimand. And the list keeps expanding" (Armbrister 1998).

The fears and frustrations of business have been amplified by the media, including *60 Minutes* and *20/20,* two of television's most popular programs. Several highly questionable and eventually notorious ADA lawsuits have caught the public's attention and fed its skepticism about the law. Among them:

- A visiting nurse in St. Louis demanded that her employer, Cigna Health Care, reassign her to another area. She claimed protection under the ADA, arguing that being assigned to patients in unsafe neighborhoods "made her fearful and depressed." However, the U.S. appeals court ruled that her "depression" did not reach the level of a disability (Wolfe 1998).
- When a law student failed the New York bar exam five times, she requested special testing accommodations under the ADA, claiming that she had a severe learning disability that interfered with her reading. The judge ruled in her favor, saying that she had a "defect that significantly restricts her ability to . . . decode the written word" (Leo 1998).
- In Seattle, a woman sued the owner of a small clothing shop when he refused to allow her to enter the store with her dog. The woman was not blind or deaf, nor did she exhibit any other sign of a disability. However, she claimed that she was "emotionally dependent" on the dog, and the Seattle Office of Human Rights accepted her charges of discrimination based on disability. The shop owner was eventually forced to pay a $650 fine and attend sensitivity training.[5]
- A seventeen-year-old high school varsity basketball player was convicted of driving under the influence of alcohol and was kicked off the team. He sued his school under the ADA, seeking reinstatement and $100,000 in compensation. Said his attorney: "The boy has a recognized medical condition for which he has sought treatment."[6]

Whether or not the plaintiffs prevailed, these notorious cases created in the public's mind the impression that the ADA was yet one more misguided piece of federal legislation. Paradoxically, people with real disabilities inevitably suffered along with wrongly charged businesses, since the most notorious cases were filed by people who arguably were not really disabled at all.

With abuse of the law so readily apparent, it was inevitable that changes would be made. Two Supreme Court cases decided in 1999 began to reverse the trend toward sweeping protections under the ADA. In the first, a terminated UPS driver claimed protection under the ADA—that is, claimed that he was disabled—because he had seriously high blood pressure if he did *not* take his medication. He *did* take his medication; but his lawyers argued, what if he *didn't*? The Supreme Court ruled against him, saying that treatment offered "mitigation" of his condition, leaving him without an actual "substantial" impairment.

The same day, the court also ruled against sisters Kimberly Hinton and Karen Sutton. They had sought protection under the ADA because of their "poor eyesight." Like many others, however, their eyesight could be corrected to nearly normal when they wore glasses, so the court denied their claim.

The latter case in particular faced a formidable obstacle: seven of the nine Supreme Court justices wore glasses. There was no report of what either case did to the justices' blood pressure. However, during oral arguments Justice Stephen Breyer commented, "I don't see how to get this statute to work." Said Justice David Souter, "I'm at sea" (Olson 1999).

These Supreme Court rulings received very different interpretations from disability advocates and business representatives. Said Professor Chai Feldblum of the Georgetown University Law Center, who had been closely involved in the drafting of the legislation: "It's as devastating a cut to the ADA as one could imagine" (Coyle 1999). Others pointed out that, using the plaintiffs' own logic, fully 160 million Americans would have been covered by the law, not the 43 million originally estimated during legislative hearings. Businesses saw the decisions as the only reasonable outcomes.[7]

In 2002 a Supreme Court ruling, *Toyota v. Williams*, further tightened eligibility under the law. In this case, the plaintiff had argued for protection under the ADA because her carpal tunnel syndrome prevented her from performing specific actions related to her assembly line job. The court unanimously held that her arm and wrist pain did not "substantially limit" any "major life activities" as required for eligibility under the law. Disability advocates once again decried the ruling as representing an important loss of rights. Kathleen Blank, an attorney-adviser with the National Council on Disability, said the ruling would "embolden employers who are already disinclined to make accommodations" (Walsh 2002). This time advocates' criticisms were undermined by their lack of a single supporter among the justices. Businesses saw the court's ruling as a hopeful sign that the court would continue to hold a more reasonable interpretation of the law than had sometimes prevailed in both lower courts and enforcement agencies. Toyota Senior Vice President Dennis Cuneo commented: "When the law was passed, no one said it was going to apply to normal workplace injuries. It was for major disability."[8]

Also in 2002, the Supreme Court ruled in *Chevron v. Echazabal* that employers could refuse to hire a disabled job applicant if they concluded that the work would threaten the individual's own life or health. Mr. Echazabal had applied for a job working in an environment sometimes containing airborne toxins, despite the fact that he has hepatitis C, a chronic liver disease. He contended that he was the best judge of risks to his own person, but the justices sided 9–0 with Chevron. Though disability advocates decried the decision, most observers viewed it as another step by the judiciary toward a reasonable elucidation of the ADA. Said Ann Elizabeth Resman, general counsel of the Equal Employment Advisory Council, a business organization, "This was a victory for common sense" (Lane 2002).

Since it is likely that future court decisions will further clarify eligibility under the law, businesses should stay informed of important legal developments.

Inmate Suits

One particular type of frivolous litigation merits special consideration: actions brought by those who are incarcerated, usually referred to as "inmate suits"— the legal kind, not the wool striped. In *Pennsylvania Department of Corrections v. Yeskey* the U.S. Supreme Court considered the claim by a prisoner that, in violation of the ADA, he had been excluded from a motivational boot camp because of his hypertension. When the court ruled 9–0 in the plaintiff's favor, the ruling established clearly that "qualified individuals with disabilities" under the ADA included even those in prison.

Two considerations are important here. First, the ADA's broad definition of disability includes a largely unspecified variety of psychological, emotional, behavioral, and learning difficulties. Arguably, by this definition a high proportion of prison inmates could qualify for protection under the law, and virtually *all* of them could *claim* protection. Second, many of them do just that.

Since *Yeskey* there has been a flood of copycat inmate litigation, demanding such provisions as special mattresses, protection from "environmental pollutants," an increased supply of underwear, work assignment accommodations, and more time for lunch.

As Roger Clegg wrote in the *Weekly Standard:* "The ADA is an open invitation to any or all of these inmates to sue their wardens. And since 'jailhouse lawyers' are notoriously litigious—prisoners, after all, have lots of time on their hands and some familiarity with the legal system—a great number of inmates are accepting that invitation every year" (Clegg 2000).

If advocates intended prison inmates to be covered by the ADA, they failed to mention it during legislative hearings on the proposed legislation. Although some basic protections are certainly arguable, the current sweeping application of the law to the incarcerated must be considered a major flaw of the ADA as currently written. Inmate suits present disability advocates with one more public relations problem that could easily precipitate "corrective action" from Congress.

Direct and Indirect Threats to Health and Safety

As we have seen, in the area of employment, qualified individuals with disabilities are protected from discrimination, including termination, unless their disability poses a "direct threat" to the health and safety of themselves and others. The meaning of "direct" can be interpreted very narrowly, and has been by some courts. Taking action against those who pose only an "indirect threat" to health and safety can trigger heavy penalties. As a result, employers can be left in what psychologists call a double bind—what an average person calls "damned if you do, and damned if you don't." Remove an employee you regard as unsafe and you can be sued for disability-related discrimination; fail to remove the employee and, if an accident occurs, you can be sued for negligence.

The most widely known case of such a double bind involved the Exxon Oil Company. A 1998 ABC News *20/20* piece by John Stossel reported that Exxon had been forced to employ the captain of the *Exxon Valdez,* although Exxon knew he had a chronic problem with alcohol. After the notorious Alaskan oil spill, and having paid millions of dollars in restitution for the captain's negligence, Exxon changed its company policy to forbid those with similar problems from being officers on their ships, only to find themselves being sued—successfully—for discrimination against those "disabled" by alcoholism.

Other employers have faced similar dilemmas:

- Northwest pilot Norman Lyle Prouse was reported for heavy drinking the night before he was scheduled to pilot a flight at 6:30 A.M. to Minneapolis. Thus alerted, the FAA performed a blood test after he completed his flight, and the test revealed that Prouse had a blood alcohol level of .13. In Minnesota, that would qualify him as a drunk driver, let alone a drunken pilot. Facing arrest, termination, and loss of his license, Prouse immediately entered rehab and hired a lawyer, who argued that his client's alcoholism was a disability covered by the ADA. Prouse was eventually sentenced to more than one year in prison, but after his release, Northwest rehired him. Instead of contesting his status as a "qualified person with a disability," the airline allowed him to resume flying passenger aircraft (Olson 1997).
- A driver was terminated from Ryder Systems, Inc., because he had epileptic seizures and was regarded by the company as a safety hazard. Under the ADA, he sued the company for $5.5 million and won.
- The Equal Employment Opportunity Commission filed a suit against Federal Express because of its policy that drivers must have sight in both eyes—even though the Department of Transportation prohibits one-eyed drivers from operating large trucks.[9]
- The EEOC argued before a federal appeals court that a railroad employee who had a heart condition that could cause him to lose consciousness should not have been denied promotion to the position of dispatcher, a job that involves directing trains and responding to emergencies. Said the EEOC: "While consciousness is obviously necessary it is not itself a job function."[10]

Such examples represent unusual cases, but they serve to highlight some of the most obvious flaws in the ADA. In addition, they put the public on notice that the ADA may carry some hidden "costs" that they might wish to reconsider. Safety-related issues might pose the greatest single threat to the ADA as it now stands.

Prospects for Change

Current discussion about the ADA is a study in polarization—advocates on one side, critics on the other. Kenneth Glover (1999) describes the situation as follows: "To disability-rights advocates, the existence of thousands of complaints is evidence that disability-related discrimination remains a problem; to business groups, the complaints reinforce their pre-ADA belief that the law is 'a good idea gone bad.'"

Though the flaws of the legislation are now obvious, attempts are still being made to deny them or minimize their importance. Advocates routinely cite data that are stale or flawed, and gloss over uncomfortable evidence of the law's short-comings. Some even demonize those who argue that the law needs to be changed.

Consider the following message from Tony Coelho (1999), former chair of the President's Committee on Employment of People with Disabilities:

> Today, I am frequently asked how the employment scene has improved for people with disabilities. Have we made progress?
>
> The answer, without a doubt, is yes. During just the first three years after ADA was passed, more than 800,000 adults with severe disabilities went to work. As more and more individuals enter and re-enter the workforce, our example helps to erode deeply rooted stereotypes, myths and misconceptions. But for the millions of people with disabilities still waiting for the opportunity to prove themselves, statistics are not very encouraging.
>
> The staggering unemployment rate facing Americans with disabilities is a problem that affects all of our citizens, and it is up to everyone to confront his or her own attitudes.

Obviously, this statement glosses over the troubling data from the government's own Census Bureau. Why do proponents downplay the fact that the employment picture for people with disabilities has remained virtually unchanged since the passage and implementation of the ADA? Is it more likely that the design of the law was flawed, or that people's negative "attitudes" are to blame?

Chairman Coelho's comments also demonstrate that statistics can be used selectively and "creatively" to defend the legislation. The figure of 800,000 individuals with severe disabilities becoming employed sounds impressive. But how many could have become employed *without* the ADA, how many *in spite of it,* and how many *never were employed,* because of its flaws?

The "official" line of the disability establishment in defense of the ADA is perhaps best exemplified by the National Council on Disability (NCD) in a December 1999 report:

> Nine years later, ADA and the American disability rights movement have produced some tangible results for many Americans with disabilities. In towns and cities across the United States, ADA has produced evolutionary progress in removing barriers that exclude Americans with disabilities and their families. But

for a large segment of the population with disabilities, particularly those from diverse racial, cultural, and ethnic communities, a shameful wall of exclusion continues to hinder their ability to participate fully in all aspects of American society. Whether the exclusion stems from one's disability, one's race, one's language, one's culture, one's ethnicity, or a combination of these, the sting of rejection is just as painful. As we mark the ninth anniversary of the signing of ADA, the declaration of equality made in 1990 remains hollow for many people with disabilities from diverse cultural backgrounds in their continuing struggle against the persistent barriers of poverty, inequality, and dual discrimination.

The message from the NCD is that the failures of the ADA simply indicate that more of the same is needed—beginning with an even greater appreciation of the role of discrimination in the plight of people with disabilities. No credence is given to those who suggest that major changes are needed because of some demonstrable failures of the legislation and the possibility that it failed to address some of the real causes of the socioeconomic disadvantages of disabled people.

Suggest otherwise, and you are likely to be demonized, judging by the same NCD report responding to the ADA's critics:

> The backlash against civil rights for people with disabilities continued to show its face in the last year. Commentators and pundits continue to complain about the "wrong people" benefiting from ADA and about the extraordinary costs being incurred by employers, particularly for litigation. Critics argue that ADA is a failure because the employment rate for people with disabilities has not increased significantly since the law's passage and because of the perception that the law is vague and difficult to interpret with certainty. None of these arguments withstand close scrutiny, yet they resurface consistently.

Unfortunately, the "close scrutiny" of arguments critical of the ADA is almost totally lacking within the NCD and elsewhere in the disability community. Statisticians, economists, and political commentators can make their arguments, present their data, and draw their conclusions, but advocates strongly resist any change, and accuse their critics of having "attitude" problems.

Despite the opposition of disability activists, the certainties that prevailed in 1990 when the ADA was passed are beginning to give way to the lessons of experience, and there are now some indications that fundamental changes in the law, or at least the interpretation of the law, will be made. Recent Supreme Court decisions clearly indicate that interpretations of the law will not be so sweeping in the future.

Other trends to watch:

- Rational limitations to the definition of disability, reasonable accommodations, and readily achievable efforts seem increasingly likely. Original definitions will be made more explicit, and inappropriate interpretations are likely to be modified, as courts and legislators face the consequences of the original language of the law.
- There is a growing realization that the economic plight of disabled people, the prime focus of the law, is not simply a result of "shameful" discrimination. The recently passed federal "Ticket to Work" law begins to remove medical insurance–related economic disincentives to employment, and may represent a major step toward the government's acceptance of its own responsibility for the vast rate of unemployment among disabled people. In addition, as the first generation of well-educated job candidates with significant disabilities enters the workforce, it will become more evident how much was lost by earlier generations because of educational neglect. If unemployment now begins to decrease, as many think it will, the "Ticket to Work" program and mandated special education services will offer further evidence that the employmet provisions of ADA were flawed in their original design.
- Competing interest groups, especially elderly citizens, will increasingly question the scope of the legislation. For example, in the area of housing, the ADA's antidiscrimination provisions have opened up formerly all-elderly facilities to "qualified" individuals with disabilities, including, of course, some young people with a history of substance abuse—a move highly unpopular with seniors. Paratransit services, formerly dedicated solely to elderly citizens, must now be shared with newly eligible individuals with disabilities, further straining already scarce resources. Such conflicts portend serious political problems.
- People with disabilities will become increasingly concerned as proof mounts that the ADA has failed to promote employment. They will be forced to adopt a more pragmatic and conciliatory tone, and less monolithic political positions. As Kathi Wolfe (1998), a person with a visual disability, has said: "I used to dream of a law that would dispel prejudice toward folks like me. Now, despite the good it does, the ADA is becoming a nightmare. If people don't stop using it to clog up the courts and excuse imcompetence,

the Americans with Disabilities Act will wind up reinforcing the discrimination it was designed to eradicate."

- Safety could be the issue that will catalyze major amendments to the
ADA. Although the Supreme Court has taken some preliminary steps to
limit those covered under the law, to date Congress has shown little enthusiasm for major amendments. This is undoubtedly due in part to the
political clout of the law's proponents. That could change quickly. If the
range of people protected by the law is not more rationally limited, and
if employers are not given greater latitude in matters involving health
and safety, it is only a matter of time before a public backlash forces
changes in the ADA. Every person is just "one accident away" from
being disabled. The same might be said of the law itself. To date there
has been no major catastrophe involving a loss of human life that is directly traceable to the ADA. If such a tragedy should occur, the public
would demand that Congress make major amendments to the law. In
such an environment, politicians would not be deterred by the political
clout of the nation's largest minority.

More than a decade after its passage, the ADA seems to have been a mixed
blessing, providing at long last some comprehensive provisions and protections to those with great needs, but also creating serious problems and ambiguities. Also of importance is what the law did *not* do: remedy government's
most pernicious failures in disability-related policy—inadequate educational
services and economic disincentives to employment.

In retrospect, the ADA could have been drafted with greater reason and
less righteousness. Attributing the economic and social plight of those with
disabilities primarily to discrimination was an oversimplification. Thomas
Sowell (1998) has summarized the principle involved as follows: "The fact
that discrimination deserves moral condemnation does not automatically make
it causally crucial. Whether it is or is not in a given time and place is an empiri-
cal question, not a foregone conclusion. A confusion of morality and causation
may be politically convenient, but that does not make the two things one."

The vehemence of the ADA's proponents, as they addressed the "shameful" practices of presumed bad people, overpromoted issues related to discrimination, while paying insufficient attention to other factors, especially federal
policy. Legislators accepted the reasoning of advocates too unquestioningly. It
was far too easy for government to target business and other presumed sources

of discrimination before fully understanding the problem and getting its own policy house in order. The ADA reflects the enlightened determination of Americans to promote the integration of the nation's largest minority. It is hardly indicative of a "shameful" national attitude toward disabled people.

All parties involved should participate in an effective amendment of the law. If businesses find their objections to some of the more burdensome aspects of the ADA taken more seriously, and if critics of the law are no longer vilified, they may be more willing to think proactively, and speak more honestly, about disability issues. Honest communication, always a rare commodity, would benefit all parties involved. Although a climate of litigation does not encourage them to admit it, business leaders' dread of burdensome regulations and increased expenses has undoubtedly contributed to the lack of economic progress by people with disabilities during the last decade. Immutable disability unemployment statistics may indicate, among other things, that for each qualified person hired in compliance with the ADA, another was passed over out of a fear of compliance expenses and employee litigation. Business leaders can join disability advocates in admitting some past mistakes and beginning an effort toward cooperative improvement of the law.

Resources

Americans with Disabilities Act Document Center
http://www.jan.wvu.edu/links/adlinks.htm

http://www.disabilitydirect.gov/
A website of the Office of Disability Employment Policy designed to pull together a wide variety of disability information, especially from federal government sources.

Equal Employment Opportunity Commission (EEOC)
http://www.eeoc.gov/
For technical assistance:
(800) 669-4000 Voice
(800) 669-6820 TTY
To obtain documents:
(800) 669-3362 Voice
(800) 800-3302 TTY

The National Organization on Disability (NOD)
http://www.nod.org/
910 Sixteenth St. N.W.

Suite 600
Washington, D.C. 20006
(202) 293-5960 Voice
(202) 293-5968 TTY
(202) 293-7999 Fax

U.S. Dept. of Justice ADA Home Page
http://www.usdoj.gov/crt/ada/adahom1.htm/
U.S. Department of Justice
950 Pennsylvania Ave. N.W.
Civil Rights Division
Disability Rights Section—NYAVE
Washington, D.C. 20530
(800) 514-0301 Voice
(800) 514-0383 TTY
(202) 307-1198 Fax

ADA ON CD-ROM

The U.S. Department of Justice offers a free CD-ROM containing extensive technical information on the ADA. The CD-ROM is in a variety of formats, including WordPerfect, HTML, and text (ASCII). The CD-ROM includes:

- The new electronic version of the ADA Standards for Accessible Design;
- The ADA Guide for Small Businesses;
- Common ADA Errors and Omissions in New Construction and Alterations;
- The Americans with Disabilities Act Checklist for New Lodging Facilities;
- The ADA Guide for Small Towns;
- A series of commonly asked question and answer publications; and
- Technical Assistance Manuals for Titles II and III of the ADA.

Single copies can be ordered online at:

http://www.usdoj.gov/crt/ada/cdrequestform.htm
or by calling the Department's ADA Information Line:
(800) 514-0301 (Voice) or (800) 514-0383 (TTY).
Internet users can access the same information at: http://www.usdoj.gov/crt/ada/adahom1.htm

3

Diversity, Disability, and Inclusion

One of the greatest challenges business managers faced during the second half of the twentieth century was adapting to the radical changes in American society that followed the civil rights movement of the 1960s. A combination of factors—including legislation, public awareness, and immigration patterns—forced businesses to devote more attention and resources to issues relating to the rights of people previously marginalized. An understanding of this era is critical to a discussion of disability because the civil rights movement, which initially focused on racial issues, led eventually to the disability rights movement.

During the early 1960s, the attention of civil rights activists focused primarily on concrete issues affecting African Americans, such as voting rights and educational segregation. Soon, however, their attention broadened to encompass larger concerns, especially economic issues. Particular attention was devoted to the issues of poverty, unemployment, and discrimination in hiring. The Civil Rights Act of 1964 prohibited employers from discriminating on the basis of race; it represented a milestone in American political history, one of the most important advancements in civil rights since Reconstruction.

Although the expectations of civil rights leaders were high, real progress in the status of racial minorities was slow in coming. With the assassination of Rev. Dr. Martin Luther King Jr. and the widespread rioting that followed his death, the nation seemed to sense that much more than legal changes needed to be made. Steps had to be taken not only to eliminate discrimination, but also to remedy the economic injustices that were the remnant of decades of mistreatment.

During the 1970s a consensus developed, both popular and political, that businesses needed to take action to increase the number of minorities they employed. Eventually, this imperative became public policy as both federal and state courts began to hold employers responsible not just for individual acts of discrimination, but for "patterns" of discrimination over time as indicated by records of hiring and promotion. Such statistics became known as "tests" of nondiscriminatory practice.

In response to widespread public expectations, and to protect themselves from charges of discrimination, most large corporations eventually adopted strategies known as "affirmative action." Affirmative action initiatives were originally intended to increase the number of employees from racial minority groups and to provide concrete evidence that the corporations were not discriminating in hiring. Although the primary intent of such efforts was often to avoid charges of discrimination, most businesses also recognized a social and moral responsibility to respond. Over time, most businesses also came to view employment integration as a business opportunity—a chance to adapt effectively to the uniquely heterogeneous American marketplace.

As the effects of the civil rights movement permeated American society, groups other than African Americans began to express similar concerns and demand similar remedies. In response, many affirmative action programs broadened to include other racial and ethnic minorities and women.

In her autobiography, *Personal History,* Katharine Graham, the first female publisher of a major American newspaper, describes her experiences and frustrations with affirmative action at the *Washington Post* during this era:

> Like all businesses and editorial companies, in fact all white- and male-dominated institutions, we had a lot to learn in this period. At both the *Post* and *Newsweek* there was a great deal right and a great deal wrong about some of our procedures and some of our responses to the issues. Prior to the late 1960s, our intention had been good but our accomplishments only so-so. . . . When the 1970s brought infusions of blacks and women, neither the *Post* or *Newsweek* at first dealt with the new employees with much sensitivity, understanding, or skill, but this was also true of almost every organization in mainstream America. Adding to the problem was that our beginning efforts to hire "qualified" women and minorities were carried out inadequately. When saddled with inadequate talent or failures whether women or blacks, we didn't know either how to work with them to bring them along or how to let them go. (1997, 426)

Although Graham's perspective is unique, her experience was typical of many business leaders. Antidiscrimination and affirmative action efforts often proved to be problematic, and business leaders continued to search for better ways to address social inequalities.

The Concept of Diversity

From mandates for affirmative action in the hiring of minority groups and women, the concept of a diversified work force began to emerge during the 1980s as an almost universally accepted social goal. During the 1990s a diversity consulting and training industry came into being. Today, most medium-size to large corporations have a formal commitment to promoting "corporate diversity," and diversity initiatives are commonplace.

Despite almost universal acceptance in the business world, diversity theories and practices have received relatively little attention from management researchers and academicians, and are often treated with what some critics have termed "distant cheerleading" (Prasad and Mills 1997, 5). This lack of critical analysis helps to explain some of the problems associated with current initiatives, and indicates the importance of taking a careful look at the concept.

The Meaning of the Term

In corporate America, "diversity" has a significance that, although unique to the context of business, has different meanings depending on the source. R. Roosevelt Thomas Jr., a leading diversity theorist, offered the following definition in his book *Beyond Race and Gender:*

> Diversity includes everyone; it is not something that is defined by race or gender. It extends to age, personal and corporate background, education, function, and personality. It includes life-style, sexual preference, geographic origin, tenure with the organization, exempt or nonexempt status, and management or nonmanagement. (10)

Thomas's definition, published in 1991, typified a shift in focus away from affirmative action and hiring quotas toward more expansive issues. Even so, it was unusually broad for its time, and was, in fact, broadened even further by the author in his later writings (e.g., *Redefining Diversity,* 1996).

While understandings of diversity are almost always wider ranging than previous notions of affirmative action, there is today no definitive interpretation of what the term means. Many corporations and employer organizations have created their own definitions of diversity, and many more express a commitment to the issue without defining precisely what they understand it to mean. (See "Some Definitions and Quasi-Definitions of Diversity" in this section.)

For example, the Microsoft Corporation says:

> At Microsoft, we believe that diversity enriches our performance and products, the communities in which we live and work, and the lives of our employees. As our workforce evolves to reflect the growing diversity of our communities and global marketplace, our efforts to understand, value and incorporate differences become increasingly important. At Microsoft, we have established a number of initiatives to promote diversity within our own organization, and to demonstrate this commitment in communities nation wide. (2002)

Since many corporations view the issue of diversity almost exclusively as a

SOME DEFINITIONS AND QUASI-DEFINITIONS OF DIVERSITY

Webster's Collegiate Dictionary
"the condition of being diverse: variety."

BankBoston
Diversity at BankBoston is defined broadly to include group differences (based on age, race, gender, sexual orientation, disabilities, parental status or job group, for instance) and individual differences, including communications style, career experience, and other variables.[1]

General Motors
Managing diversity is "the process of creating and maintaining an environment that naturally enables General Motors employees, suppliers and communities to fully contribute in pursuit of total customer enthusiasm." (Thomas 1996, 235)

Honeywell
"The belief, philosophy and recognition that each individual is unique and valuable, melding into and conflicting with established norms. The necessary skills and energy for business success will be drawn from this array of people." (Hayles and Russell 1997, 12)

The Pillsbury Company
"all the ways in which we differ" (Hayles and Russell 1997, 11)

human resources issue, the Society for Human Resource Management (SHRM) definition is an important one:

> To celebrate diversity is to appreciate and value individual differences. SHRM strives to be the leader in promoting workplace diversity. Although the term is often used to refer to differences based on ethnicity, gender, age, religion, disability, national origin and sexual orientation, diversity encompasses an infinite range of individuals' unique characteristics and experiences, including communication styles, physical characteristics such as height and weight, and speed of learning and comprehension.[2]

SHRM's "workplace" focus is understandable given the purpose of the association. Some organizations and corporations broaden the issue to include matters such as customer service and community relations. SHRM's inclusion of groups other than racial minorities and women is also increasingly common today, in theory if not in practice.

The influence of diversity has not been limited to the private sector. The federal government is also heavily committed to the issue. For example, the U.S. Department of Energy defines diversity as follows:

> Diversity at the Department of Energy has internal, external and global meanings. It encompasses all differences in individuals and groups, moving well beyond race and gender to the broadest definition of inclusiveness for employees, contractors, suppliers, and our customers. Diversity at the Department of Energy is about establishing superior performance. (Hayles and Russell 1997, 13)

Many other federal, state, and local governmental departments have similarly endorsed the concept. The Equal Employment Opportunity Commission uses the term frequently, often as a synonym for "equal opportunity"; however, even the government agency charged with enforcing antidiscrimination employment law offers no formal definition. In fact, despite the connection between diversity and such issues as discrimination and affirmative action, the federal government has established no legal definition of the term, another reason why it tends to be a very fluid concept.

Including Disability

Although most definitions of diversity include disability as a consideration, some corporate diversity initiatives pay it little or no attention. One critic of such programs recently said: "By and large, most [diversity] training efforts are strictly about race and gender. Their information, their discussion, and their exercises all relate to these two issues."

The reluctance of some diversity practitioners to pay sufficient attention to disability issues is difficult to understand. The minority group that most people have some knowledge of, and the one that all are likely to join at some time in their lives, is that of people with disabilities. If an educator desiring to promote tolerance were looking for a strategic issue with which to begin a training session, this would be the one to choose. Yet few diversity initiatives take this approach.

Why would diversity trainers largely ignore a minority most likely to be familiar to the public, a group much less likely than others to foster contentiousness, and one most likely to appeal to the public's self-interest? Even apart from educational considerations, there is the matter of litigation—a concern of most businesses. The statistic that about one-quarter of charges filed with the Equal Employment Opportunity Commission involve disability issues, and the fact that the cost of the average settlement is increasing, alone ought to inspire corporate diversity trainers to emphasize disability issues, but many still do not. Why is this the case?

There may be several reasons. The first is habit. During the 1970s and 1980s, while companies were moving from mandates against discrimination to requirements for affirmative action, the concept of diversity was evolving. While racial and ethnic issues still dominated matters involving discrimination, there was also an increased emphasis on women's rights. Although a constitutional "Equal Rights Amendment" for women failed to be passed into law, the right of women to equal pay for equal work, fair treatment, and matters of equity became a pervasive part of the public consciousness. Racial and gender issues were well established as civil rights concerns before disability was added to the list.

It may be that, despite recent litigation trends, racial and gender issues are still those most feared by employers. They are also easily subject to numerical analysis—still a common vestige of the era of affirmative action. Few companies have numerical quotas or hiring goals for those with disabilities. Not only is it more difficult to "count" people with disabilities, but when considering a job candidate who has a disability, it is relatively easy to explain that another candidate was simply more qualified. Without any pressure for numerical goals or quotas in the hiring of disabled job candidates, some employers may feel relatively free from compulsions to hire them.

Second, in matters relating to the employment of disabled people, the focus is on the individual, not the group. In regard to disabilities, employers are obligated not to discriminate in each *individual* case. Each case must be decided according to whether or not the job candidate is qualified, what "reasonable accommodations" are required, and so on. Not only must each case be considered individually, but also the number of people with significant disabilities currently in the work force is so small—and virtually the same as it was before the ADA was passed—that employers might perceive little pressure to employ disabled job candidates. To date, class action litigation against employers for disability-related discrimination has not been a major threat. Unlike women and other minorities, people with disabilities are feared as an employment litigation threat individually, but less so as a class.[3]

One of the few trainers to address the issue of including disability in diversity programs, Karen Roberts, maintains that it makes good sense *not* to: "While it may be convenient for the purposes of devising social programs or assigning what may be socially useful labels to refer to 'the disabled' as a group, individuals with disabilities do not form an internally homogenous group with respect to having common experiences in the workplace or larger community" (1995, 316). Roberts goes on to explain, somewhat apologetically, that it is precisely these individual differences that make people with disabilities unlike others who can properly be considered in groups: "The nature of disability is more insistent on attention to the individual and recognition of the contribution of culture and context to how a problem is defined than with most other sources of diversity" (328). In other words, people with disabilities don't really belong in discussions of diversity because their "experiences" tend to be individual and unique! To traditional diversity approaches, the fact that people with visual impairments might have needs and interests different from those of people with mobility or learning impairments is a major obstacle. People with disabilities have too many individual differences to be included. So, traditional diversity initiatives, which their advocates maintain are all about respecting "individual differences," are in reality only for those who are homogenous.

Third, diversity efforts are largely developed and implemented by the diversity industry. Corporate programs have now been around long enough that they have developed their own traditions, ideologies, customs, and leaders. Many of those personally involved in diversity efforts—as human resources professionals, diversity managers, or personnel trainers—are themselves members of racial minorities, women, or both. Their personal interests and experience may not include disabilities, and that may help to explain a more limited focus in practice than is sometimes described in theory.

Despite a relative lack of emphasis from diversity practitioners, the issue of disability holds great promise in helping businesses promote diversity. To understand why, we must look more closely at the current status of corporate diversity efforts.

Corporate Diversity Initiatives

In business, diversity initiatives can include not only establishing numerical goals for employment, but also recruitment strategies, community initiatives, mentoring partnerships, integrated advertising, and so on. Just as there is no commonly accepted definition of diversity, there is great variation in the ways in which employers attempt to promote the concept.

One of the most common diversity practices is employee education. Diversity training has become so widespread that it has created a sizable industry of diversity consultants and trainers, as well as its own literature, commonly accepted practices, and leadership. According to *Training* magazine, in 1999 approximately 57 percent of American companies participated in some sort of diversity training, spending a total of almost $10 billion (1999, 58).

Diversity training can consist of anything from employee group discussions to comprehensive corporate programs. Often, diversity initiatives are headquartered in the human resources department of a company, and activities may be limited to that section. Such programs frequently begin with a corporate diversity "audit" intended to determine the presence of disadvantaged groups in the work force as the basis for developing goals, a corporate strategic plan, and an employee education program.

Many diversity training curricula include a review of the status of minorities throughout American history, including such issues as racial segregation, employment discrimination, the treatment of Native Americans, and so on. Games, role-playing, and discussion activities are also used frequently. In some classes, trainers have been known to require participants to list all the epithets they have heard used to describe members of disadvantaged groups; others have asked trainees to recount instances of unfair treatment they have personally witnessed. In some sessions, participants have been assigned roles—for example, one person will be asked to play the part of a job interviewer and another the part of a minority job candidate—and asked to act out how they think such an encounter might go.

Other instructional activities may be much more abstract. Training participants occasionally report being asked to engage in unusual "learning" activities, such as drawing pictures of problematic social situations, and mimicking the linguistic styles of various groups. One leading diversity training organization routinely uses multicolored pop-it beads, which participants are instructed to string together to represent the multiracial makeup of a "diversified work force." *Forbes* magazine reported: "A marketing manager forced to endure American Express' diversity training says one exercise involved continually crossing and uncrossing his arms in an unusual way, supposedly to teach him about different ways of looking at things" (Lubove 1997).

Such practices help to explain why diversity training, though widely used, is also often held in low regard by those who participate in it.

Common Characteristics of Traditional Diversity Programs

As we have seen, there is great variance in understandings of what exactly diversity is and how it can, and should, be promoted. Yet traditional diversity initiatives share some characteristics (fig. 3.1).

Almost all diversity initiatives are concerned with avoiding litigation. As an outgrowth of the civil rights movement, business diversity became a prominent issue when legal authorities began to hold employers responsible for "patterns of discrimination." Since compliance with antidiscrimination laws was to be measured numerically, it became increasingly important for employers to be able to demonstrate good-faith efforts in hiring and promotion, that is, affirmative action.

While many companies are committed to the issue because they recognize diversity as both a business necessity and a societal obligation, the connection between litigation and diversity initiatives has become stronger as courts and

Fig. 3.1. The traditional diversity model

THE TRADITIONAL DIVERSITY MODEL	
Rationale	Problem Prevention
Process	Social Engineering
Unit	Group
Focus	Differences
Emphasis	Weaknesses
Outcome	Enhanced Economic Status

60

The Inclusive Corporation

the EEOC have mandated diversity training as part of settlements in discrimination cases.

Commenting on the popularity of diversity training, Seth Lubove (1997) observes:

> Many companies come to this game under duress. It's not enough for them to shovel out millions to settle discrimination or harassment lawsuits or settle with the Equal Opportunity Commission or some other federal agency. More often, the plaintiffs' lawyers also demand that a company do penance by forcing every employee through some kind of sensitivity-training program, even tying management's compensation—or careers—to achieving diversity goals.

Today, diversity training clearly is used both preemptively and remedially in response to litigation. For obvious reasons, few businesses identify litigation as the primary reason for their diversity efforts. Within companies there may be a wide variety of opinion on the issue—some employees viewing the issue as a bothersome necessity, others seeing it as an important opportunity. In general, the more traditional a company's approach to diversity, the more concerned it is with preventing problems—especially discrimination charges.

Traditional diversity initiatives promote social engineering. In attempting to increase the presence of particular groups in the workplace, especially women and racial minorities, traditional diversity initiatives are intended to change fundamentally the human makeup of the business world. In addition, by focusing on the discriminatory behavior of business, both past and present, such initiatives attempt to change fundamentally the values and, ultimately, the behaviors of employers and employees alike.

The *macro* level of such social engineering is employment and promotion statistics. These are relatively easy to quantify, and therefore a focus of much attention. The *micro* level—much more difficult to quantify—is changes in "objectionable" attitudes in the workplace. The difficulty of measuring this variable contributes to the confusion over what distinguishes effective from ineffective traditional diversity initiatives.

Traditional diversity initiatives focus on groups. With their origins in a social engineering model and their intent to provide statistical proof of nondiscrimination, traditional business efforts at promoting diversity necessarily deal

```
1. Are you        _____ Hispanic
                  _____ Asian American
                  _____ American Indian
                  _____ White
                  _____ Black
                  _____ Other (Please specify: _____)
2. Are you        _____ Female or _____ Male?
3. How long have you been with the ORGANIZATION NAME?
```

Fig. 3.2. The first three questions from a culture audit "interview guide"

primarily with the status of groups of people, especially racial minorities and women.

Most employers sponsoring diversity initiatives maintain statistics on the status of various groups identified in their employment population, and many diversity initiatives begin with the kind of quantitative analysis evident in the culture audit "interview guide" shown in fig. 3.2 (Thomas 1991, 61). The success or failure of diversity initiatives is often measured by the change in the number of members of particular groups who are hired or promoted. Although formal numerical "quotas" have recently met numerous legal challenges, many companies establish less formal "goals" that amount to much the same thing.

Despite oft-repeated admonitions that "individual differences should be respected," traditional diversity programs invariably stress group status, and in so doing may even promote the process of categorization—forcing the issue of labeling and grouping. (Young Americans are showing increasing resistance to this process, the most prominent example being the golfer Tiger Woods.) They may also foster generalizations about various groups, such as that all members must be underprivileged, or that they are at risk of mistreatment and desirous of protections. Many diversity programs assume, for example, that all African Americans are economically disadvantaged, despite the emergence of a sizable and affluent African American middle class.

Traditional diversity initiatives focus on differences. While most definitions of diversity recognize the importance of human similarities, traditional programs tend to place a greater emphasis on differences that exist, or are presumed to exist, between the sexes and among various races, cultures, economic groups, and so on. Most diversity initiatives attempt to reduce or eliminate discriminatory behavior related to those perceived differences.

The emphasis upon differences entails some significant dilemmas. By defining conditions such as race, age, ethnicity, and gender as important factors worthy of attention, practitioners are, in effect, supporting the reality and importance of those characteristics. For example, in order to categorize individuals by various racial groups, some definition of what constitutes that race must be employed, no matter how nebulous and illogical commonly accepted definitions may be: many people consider an individual to be a member of a racial minority even if only one of the peson's ancestors came from that group.

If the ultimate message of diversity programs is intended to be that people's similarities outweigh their differences, that message is undermined by a constant preoccupation with what distinguishes one group from another. At the very least, the idea that an appreciation of human commonalities can be promoted by a preoccupation with differences is an unproven pedagogical premise.

Traditional diversity initiatives explore weaknesses. Traditional diversity programs are created in response to problems, and therefore tend to be problem-oriented. Within this approach, emphasis is usually placed on past patterns of offensive behavior, misunderstandings and ignorance, objectionable societal values, and so on.

In many diversity programs, preoccupation with human weakness is reflected in an attempt to promote "awareness" of imperfect human behavior. Frequently, the behavior under consideration is that of members of traditionally powerful groups—Caucasians, males, the affluent—sometimes referred to as "the dominant culture"—and their tendencies to discriminate against others.

Responding to criticism that they have been too negative, some diversity trainers have begun to change their emphasis. These trainers now offer programs that are more prescriptive than in the past, promoting acceptable behaviors in the workplace, rather than rehashing old mistakes or engaging in sensitivity exercises. According to Stephen Paskoff of Employment Learning Innovations, an Atlanta-based firm that offers diversity training, "What we do is identify the kinds of behaviors the laws are designed to manage and focus on that without a lot of social theory" (Lubove 1997).

Traditional diversity initiatives seek enhanced economic status.
Most diversity programs would not be considered successful unless they promoted the increased employment of racial minority groups and women. In addition, most programs also look at other measurements of the economic status of various groups within the organization, issues such as pay, retention rates, promotion patterns, and the number of people in administrative or executive positions.

The economic status of the business is another important consideration. As legal challenges to "affirmative action" increase, many employers are feeling less pressure to meet numerical quotas and for the first time are asking for evidence that diversity initiatives, like other company activities, contribute to the bottom line. Although the research on diversity outcomes is not extensive, there is evidence to support advocates' enthusiasm. During the 1980s, a study by Rosabeth Moss Kanter concluded that businesses with "progressive" human resources practices enjoyed significantly greater profits than their less progressive competitors (Hayles and Russell 1997, 4–5). In 1993, a front-page article in the *Wall Street Journal* reported that companies with diversity initiatives had stock price increases that were 2.4 percent greater than those of average companies.[4] In his book *Cultural Diversity in Organizations,* one of the most highly regarded publications in the field, Taylor Cox Jr. reviews the research related to the impact of diversity initiatives and finds support for several direct benefits, including improved employee recruitment, increased marketing effectiveness, and improvements in workgroup creativity and problem solving. Cox also identifies two potential problem areas related to diversity: communications and group cohesiveness (1993, 27–39).

Some of the evidence often cited in support of diversity training is open to question. Some studies equate the apparent effectiveness of diverse work forces with effective diversity employee education. One prominent report, the "SHRM/Fortune Impact of Diversity Initiatives on Bottom Line," based its findings on a survey of 121 human resources professionals at Fortune 1000 companies. The significance of the positive data provided by this study is undermined by the fact that it measured only the opinions of those likely to be responsible for the programs being evaluated (SHRM 2001).

Problems Encountered in Traditional Diversity Programs

Corporate diversity programs are likely to reflect many, or even all, of the characteristics listed above. These characteristics, of course, are often at odds with what companies claim their initiatives are all about. In addition to the disparity between what companies say and what they actually do, there can be a significant difference between what they expect to achieve through their diversity programs and what actually happens. For both these reasons, the story of Texaco and its problems with diversity—often mentioned and rarely understood—is a cautionary tale.

The Texaco Story

At the beginning of the 1990s, Texaco had well-established policies prohibiting various forms of discrimination, and had conducted employee diversity education sessions. Despite these factors, the company's own Equal Employment Opportunity statistics indicated that the company was actually becoming less diverse, and identified minorities were decreasing. Employee dissatisfaction was growing, and many questioned the sincerity of the company's commitment to diversity.

A group of minority employees eventually filed suit against the company, alleging discrimination. In addition, the plaintiffs charged that company executives tolerated a culture of intolerance against minorities. Specifically, they alleged that one executive had referred to minorities derisively as "jelly beans." In the media, the accusation relating to the alleged abusive language soon became the focus of attention. The charge was quickly sensationalized, and the public quickly began to see the company in an extremely negative light.

The accusations against Texaco that were most ballyhooed by the media were in fact inaccurate. In court, the company showed that during some of their training sessions, diversity instructors used different-colored jelly beans to represent employees of different racial groups (SHRM 2001), a common training practice at the time.

> When you are dealing with diversity, you are focusing on the collective mixture, not just pieces of it.
>
> To highlight this notion of mixture, visualize a jar of red jelly beans; now imagine adding some green and purple jelly beans. Many would believe that the green and purple jelly beans represent diversity. I suggest that diversity instead is represented by the resultant mixture of red, green, and purple jelly beans.
>
> It is easier to see these jelly beans as a metaphor for the company's employees, in other words, for workforce diversity. (Thomas 1996, 7)

Although Texaco was not innocent of all of the charges made against it, it may have been innocent of the alleged offense that became most notorious. In 1996, after extensive litigation and extremely damaging publicity, the company settled the case for $176 million. Undoubtedly to Texaco's chagrin, the settlement mandated additional "diversity training" for company officials.

Texaco's experience with diversity training is not unique. Another example: As a component of its diversity training, the R. R. Donnelley and Sons Company showed a movie depicting lynching in the old south. The experience so offended one employee, who had to view the film four times, that he filed charges against the company on behalf of 3,500 minority employees. The training module in which the "offensive" material was contained had been developed as part of a settlement of previous discrimination charges (Lubove 1997).

Though not common, such infamous disasters help to explain why some business leaders, public pronouncements notwithstanding, abhor the entire concept of diversity training. In private, some managers will admit that, at best, their diversity training program may be useless; at worst, it can cause major problems. Many fear that it will create problems even larger than the ones it is supposed to address.

Weaknesses Inherent in Traditional Diversity Programs

Business executives and employee managers who want to avoid diversity training–related problems would do well to understand some of the underlying reasons why such programs can be so precarious:

- *The first is the issue of true intent: the company's own description of the rationale and goals for its diversity initiatives versus the underlying reality. The two are often very different.*

   While most companies talk about how they hope to foster an appreciation of "all differences" in their company, what many really want most of all is to reduce the costs associated with litigation. According to one vice president for human resources at a major midwestern corporation: "One of the things that is most frustrating to me is that what companies *say* and what they *mean* is very different. Companies *say* they are committed to a diversified work force because that's a 'good'; but in reality, I'm afraid that most companies are simply concerned about litigation. They don't want to be sued, so they commit to diversity to protect themselves."

   The hidden agenda of avoiding litigation can foster the type of bad feelings that most companies claim they want to eliminate or avoid through diversity programs.

• *The second problem, closely related to the first, is that the objective, nonjudgmental approach that claims to "value" or even "celebrate" all differences is as unattainable as it is undesirable. Human beings are judgmental creatures. In addition, common sense dictates that some differences are better than others, and that not all differences are good. Many people disbelieve diversity dogmas that demand value neutrality, although the pressures of "political correctness" can make them reluctant to share their misgivings.*

Occasionally, some do anyway. During a discussion of "diversity" theory, one executive remarked: "Celebrate *differences?* Mass murderers are *different!* I don't think we want to celebrate *them!*"

One diversity consultant described the "value-free" approach as follows:

> Human beings simply aren't going to "appreciate, celebrate and value the gamut of cultural differences" in the undiscriminating, judgment-free manner proposed by many diversity trainers—never have, never will. As a society (and like any other society in history), we will continue to make value judgments about what is appropriate or inappropriate, right or wrong, good or bad.
>
> Diversity advocates routinely underscore the folly of their own premises by serving, themselves, as people who judge right and wrong. They are the first to point out that if what you think is not in keeping with what they think, you are wrong and you need to be fixed. (Beekie 1997, 122)

• *A third problem is that, although they claim to concern themselves with a wide variety of differences among various groups, in practice many diversity initiatives tend to have a much more limited scope. Over time, the scope claimed by diversity initiatives has broadened; the reality, however, has not kept pace.In Redefining Diversity (1996), R. Roosevelt Thomas Jr. laments this trend:*

> At one time *diversity* simply meant variety, the existence of multiple versions of the thing in question. In the last decade or so in the business world it has been applied mostly to personnel issues. Despite the protests of a few of us who have always interpreted the word more broadly, it has come to be a shorthand descriptor for a workforce made

up of people from several racial and cultural groups. As business organizations began to develop specific human resources programs under the
label of "affirmative action" or "understanding differences," focused on
employees who were in some way different from the main group, the
meaning subtly shifted. *Diversity* became a more delicate way of saying
"minorities." In some situations, it has narrowed down even further, to
a sort of code word for "African-American"; when certain organizations
and certain individuals say "diversity," they mean "black." (xi)

Diversity initiatives that consider matters other than race may add
only "gender" issues. One diversity professional has said, "Unfortunately,
too many programs are simply focused on 'black/white-man/woman.'"
Paradoxically, initiatives that claim to be about appreciating "all differences" in reality may consider only one or two.

- *The last and most important flaw in traditional diversity initiatives,*
  however, relates to their overall design and implementation strategy.
  Figure 3.3 represents the way most such initiatives are constructed.

As the figure indicates, traditional diversity programs tend to be constructed on the weakest possible base. They concern themselves first and
foremost with issues most likely to arouse contention—namely race and
gender—and they postpone attending to, or never address, other related
but much less divisive subjects—such as disability and age. The problem
with such a design is that, while it may direct attention quickly to problematic topics, it does so in a way that lays a very shaky foundation for further
progress.

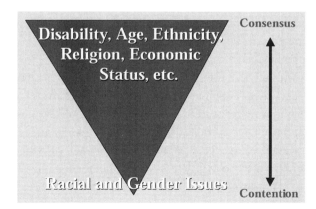

Fig. 3.3. A traditional
diversity model

Such an approach may be politically expedient, but it makes no sense pedagogically. In virtually all other areas of learning, students proceed from the known to the unknown, and from areas of agreement to areas of uncertainty. For example, history teachers do not critique important past events before students know basic facts and terms. Nor do medical educators teach controversial theories of neurology before students have mastered the anatomy of the brain. First things first. Traditional diversity training reverses this strategy, focusing on the most contentious issues before moving on to ones less so—if those issues are *ever* attended to.

Americans are fully aware of the racial tensions inherent in their society, and of discord in the women's movement, with its plethora of hotly debated issues—from harassment and pay inequity to abortion. A diversity effort that focuses first and foremost on these topics of least agreement—and most do—virtually guarantees that the process will be frustrated by contentiousness and resistance to change. It will not be one that effectively promotes tolerance.

Promoting Inclusion

Legal, political, and social changes are today providing business leaders with new options for corporate development. According to R. Roosevelt Thomas Jr., until very recently "affirmative action has been the chief, often the exclusive, strategy for including and assimilating minorities and women into the corporate world" (1991, 17). During the past decade, however, successful legislative and judicial challenges have overturned affirmative action practices that provide "racial preferences," or quotas, and public support for such practices has declined significantly. The public increasingly believes that affirmative action strategies often represent "reverse discrimination" against unfavored classes on the basis of race, sex, or other criteria—discrimination similar to that which affirmative action strategies were originally designed to counteract. Dissatisfaction with such practices has even spread to the minority groups they were originally intended to benefit. According to Thomas, some members of minority groups "say that affirmative action stigmatizes 'qualified' minorities and women who would have been hired on their own merits, and compromises their credibility and ability to move up the organizational ladder" (1996, 81).

While quota-based affirmative action procedures seem increasingly *passé,* and diversity proponents downplay the importance of quotas and group preferences, efforts to promote the same goals using other strategies continue. The movement away from affirmative action, while very threatening to traditional diversity programs, presents new opportunities to businesses not just interested in avoiding litigation, but truly committed to fostering a corporate culture that values the contributions of all members of its work force.

In response to this opportunity, some corporations, educational institutions, and not-for-profit organizations have begun to reformulate their approach. In so doing, some have begun using an approach that treats disability not as an afterthought, but as a centerpiece of their diversity initiatives. That practice has become known as *inclusion.*

Inclusion is an outgrowth of educational theory, which first used the term to refer to the integration of children with disabilities into regular classrooms. The expansion of the concept of inclusion to encompass larger social concerns has been promoted primarily by a handful of nonprofit organizations, especially the Inclusion Network of Cincinnati, and it is receiving increased acceptance in the business world. Companies that have begun to consider inclusion as an important corporate goal include Broadwing, Federated Department Stores, and The Limited, Inc.

In order to understand how promoting inclusion differs from traditional diversity initiatives it is necessary to define the term:

Inclusion is the valued participation of all people with disabilities in every aspect of community life.[5]

Each of the components of this definition is important.

1. The term "valued" means that people participate because others think their involvement has importance. There are many other reasons to include people—tradition, legal compliance, or fear that you will be embarrassed if you do not. But inclusion mandates an appreciation for others that is genuine. People are to be appreciated for the good they can bring to others.

2. "Participation" means active involvement, not just physical presence (the "illusion of inclusion"). The danger of evaluating the quality of an environment by means of a census is that tokenism—mere physical presence—will be equated with true progress.

   Inclusion demands that people be involved as much as they want to and can be. Participation also requires that activities be truly accessible, and that unnecessary barriers to involvement be removed. For example, a business that claims to welcome all people, but is located in a physically inaccessible facility, is not practicing inclusion.

Active involvement is of great importance to those with disabilities because, according to a recent survey conducted by the National Organization on Disability, there are "persistent gaps in levels of participation between people with disabilities and other Americans in employment, income, education, socializing, religious and political participation, and access to healthcare and transportation."[6]

3. The phrase "all people with disabilities" indicates that the process of inclusion begins with those who have physical, mental, or emotional impairments, without regard to the severity of those impairments. In contrast to various approaches to diversity that claim to be about "all differences" but in actuality are much more circumscribed than that, inclusion-based initiatives are intentionally limited, at least initially, to issues related to disabilities.

4. Finally, the stipulation that participation must be in "every aspect of community life" requires that any community activity should be equally accessible to those with disabilities. This includes education, business, religious worship, recreational activities, clubs—any valued activity available in the community.[7] This part of the definition eschews separate, segregated activities that are sometimes presented to people with disabilities as alternatives, equivalent to those commonly available to others. The philosophy of inclusion, like the U.S. Supreme Court decision *Brown v. Board of Education,* is that "'separate but equal' is inherently unequal."

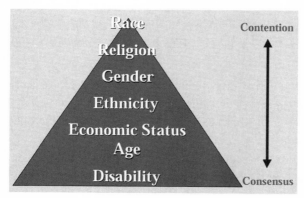

Fig. 3.4. The inclusion model

Figure 3.4 symbolically portrays the concept of inclusion building. As the figure indicates, inclusion-based programs attempt to build upon human strengths —the things we are most likely to have in common—proceeding to progressively more challenging issues. Since anyone can become disabled at any time, this issue is the first to receive attention. The order in which secondary issues should be addressed is, of course, variable. For example, ethnic tensions might be inflamed in a particular society, but of no great consequence in another. If so, treatment of such issues might be delayed until less contentious matters are covered. But the presumption is that the starting point should be the subject most likely to promote consensus—the subject of disability.

The tapering of the pyramid as it ascends implies the increasing difficulty of achieving consensus as more challenging issues are faced. With this model, however, as more difficult topics are addressed, participants can build upon a basis of previously acquired knowledge and skills.

Advantages of the Inclusion Approach

What are the advantages of promoting inclusion rather than diversity? Consider the inclusion model represented in figure 3.5.

Inclusion is based on an educational model. By definition, education is a developmental process, building upon capabilities and moving from the known to the unknown in order to gain knowledge and skill.

The process of inclusion-related learning is similar to other disciplines, and is based on educational theory. Inclusion begins with a focus on people with disabilities not just because the agenda is to promote the interests of those with disabilities (which it is) but also because a focus on disabilities is the logical starting point for learning.

Although people on average are unlikely to have much personal knowledge

Fig. 3.5. The inclusion model

THE INCLUSION MODEL	
Rationale	Education
Process	Skill Building
Unit	Individual
Focus	Similarities
Emphasis	Strengths
Outcome	Valued Participation

of other minorities, they are very likely to have some personal knowledge of disability. People with disabilities are the largest minority group in any population. To reiterate, almost 29 percent of American households include at least one person who has a disability, and at least half of the people in the world have a personal connection to someone who is disabled. "The disabled" are the minority group to which most of our grandparents have belonged.

There is another advantage of an educational model—it's not a political one. The traditional diversity model is a political construct, dictated by the *realpolitik* demands of society. As a political entity, its effectiveness can wax or wane according to the political trends of the times. For example, as popular sentiment increasingly rejects traditional affirmative action initiatives because they represent "racial preferences," diversity programs experience mounting pressure to reject such measures.

Inclusion initiatives are not as easily subject to the influence of political correctness and societal pressure. They must pass rational scrutiny, not tests of popularity.

Inclusion involves building skills. Promoting the valued participation of disabled people is not just an esoteric concept; it invariably involves very practical challenges such as providing accessibility modifications and job accommodations. Inclusion participants can devote their attention to such concrete issues while building their capacity to understand and address more complex concerns. Inclusion participants can be confident that they are expanding their capabilities, not just emoting or "spinning their wheels."

While some inclusion-related skills, such as rejecting stereotypes and appreciating the value of others, are less concrete, they need not be the initial focus of attention. Inclusion involves immediate, practical issues that can be addressed until it is appropriate to work on more complex skills. For example, inclusion participants can begin immediately to analyze the practical needs of an employee who requires an accommodation, rather than simply discussing their feelings about people with disabilities.

Inclusion is concerned with individuals. The inclusion model considers the uniqueness of each individual. There is no attempt to lump people together into groups or categories such as "schizophrenic" or "amputee"; in fact, such categorization is antithetical to inclusion. Whether the issue is capabilities, accommodations needed, or any other concern, attention is always focused on the person rather than the group. This is the opposite of traditional approaches that promote, and sometimes even require, group categorizations.

The inclusion approach benefits from the historical experience of disabled people who have often endured being "labeled" and otherwise put into categories without their approval. Their resistance to a "group mentality" promotes a focus on the individual.

An additional factor has been particularly beneficial. The Americans with Disabilities Act requires that, among many other things, employers provide "reasonable accommodations" to qualified workers with disabilities *as determined on a case-by-case basis.* The mandate to look at the needs and capabilities of each individual worker with a disability, while it might at first have appeared burdensome, was really a blessing in disguise. Because of the accommodation provisions of the law, businesses are increasingly inclined to look at disability issues as individual matters, rather than group concerns.

Inclusion stresses similarities. Instead of focusing on what makes people seem to be different, much less celebrating those differences, inclusion concerns itself with what people have in common. We all have strengths and weaknesses, we all have abilities to contribute to the community, we all need the help of others from time to time. A fundamental precept of inclusion is that the better we understand the things we have in common, the more willing we will be to tolerate our differences.

Inclusion does not attempt to demonize anyone or to impute blame for what is wrong with the world. Imperfection is the most obvious characteristic that all people have in common, and a reality with which disabled people are quite familiar. Inclusion encourages everyone to accept that fact and move on.

Inclusion stresses strengths. Although inclusion can also be promoted by eliminating misunderstandings related to disabilities (for example, the disability myths and stereotypes discussed in chapter 4), the dominant emphasis is not on "What have we done!" or "How guilty we should feel!" Because it is based on an educational model, inclusion moves developmentally from the question "What can we do now?" to "What can we do next?" This positive emphasis can help make learning less threatening and more pleasurable.

Inclusion stresses values. Inclusion initiatives are overtly value-based without being excessively dogmatic. People are to be included not because they are

CONTRASTING MODELS		
	DIVERSITY	**INCLUSION**
Rationale	Problem Prevention	Education
Process	Social Engineering	Skill Building
Unit	Group	Individual
Focus	Differences	Similarities
Emphasis	Weaknesses	Strengths
Outcome	Enhanced Economic Status	Valued Participation

Fig. 3.6. Contrasting models of diversity and inclusion

"different," but because of their value to the community. Inclusion demands that practitioners expand their appreciation of the gifts that others can bring, but it requires no sweeping presumption of excellence in all regards, nor does it require that participants pretend to be "value-free."

Inclusion builds upon personal self-interest. People tend to be interested in what affects them. Most people understand that they could become disabled at any time, and many appreciate the fact that they are likely to experience a disability at some point in their lives, especially as they grow older. Inclusion can, therefore, engage people's attention for practical reasons, and before they have any moral or spiritual commitment to the issue.

The philosophy of inclusion maintains that people of all racial, ethnic, and economic groups can discuss issues such as "How would you handle getting to work if you broke your leg?" more profitably than "How would you feel if you were a Native American?" Participants understand that promoting inclusion can benefit them personally.

While rooted in self-interest, inclusion programs are not selfish; in fact, they can promote real community-building skills. During inclusion training, developing inclusion solutions typically involves individuals from many backgrounds—young and old, black and white, male and female, top management and lower-level staff—challenging them to work together on issues they have in common. The process of working together on inclusion can lay the foundation for better cooperation when addressing other concerns.

Choosing Inclusion over Diversity

In the latter half of the twentieth century, societal trends, antidiscrimination legislation, and litigation led to calls for affirmative action and employment diversity. Over time, traditional diversity programs have become known for their uneven quality, unproven effectiveness, and occasional counterproductivity. Many businesses leaders have resented being forced to participate in programs they regard as being of questionable value. Some have regarded diversity itself as an unpleasant issue.

The terrorist attacks of September 11, 2001, may have changed all that. Following the harrowing events of that day, many Americans concluded that their country had been victimized by those who epitomized intolerance and that Americans had been targeted because they lived in a free society. While knowing that they were far from perfect, Americans had long felt a sense of pride in their country as a "melting pot" of races, religions, ethnicities, and groups of all sorts. The events of 9/11 deepened the nation's appreciation of its cultural richness. There is nothing like sharing an experience of being targeted to bring a group together; there is nothing like a burglary to make you appreciate what you have. If any Americans had ever taken their country's strengths for granted, they would be loath do so again.

The terrorist attacks of 9/11 may have provided the United States with a unique opportunity to rededicate itself to promoting tolerance. Today, businesses may be much more inclined to promote tolerance out of a sense of national pride, rather than as a simple obligation. A strategy based on inclusion can be of particular value in pursuing this goal. It is more reasonable, educationally sound, and much more likely to provide lasting benefits.

Businesses that learn to include workers and customers with special needs, looking at the capabilities and needs of each individual, will begin to promote basic capacities of understanding, tolerance, and appreciation that can potentially benefit everyone. Skills developed in advancing the inclusion of people with disabilities are transferable to other issues as well, to the eventual benefit of business, employees, and society in general. While traditional diversity training is a tired concept, promoting tolerance may well be an idea experiencing a renaissance.

Resources

The American Institute for Managing Diversity
http://www.aimd.org/
50 Hurt Plaza, Suite 1150
Atlanta, Ga. 30303
(404) 302-9226 Voice

The Inclusion Network
http://www.inclusion.org/
312 Walnut Street, Suite 3600
Cincinnati, Ohio 45202
(513) 345-1330 Voice
(513) 345-1336 TTY
include@one.net

Society for Human Resource Management
http://www.shrm.org/
1800 Duke St.
Alexandria, Va. 22314
(703) 548-3440 Voice
(703) 535-6490 Fax
shrm@shrm.org

4

Disability Stereotypes
and Myths

What we don't know *can* certainly hurt us; but what we *think* we know that happens to be untrue can be equally damaging. Few people are ever adequately prepared for the reality of a disability, but all of us, whether we realize it or not, receive a great deal of education in the subject. Much of that education is erroneous.

Some people learn about disability in a direct, personal way—with the birth of a disabled child, the experience of an accident, or the gradual progress of debilitation or disease. Coping with a disability can shock us and change us to the very core; few things in life can compare. Some people confronting disability are devastated and may never adjust to their loss; others consider disability to be one of life's challenges that they meet and deal with.

If disability does not have a direct impact on us, it is sure to influence us indirectly at many times during our lives—through our families, our schools, our neighborhoods, and our jobs. Such a large portion of the population has a disability that virtually everyone comes into contact with disabled people throughout life.

Like all other experiences, our perception of disability is shaped by all of the information, both true and false, that we acquire. If we have received accurate information about what disabilities are and aren't, we may be able to address disability matters as they arise. But all too often, our misinformation and misunderstanding can make situations much worse than they need to be.

In business, the information about disability that each of us takes into the workplace can have profound influences on virtually anyone involved in the business—executives, supervisors, disabled and nondisabled workers, job applicants, marketers, and customers. Eliminating misunderstanding and providing accurate information about disabilities can benefit any business, allowing it to take maximum advantage of the work force and appeal to the widest possible customer base. Failing to do so can mean lost opportunities, at best; at worst, it can mean a host of serious problems.

This chapter is about all the misinformation that our culture conveys about disabled people, how it can hurt businesses, and how to substitute knowledge and understanding for the stereotypes and myths about disability. Businesses need to know this information. It is critical to at least 20 percent of their potential employees and customers.

Sources of Misinformation

From our earliest days, perhaps long before we meet a person with an impairment, our culture communicates a great deal of information to us about disabilities. Only a very small portion of the information we receive is both accurate and helpful. Messages about disability may be so subtle or pervasive that we are unaware of their influence on us.

Consider the following ways in which we receive inaccurate information about disabilities:

Children's Literature

Disability stereotypes appear frequently in works of children's literature. Misbehaving characters often incur a disability as punishment for their immorality. Captain Hook's amputation is a well-known example (Shapiro 1993, 31). Witches are commonly described as having physical deformities; they are almost never physically appealing. Even in classic works, such as *Hansel and Gretel* as told by the Brothers Grimm and Robert Louis Stevenson's *Treasure Island,* a physical disability is often used as a metaphor for moral corruption.

In other stories, disabilities may represent to children imperfections to be avoided. Thus "Simple Simon" (fig. 4.1) is depicted as naive, unintelligent, or both as he attempts to purchase a pie although he has no money. Whatever else

Fig. 4.1. A drawing of "Simple Simon" by G. J. Pinwell (1870)

they may learn, children hearing this story are taught to laugh at the ridiculous behavior of the "simple"—those who are mentally deficient.

Children's jokes can also be profoundly damaging. For example:

Question: Why did the Little Moron throw a clock out of a window?
Answer: He wanted to see time *fly!*

Parents who wonder how children "can be so cruel" to disabled people can often find an answer in some of the jokes and stories they have shared with their own children.[1]

Adult Literature

Literature for adults is frequently concerned with disabilities. So common is the treatment of the issue that it is difficult to think of a classic work that does *not* involve a disability of some sort.

Homer's *Odyssey* graphically describes the grotesque physical deformity of the fearsome Cyclops. (Paradoxically, Homer was blind.) Shakespeare peopled his plays with countless disabled characters, including court "fools" who, according to scholars, were people with mental illness or mental retardation. The Bard endowed Richard III with a hunchback to symbolize his wickedness, although the real Richard III had no such characteristic. In *Don Quixote,* the world's first novel, Cervantes relates the adventures of a delusional knight errant whose bizarre behavior he intended to be both instructive and entertaining.

Some of American literature's greatest works also deal with disabilities. In Herman Melville's *Moby Dick,* an injured and obsessed Captain Ahab pursues the great white whale. In William Faulkner's *The Sound and the Fury,* a mentally deficient young man, Benjy Compson, serves as both a prime character in, and a co-narrator of, the novel. In John Steinbeck's *Of Mice and Men,* the character

Lenny is portrayed as both mentally deficient and dangerous. Tennessee Williams's best-known plays, *A Streetcar Named Desire* and *The Glass Menagerie,* deal with both mental and physical illness.[2]

Only recently has it become common for works of literature to portray those with disabilities in a favorable light. Examples include John Irving's novel *A Prayer for Owen Meany* and the murder mysteries of best-selling author Jeffrey Deaver.[3] Some of the best portrayals of characters with disabilities have come from authors who are themselves disabled, including novelists Christopher Nolan and Christy Brown.

Movies and Television

In the early days of both cinema and television, the images of those with disabilities paralleled those of adult literature, and they usually conveyed negative or ambiguous messages about disabled people. In *The Hunchback of Notre Dame,* Lon Chaney was terribly disfigured but also cruelly treated. The heroic title character in *The Lone Ranger* incurred a facial disfigurement due to his crime fighting, and thereafter wore a mask both to hide the scar and to conceal his identity.

The Second World War, which brought about so many changes for people with disabilities, also changed how visual media portrayed them. The Academy Award–winning *The Best Years of Our Lives* realistically portrayed the struggle experienced by a disabled veteran returning home; moreover, for the first time Hollywood actually employed an actor with a visible disability—Harold Russell, who had lost both of his hands in the war (Agee 1995).

In recent years television has joined the movies in offering many positive depictions of disabled characters, from Raymond Burr as a detective who uses a wheelchair in *Ironsides,* to Chris Burke, a young man with Down syndrome who was a regularly featured character in the series *Life Goes On.* On public television, *Mr. Roger's Neighborhood* and *Sesame Street* were among the first programs to offer children positive images of their disabled peers.

Despite some progress, negative depictions in visual media are still common. In the 2000 hit film *Unbreakable* starring Bruce Willis, the villain is a character deeply embittered by his *osteogenesis imperfecta,* also known as "brittle bone disease." At the end of the film he is said to be "in an institution for the criminally insane."

Little people continue to receive poor representation in the visual media, invariably being assigned only comedic or trivial parts, such as elves, fairies, or leprechauns. The late Billy Barty, one of Hollywood's best-known actors of short stature, was offered almost exclusively comic roles during his career lasting more than seventy years.

Parts given to people of short stature are a good example of the media's tendency to employ actors having, or assuming, disabilities only when the subject is disability itself. Very rarely will an actor with a disability be portrayed "incidentally," in situations involving a subject other than his or her condition.

Religious Teachings and Practice

Leviticus **13:45–46:**
The one who bears the sore of leprosy shall keep his garments rent and his head bare, and shall muffle his beard; he shall cry out, "Unclean! Unclean!" As long as the sore is on him he shall declare himself unclean, since he is in fact unclean. He shall dwell apart, making his abode outside the camp.

Martin Luther, *Colloquia Mensalia:*
Eight years ago, there was one at Dessau whom I, Martinus Luther, saw and grappled with. He was twelve years old, had the use of his eyes and all his senses, so that one might think that he was a normal child. But he did nothing but gorge himself as much as four peasants or threshers. He ate, defecated and drooled and, if anyone tackled him, he screamed. If things didn't go well, he wept. So I said to the Prince of Anhault: "If I were the Prince, I should take this child to the Moldau River which flows near Dessau and drown him." But the Prince of Anhault and the Prince of Saxony, who happened to be present, refused to follow my advice. Thereupon I said: "Well, then the Christians shall order the Lord's Prayer to be said in church and pray that the dear Lord take the Devil away." This was done daily in Dessau and the changeling died in the following year.

Disability is a subject dealt with by all the world's major religions. Their interpretations vary greatly, and can change significantly over time.

Like other ancient civilizations, the Jewish people struggled to understand the origin and nature of various impairments, and how to treat those who had them. The book of Leviticus describes various conditions and diseases, and prescribes how the Jewish people and their religious leaders were to deal with them.

The New Testament depicts numerous interactions between Jesus Christ and those with various types of disabilities. Although in the "healing narratives" Jesus cures many of their impairments, he constantly emphasizes that their spiritual status is much more important than their physical condition (Wilke 1999, 54). The Christian gospels also tell the story of a paralyzed man who, unable to get near Jesus because of the crowds around him, had himself lowered through a hole in the roof into the house where the Messiah was residing—one of the first recorded examples of disability activism (Mark 2:1–5).

Islam teaches that "It is no fault in the blind nor in one born lame, nor in yourselves" (Qur'an 24:61). Buddhists are taught that the Buddha ministered to the sick and disabled (Mahavagga VIII.26.1–8). While Hinduism teaches tolerance and compassion, some practitioners view disabilities as punishments from the gods and goddesses for transgressions in this world or in past lives (Schubert 1998). In all religions, there is often a great disparity between the dictates of sacred scripture and the practice of the faithful.

Public Policies, Professional Standards, and Procedures

In addition to the informal ways that cultures convey their valuing, or devaluation, of those with disabilities, societies also overtly convey their standards through laws and established procedures. The ancient civilizations of Greece and Rome viewed those with severe disabilities as intolerable economic burdens on the rest of society, and so sanctioned abandoning or outright killing them. At the opposite extreme, other cultures, such as some Native American tribes, have considered some people with disabilities to be divinely blessed or gifted, and have treated them accordingly.

Public policies can change significantly over time. After seeing atrocities against the Jews in German concentration camps, returning GIs viewed anew conditions in their country's institutions for those with mental illness and mental retardation, and were instrumental in creating a national crusade for institu-

Fig. 4.2. The Public Hospital, Williamsburg, 1773. America's first institution for those with mental retardation and mental illness predated the Declaration of Independence. *(Courtesy of the Colonial Williamsburg Foundation)*

tional reform. That movement led eventually to further changes in governmental policy, such as the Education for All Handicapped Children Act in 1974, and the Americans with Disabilities Act in 1990.

Many other cultural authorities contribute to determining cultural values. Medical professionals have a great influence on public attitudes toward disabled people. Their approach to issues such as appropriate treatment regimens, resource allocation, and quarantine both reflect societal values and help shape them. Likewise, educators exert a major influence. For decades, children with severe disabilities were routinely excluded from public education, and little professional attention was devoted to them—all with the sanction and participation of teaching professionals. All of that changed when more ambitious professionals challenged and eventually disproved previous dogma about "uneducatable students." The late Dr. Gunnar Dybwad, in a personal communication, summarized that educational revolution as follows: "For years we thought it was they who could not learn; now we know it was we who could not teach."

Major Stereotypes

A stereotype is a commonly held, oversimplified, and generally misleading image. There are many disability stereotypes.[4] Below, we consider some of the most common, along with examples of how they sometimes influence the world of business.

The Sick

Example: An interviewer in the human resources department passes over a qualified job candidate who has spina bifida, partly because of a sense of uneasiness, and partly because of a vague fear that the condition might be contagious.

Disabled people are frequently treated as if they are unwell, even when they enjoy perfect health. Like everyone else, those with disabilities may be ill, but the assumption that they are sick or diseased simply because they have a disability is a common misconception.

The "sick" stereotype is often evidenced in the way services are provided to disabled people. For example, in educational and rehabilitation programs, medical personnel often occupy leadership positions. Many residential services for people with developmental disabilities—including group homes and supervised apartments—are controlled and paid for by the federal Medicaid program, and many of their operating regulations are virtually the same as those for nursing homes. Healthy residents who work full-time in competitive employment often find themselves being referred to as "patients" when at home. Even when they are enjoying themselves, disabled people can be treated as if they are sick: when they go swimming it's called "aquatic therapy"; when they go for a hike it's referred to as "mobility training."

In business, the "sickness" stereotype can cause disabled people to be overprotected, segregated, or avoided completely. Out of fear of "sick" people, a supervisor might demand safety precautions that go far beyond real needs—for example, stocking an emergency oxygen supply because someone once had a mild epileptic seizure, or insisting that an employee who has a mobility impairment not venture into a busy part of a manufacturing facility. More commonly, this stereotype is expressed simply as a shunning of an individual because of a feeling of awkwardness. Unfortunately, shunning can include not hiring.

Many of those with HIV, the virus that causes AIDS, have reported such discriminatory treatment, from being denied job interviews, to being avoided by co-workers, and even being fired.

Regrettably, healthy disabled individuals are not immune from accepting this stereotype, and may occasionally demand unwarranted treatment because they wrongly consider themselves to be ill, or enjoy the special attention they can receive by feigning illness.

The Subhuman

Example: A person who uses a wheelchair applies for a data management position. That individual is highly trained, technically qualified, even highly experienced. But the interviewer or decision maker is convinced that a person with a disability couldn't possibly do the job, and the applicant is quickly rejected.

No stereotype of people with disabilities has been more outrageous or harmful than the subhuman. From the Spartan city-state, where "defective" infants were destroyed or allowed to starve, to Nazi pogroms that targeted those with physical and mental defects, and contemporary assaults disguised as "humane" medical practices, people with disabilities have often, overtly or covertly, been treated as less than human beings.

Remedying the effects of this stereotype has long been a concern of dis-

Fig. 4.3. German disabled citizens were the first victims of the Third Reich. *(Photo courtesy of the United States Holocaust Memorial Museum)*

ability activists. One of the main reasons for the reform of residential institutions for those with mental retardation during the 1950s and 1960s was the conclusion that the residents were being treated "like animals"—they were warehoused in filthy conditions, fed slop, and hosed down, among other indignities. Yet dehumanizing treatment still occurs. Although many state institutions have been closed or downsized, instances of neglect and abuse still occur frequently. Some community residences—group homes, foster services, and apartments—are no better than the institutional services they replaced.

Today, the subhuman stereotype is most evident in the terminology used to describe people with disabilities. Those with severe impairments are sometimes referred to as "vegetables," "rocks," or "animals," even by those who have received professional training. Medical personnel commonly refer to comatose patients as being in a "persistent vegetative state." Some well-known ethicists (e.g., Fletcher 1972) have suggested seriously that at some point along the continuum of capability those with serious impairments should not be considered human beings at all.

Such outrages represent extreme examples. More often, believers in this stereotype do not blatantly deny the humanity of disabled people. Instead, they treat them in a way that expresses a subtler, unconscious denial of their humanity. They might not injure or even insult people who have a disability, but they treat them as if they are immune to pain, cannot think, do not feel embarrassment—all indications that the other is not seen as a fellow human being.

In business, employees or customers with disabilities may react strongly to indications that they are receiving substandard treatment. They realize the assumptions that such treatment represents.

The Pitiful

> **Example:** An advertising agency is asked by a client to come up with a thirty-second television commercial that highlights the client's support of community nonprofit organizations. The agency presents a concept that features a famous football player as the company spokesperson. The proposed ad would feature the football player with his arm around a nine-year-old boy who walks with crutches because of juvenile arthritis.

The "pity" stereotype associated with disabled people is one of the most widespread. This stereotype firmly establishes the pitied individual in a lower, clearly undesirable position, in contrast with the superior status of the perceiver. The perceiver thinks: "What a horrible thing is happening to him or her (and not to *me*)." The "pity" perspective depends on condescension, and may also involve fear, guilt, and relief. It always produces distanciation—creating psychological distance between "them" and "us." Since distance is precisely what people often want to put between themselves and disability, pity has an immense popular appeal.

Conversely, if the condition of another is viewed in connection with oneself, the effect produced is not sympathy but *empathy*—literally *feeling with*. Empathy involves a consideration of the suffering of another in a way that reduces the psychological distance between the perceiver and the perceived. It may lead to better understanding, remediation, and even association.

Nonprofit organizations have long known that one of the most efficient methods of raising funds is to appeal to the public's sense of pity for those with disabilities. From this stereotype have come such concepts as the "charity drive" and "poster child." The efforts of actor/comedian Jerry Lewis on behalf of individuals with muscular dystrophy are the best-known example.

In the workplace, pity is often reflected in diminished expectations, exclusion, and other forms of condescension. Those with disabilities tend to be very sensitive to such treatment. Recently, disability advocates have rebelled at the image of themselves as deserving the pity of the rest of society. They reject the idea that they are "victims," "afflicted," or "unfortunate," or any assumption that their disability is a disaster and the most important thing about them. Instead, they demand recognition of their rights and capabilities. The pity model remains a commonly encountered stereotype, however, largely because of its psychological appeal and demonstrated effectiveness in fundraising.

The Ridiculous

Example: A supervisor in a candy manufacturing plant has slurred speech due to her cerebral palsy. Some of her employees mock her speech patterns behind her back.

Most people have experienced the intolerance of children, such as those who taunt a peer who happens to be disabled or disfigured. Perhaps we ourselves have been a victim or perpetrator of such treatment. We have all heard adults bemoan the insensitivity that allows children to commit such acts. How, they ask, could children be so cruel?

Adults can be equally cruel. Although the general expectation is that adults should acquire greater tolerance and understanding as they age, this is not always the case. Individuals with disabilities know only too well that they are often held up to ridicule by adults who ought to know better. Some well-known examples:

- The 1998 20th Century Fox hit movie *There's Something about Mary* contains several running "jokes" about those with disabilities, including a figure referred to as a "retard," and a wheelchair user referred to as "roller-pig."
- On a November 16, 2000, broadcast, comedian Bill Maher, host of ABC's "Politically Incorrect," said that a key to a George W. Bush victory was "the retard vote." On January 11, 2001, Maher commented on children with mental retardation: "They're sweet. They're kind. But they don't mentally advance at all." Maher later apologized for his remarks.[5]

• A television ad for a dental insurance company opened with the line: "I suppose you think I'm a moron . . ."

In the workplace, ridiculing of disabled people can take the form of outright taunting, joking, teasing, or similar forms of abuse. Disabled people are one of very few minorities still routinely held up for ridicule in American society, and the popular acceptance of this practice makes it an especially pernicious problem.

The Inspiration

> **Example:** A company newsletter runs a profile of a relatively new employee who is blind. The author calls particular attention to the fact that the employee can travel to work independently, and even found his way to the company cafeteria his very first day on the job! The article concludes: "Juan's courage and determination set a fine example for all of our employees."

One of the most interesting aspects of stereotypes is that they can coexist with their seeming opposites. And so, after noting that some people view those with disabilities with extremely negative biases, we must recognize that others prefer to see them as an "inspiration," to be held up for high praise. The "inspiration" stereotype often involves the exaggeration of ordinary accomplishments, and a preoccupation with the few people with disabilities who "triumph over adversity" to make noteworthy accomplishments.

Some disabled people refer to this stereotype as the "supercrip." The "inspiration" or "supercrip" stereotype is a favorite of the media, the source of endless stories of "triumph over disability"—"Blind Athlete Swims English Channel" and "Paraplegic Gets Her College Degree."

Some people with disabilities have pointed out that one of their most difficult challenges is to be seen as simply *ordinary*—not a hero, not a loser— just someone more like others than unlike them. Journalist Gary Presley, who has paraplegia, tells of his experience with this stereotype:

> "You're such an inspiration. Always smiling," says a woman I see regularly in church. I don't want that burden. I want to be a jerk once in a while. I'm just an average guy with his fanny planted in a wheelchair whose one minor talent is to string words together. (2000)

While it is certainly appropriate to recognize the strength and determination that people with disabilities can demonstrate—just like anyone else—it

Fig. 4.4. Anne Sullivan and Helen Keller playing chess. *(From the website of the American Federation of the Blind)*

must also be recognized that greeting their accomplishments with excessive or unwarranted acclaim is only one more way of making them seem different.

The Perpetual Child

Example: Co-workers speak condescendingly to a clerical worker who has moderate cerebral palsy. Some conversations sound like "baby talk." One employee says: "He's so cute—we all just love him to death." The disabled employee relishes the attention, and often behaves immaturely.

People with disabilities—especially those who have significant impairments—often find themselves being treated as though they were children, sometimes even by people younger than they are. The "perpetual child" stereotype may result from the fact that some disabilities involve the loss of certain skills generally associated with adulthood—like walking, speaking, or driving. Some people infer from a particular diminished ability in others that they are totally immature and incompetent. Such people talk to disabled adults as if they are children, and may ignore their sexuality, opinions, and skills.

Most disabled adults can provide endless examples of such treatment from personal experience. Many instances involve simple one-on-one interactions characterized by condescension. Other examples are more systemic. When groups of adults with disabilities gather for activities organized by typical adults, it is not unusual—in fact it seems like standard procedure—for them to be offered childish provisions and treatment. For example, a picnic organized for adults with disabilities might feature childish refreshments, juvenile games, and clowns in costume.

Fig. 4.5. Drawing by Milton Coniff ©Goodwill Industries International.

Because the "perpetual child" stereotype thrives in segregated environments, many disabled adults avoid any and all situations where those with disabilities are congregated. It's not at all that they are ashamed of their status; they just know from experience that in such situations they are likely to be treated in inappropriate and childish ways.

In response to the "perpetual child" stereotype, many adults with disabilities have become active in the disability self-advocacy movement—unwilling to allow important decisions concerning them to be made by well-meaning others who do not treat them as equals. One of the slogans of this movement is "Nothing about me without me"—an assertion of maturity, competence, and control.

The Menace

> **Example:** An employee of a defense contractor informs his supervisor that he is receiving mental health counseling for depression. The supervisor immediately recommends to the department head that the employee be transferred to a "less sensitive position."

The stereotype of those with disabilities as a threat to others is one of the oldest and most destructive. As mentioned earlier, in ancient civilizations, those with disabilities were often ostracized or killed outright in order to "protect" others. In medieval times, disabilities were thought to be contagious, and those who had them were forced to live apart from others.

The United States has a sad history with this stereotype. At the beginning of the twentieth century, the eugenics movement blamed a host of social ills on people with disabilities and called for an end to the "spread" of such conditions. In 1907 Indiana passed a compulsory sterilization law for institutionalized individuals with mental retardation and mental illness. It was the first such law that the world had ever known, and the model for a similar policy adopted by Nazi Germany (Leaming 1977). In the United States, a total of twenty-nine other states followed Indiana's example, and many such laws were not repealed for decades (Baskerville 2001).

As in the case of compulsory sterilization, those with mental illness are favorite targets of the "menace" stereotype. Many people find it easy to believe, with the eugenicists, that the problems of the mentally ill are the source of much, if not all, of society's ills. Their faulty reasoning goes something like this: most social problems originate in the "criminal class"; those who commit crimes

THE FEEBLE-MINDED

OR THE

HUB TO OUR WHEEL OF VICE, CRIME AND PAUPERISM

Cincinnati's Problem

A STUDY BY THE
JUVENILE PROTECTIVE ASSOCIATION
OF CINCINNATI
February 15th, 1915

Fig. 4.6. Cover of "The Feeble-Minded," a pamphlet distributed by The Juvenile Protective Association of Cincinnati in 1915. *(Courtesy of the Ohio Historical Society)*

must be mentally ill; therefore those who are mentally ill are most likely to commit crimes.

In the workplace, such scapegoating can involve automatic assumptions that employees with disabilities will cause more than their share of problems, or that problems that occur after their arrival are undoubtedly their fault.

The Punished

> **Example:** A human resources manager at a small southern utility company interviews a highly qualified job candidate for a position in the customer service department. The candidate uses a wheelchair, and during his interview mentions that his injury was due to a motorcycle accident. The manager decides not to hire the applicant, and confides to a co-worker: "We don't need him on our health plan. He should have thought of the consequences before he got on that motorcycle."

One of the oldest disability stereotypes, that of disabled people being punished for their sins or transgressions, may be related to the human need to rationalize the existence of suffering, or why "bad things happen" (Kushner 1989). This stereotype finds some support in the Judeo-Christian and other religious traditions. Writers of the Bible, in both the New and Old Testament, often portray the afflicted as being possessed by demons or punished for their transgressions with a physical complaint. For her disobedience of God's order not to look back on the land she must leave, Lot's wife incurs a catatonia-like transformation into salt. For his persecution of early Christians, Paul is struck temporarily blind by God.

It is all too easy to dismiss the idea of "disability as moral retribution" as a primitive anachronism lacking any power in a secular society; but there is ample evidence that its influence continues. Today, stereotypes of people with disabilities being "punished" for their transgressions are usually not encountered in a strictly religious context. Suffering is more likely to be attributed to the violation of sexual mores or secular values such as maintaining a healthy lifestyle.

In the workplace, co-workers may shun an individual who has an accident resulting in injury because she is thought to have been responsible for her own disability. A worker who has a heart attack may be said to have "brought it on himself" because of life habits that are viewed, in retrospect, as unhealthy. While unwise behaviors can indeed lead to serious health consequences, those making such judgments often conveniently overlook their own imperfections.

The Phantom Disability

Example: A supervisor constantly shouts to a data entry worker who has a visual impairment. Finally, the employee jokes, "Hey! I'm *blind,* not deaf!"

The stereotype of people who already have a disability being assumed to have other nonexistent impairments is known as the "phantom disability." This stereotype, also sometimes referred to as "disability creep," causes some to perceive those who have actual disabilities as being much more limited than they really are. To those who have never experienced a disability, this may seem far-fetched, but to the initiated it is an all-too-common phenomenon.

Syndicated columnist Deborah Kendrick (2001) describes having such an experience while traveling:

> I was once left standing in the middle of Chicago's O'Hare Airport, with only minutes to catch the late-night flight, because I refused to get into the wheelchair brought for me. "My disability is vision, not walking," I explained. What I needed was for someone to show me the route to my gate—not a ride. But nothing doing.

An adult who incurs an immobilizing injury that requires her to return to work using a wheelchair may find herself being treated with "kid gloves" as if she is emotionally precarious and likely to fly off the handle at the slightest provocation. Likewise, an employee who is rumored to be receiving counseling for an emotional disturbance may find himself being avoided because his co-workers fear he is psychotic. Legions of those with perceptual disabilities report being treated as if they were mentally deficient, and many deaf adults have had the experience of being offered the use of Braille texts and wheelchairs![6]

The "phantom disability" stereotype is probably the result of a common human tendency to view limitations out of all proportion to their real significance.

Business Myths about Disability

Disability "myths" are the ideas, attitudes, standards, practices, and habits born of misinformation, thoughtlessness, and prejudice that are often applied to those with physical or mental limitations. Just as educators, physicians, lawmakers, and writers tend to have such myths, businesspeople have their own.

There is no end to the number of disability myths, the instances of misinformation and prejudice that one can encounter in the business world. Some of the most common are the following:

The Myth of Nonexistence

Example: A line supervisor develops an antagonistic relationship with an excellent employee who has diabetes. The supervisor has no idea that people with diabetes may require more frequent breaks—for rest or medication—than a typical employee, and the employee is too resentful to discuss his or her needs.

Businesses often operate as if people with disabilities didn't exist. Corporate leaders have long tended to ignore the disability market despite its size, and because they did not understand how they could harness the talents of those with disabilities, they have not included them as employees. It wasn't until the end of the Second World War that a significant number of people with disabilities began entering the work force. Similarly, it is only recently that businesses have begun to portray those with disabilities as consumers of their products and services.

This myth is one of simple oversight, ignorance, and thoughtlessness. It can be influential systemically, if the capabilities of disabled employees and the economic impact of disabled consumers are overlooked, or at the individual level, if the needs of employees with impairments are ignored.

When the Americans with Disabilities Act entitled qualified employees to request "reasonable accommodations" in the workplace, many employers were surprised to learn how many employees with special needs were already working for them, and doubly pleased when they learned that providing such accommodations, often inexpensively, opened up a large and relatively untapped labor supply. That experience, combined with the growing market impact of people with disabilities, is today contradicting the myth of nonexistence.

The Myth of Increased Costs

Example: A systems analyst who uses a walker applies for a supervisory position with a major financial institution. Her interviewer confides to a co-worker that "her medical problems would probably cost us a fortune," and dismisses her as a viable candidate.

The analyst is actually in excellent health, has taken no sick days in three years, and is one of the most reliable employees in the department where she currently works.

One of the most common negative assumptions made in the business world about people with disabilities is that employing them will be costly. In particular, businesses tend to fear they will be saddled by increased health and disability insurance costs.

The facts do not support this theory. In study after study, conducted not only by governmental entities such as the Bureau of Labor Statistics but also major businesses such as the Bendix Corporation and E. I. DuPont de Nemours and Company, the data indicate that employing workers with disabilities creates no special insurance burdens for employers, and has no overall negative impact on compensation costs.[7]

In fact, some companies have reported outstanding cost *savings* as a result of hiring disabled workers. When Pizza Hut, Inc., initiated its "Job Plus™" program targeted at workers with developmental disabilities, it found that the turnover rate among this group was only 20 percent compared to 150 percent among employees who did not have disabilities. Carolina Fine Snacks started hiring employees with disabilities in 1988 and found that overall absenteeism fell from 20 percent to less than 5 percent, and tardiness dropped from 30 percent to 0, all of which resulted in significant cost reductions (Digh 1998).

One of the difficulties in dispelling this myth is that, to a certain extent, it is intuitively appealing. We all know that *some* people with disabilities have high medical expenses, and that by adding these costs to the experience of an employee medical insurance plan the overall average could be expected to increase. The point of the many studies that address this issue, however, is that such instances are rare, their impact on the overall cost experience of a business tends to be minimal, and they can be offset by other cost savings.

The Myth of Increased Danger

Example: A car dealership routinely rejects applicants for sales positions if those individuals appear to have any physical impairment. The owner fears that such candidates will be unable to operate his vehicles safely during test drives. Several of the rejected candidates have had perfect driving records.

Related to the fear that employing people with disabilities will increase costs is the fear that it will also cause increased danger to those around them, including fellow employees, customers, and the public.

Is someone with a disability more likely to have or cause an accident than others? Although in rare cases an individual who poses a threat to health and safety may find protection under the ADA (discussed in chapter 2), such instances are rare. In general, employees with disabilities tend to have better-than-average safety records.

A survey conducted by the Bureau of Labor Statistics compared the performance of 11,000 workers with disabilities to that of 18,000 nondisabled employees. That survey found that the safety record of workers with disabilities was actually *better* than that of nondisabled workers, and the major injury rate was actually significantly *lower.* These findings have borne up time and again in major studies conducted by the U.S. Chamber of Commerce, the Bendix Corporation, E. I. DuPont de Nemours and Company, and many others (Career Network 2000).

Why is this? Some suggest that employees with disabilities tend to be more careful because of past experience or because of the value they place on health and safety. Others believe that people labeled "disabled" may benefit from the fact that they openly acknowledge their limitations, rather than learning about them "the hard way." In any event, the evidence suggests that any employer wanting to improve the safety record of his or her workplace should actively *recruit* workers with disabilities, not avoid them.

The Myth of Maladjustment

Example: A veteran sales associate at a ladies' wear retailer tells her co-workers that she never likes to wait on customers who use wheelchairs. "They always seem to expect special treatment," she explains.

Because many people find the possibility of being disabled overwhelming and distasteful, they may assume that those who have a disability must always pay an extreme psychological price for their "affliction." This is the origin of the "myth of maladjustment"—a combination of the "phantom disability" and "menace" stereotypes.

In business this myth is often encountered in the assumption that people with any type of disability won't be able to get along with others, that they will have a negative attitude that will infect others, or—worst of all—that they will carry a disability "chip" on their shoulder, expecting special treatment and threatening retaliation if they don't get it. Employers who see a likely future litigant in every disabled employee or job applicant are believers in this myth.

The maladjustment myth is especially harmful when applied to people who have disabilities related to mental health, such as depression and anxiety.

If others assume that all people with a mental health issue are more likely to create problems than other workers, those with that disability can find themselves receiving demeaning "kid glove" treatment, being feared, or getting the blame whenever problems occur.

There is absolutely no evidence to support the myth of maladjustment, and much workplace experience to refute it. First of all, businesses must acknowledge that disabled people are, in reality, all of "us"—20 percent of the population at any one time, and most of us at some point in our lives—an enormous portion of our society. Of course the reality of disability has consequences, and some people have problems adjusting to their limitations. *Some* people have trouble adjusting to fame, athletic success, and wealth, too—*some* but not *all.*

Taken as a group, those with disabilities adjust and continue to function as well as the rest of us. In addition to any problems they might have in adjusting, they may also benefit from valuable experiences in adapting and persevering (as discussed in chapter 6).

The best refutation of this myth is the excellent performance of the thousands of disabled employees who prove their value every day. For this reason, the myth of maladjustment is least likely to be found in environments where people with disabilities are common.

The Myth of Decreased Productivity

For over 35 years, DuPont has studied the performance of employees with disabilities. We have consistently found it to be equivalent to the performance of our other employees. In 1981, we published our findings to share our experience with our employees and other employers. We were proud of our employees' performance then and we are still proud today. The results confirm what we at DuPont believe: people with disabilities are a valuable resource. (E. I. DuPont de Nemours and Company)[8]

Many of the same researchers who have looked at issues of employee cost and workplace safety have also examined the productivity of disabled workers in comparison with others. In virtually all such studies, workers with disabilities were found to have a productivity record at least as good as other employees, and in some cases even better. The Bureau of Labor Statistics concluded that workers with disabilities had a "significantly better performance;" DuPont found that 90 percent of workers with disabilities rated average or better than average in performance, and other studies have given "above average" productivity ratings to as many as 93 percent of workers with disabilities.[9]

Motivation may be the key. Because of the very high rate of unemployment among disabled people, many naturally place a great value on work. Everyone understands that good productivity is one of the keys to continued employment. Faced with the possibility of joining the 67 percent of their peers who are unemployed, most workers with disabilities logically make every effort to be successful in their jobs. In addition, because employment indicates competence in the workplace, workers with disabilities may find particular enjoyment in doing things that make use of their *capabilities.*

In all honesty, this case can be, and occasionally has been, oversold by disability advocates. Good safety and performance records do not mean that workers with disabilities are always "super employees" by virtue of their status. By and large, they tend to be much more like other employees than unlike them. However, the reality of a disability can have positive consequences on how people conduct themselves, benefiting both themselves and their employers.

The Myth of the Tarnished Image

Example: When asked why his advertising campaigns never featured disabled consumers, the marketing director of a major food product manufacturer replied: "One reason is that people might think our products *cause* disabilities!"

The idea that those with disabilities are somehow shameful or embarrassing is deeply ingrained in our culture. Because of this myth, corporations may fear that typical employees would be dispirited or embarrassed by co-workers with obvious disabilities; advertisers may fear that their products will be associated with disabilities in a way harmful to their image—from consumers assuming their products "cause" disabilities, to buyers avoiding their merchandise because disabled models do not reflect the "beautiful" image to which they aspire.

Just like the other disability myths, this one fails to stand up to scrutiny. When a major metropolitan hospital decided to hire employees with developmental disabilities, they feared that other employees would resent working with people who had mental impairments. After hiring the new workers, however, they found that employee morale actually improved. According to supervisors, most employees found they liked their new co-workers, and several stated that the positive attitude of the new workers made them appreciate their own jobs more.

Many companies that have decided to feature consumers with disabilities in their television advertising have elicited very positive reactions from the public. When Toys "R" Us first distributed a catalog for children with special needs, it expected a limited response from a small segment of the market. The company was pleasantly surprised by the catalog's positive reception. According to CEO Michael Goldstein, the catalog has become "something that our customers love, whether or not they have a child with a disability. It's good for our business because it improves how we stand with all our customers" (Digh 1998).

Marketing research further supports the idea that businesses should associate themselves in a positive way with the issue of disability: Three in four adult Americans say they are likely to switch to products associated with a "good cause" (Digh 1998). Today, more and more companies are learning that paying attention to the issue of disability is demonstrably *good* business. The idea that they would be "tarnished" by an association with the issue is not only false, but the exact opposite of the truth.

The Myth of Specialness

Example: A large hotel in a major southwestern city has an excellent record of employing individuals with disabilities in its housekeeping and maintenance departments. These employees are part of an "enclave" program operated by a local nonprofit organization under contract to the hotel. Enclave members rarely have contact with other hotel employees, and the hotel has hired no individuals with disabilities for positions in other departments.

This myth refers to the common tendency to regard people with disabilities as being more different than they really are, and requiring more unusual provisions than are necessary. Many people view those with disabilities as being so "special"—meaning unlike them—that everything associated with them has to be extraordinary.

Think of any human activity and you will find someone who provides it in a "special" way for people with disabilities. In twenty-first-century America we still have special schools, special education departments, special camps "for crippled children," special hospitals, horseback riding centers "for the handicapped," "therapeutic" arts and recreation programs, and "vocational centers" (i.e., workshops)—an endless array of services and activities specifically intended for those with disabilities *and no one else.*

With the exception of a few medical services that require unusual expertise, there is no evidence that "special" activities are in any way better than ordinary ones provided with accommodations for those who need them. And there is plenty of evidence that segregated activities can stifle the social participation of those with disabilities, and otherwise act to their detriment.

People with disabilities do not learn to bowl better or faster in their own bowling leagues; they do not learn to be better skiers or scuba divers in programs restricted to participants with disability labels. Most importantly for business, adults who happen to have disabilities do not learn how to work better in segregated "work-like" settings—completely segregated workshops, or semi-segregated "enclaves" located in real work settings. The best place for an adult to learn work skills is at work.

"Specialness" also applies to assumptions about the person, including well-meaning assumptions about their "special" abilities. Some examples: All blind people are musically inclined and have supercharged hearing; employees with mental retardation have no problem with boring and repetitive work; people in wheelchairs love jobs that keep them in one spot all day; deaf people prefer to work around noisy machinery. The list could go on.

The Americans with Disabilities Act requires employers to provide "reasonable accommodations" to enable workers with disabilities to work productively. Such accommodations should relate to *real* needs, not fictitious ones. It is easy for businesses to succumb to popular myths of disabled people requiring "special" provisions that they don't really need, or having "special" abilities or interests that they don't really possess. The myth of "specialness" may be well intended, but it is also inaccurate and ultimately harmful.

Getting beyond Myths and Stereotypes

Over the ages, human beings have acquired a survival-related sensitivity to slight differences in their environment—the sound of a twig snapping, the smell of smoke, the sight of flattened grass. Sometimes we can enter a familiar space and notice immediately the one thing that has been moved or taken away, the one thing that is not the same.

In a similar way, we tend to notice differences in people more than similarities. We may meet a beautiful, articulate, and talented artist, but come away from our introduction remembering her primarily because she had an arm in a sling or wore a hearing aid. Rationally, we understand that differences are not necessarily the most important things about people, but our nature impels us to pay them particular attention.

Our tendency to overemphasize differences in people with disabilities is often magnified by all of the stereotypes, myths, and misinformation we have learned throughout our lives. All are part of the cultural context in which we live, conveyed to us through our parents, our friends, our stories, our movies and television, and even our religions.

How do we rid ourselves of the erroneous disability "baggage" that we carry with us? The first step is to be aware that we *all* carry it—even those of us who are disabled. That is not shameful, but human. Second, we can learn to anticipate various sources of misinformation, and recognize it when it appears. Third, we can counterbalance fallacies with accurate information. The evidence presented in this chapter will help; however, the most effective way to combat these stereotypes and myths is to include citizens with disabilities in every aspect of society. Misunderstandings about disability vanish when we get to know people as they really are—not as we have been taught to expect them to be.

Resources

Business Leadership Network (BLN)
www.usbln.com/
1331 F St. N.W.
Washington, D.C. 20004-1107
(202) 376-6200, extension 35 Voice
(202) 376-6868 Fax
(202) 376-6205 TTY
dunlap-carol@dol.gov

Disability Social History Project
http://www.disabilityhistory.org/
255 3rd St., #202
Oakland, Calif. 94607
sdias@disabilityhistory.org

The National Organization on Disability (NOD)
http://www.nod.org/
910 Sixteenth St. N.W.
Suite 600

Washington, D.C. 20006
(202) 293-5960 Voice
(202) 293-5968 TTY
(202) 293-7999 Fax

The Training Institute
805 South Crouse Avenue
Syracuse, N.Y. 13244-2280

5

Language and Etiquette Strategies

During the United Nation's International Year of Disabled Persons, a national nonprofit organization invited the Rev. Dr. Harold Wilke to deliver the keynote address at its national convention. Rev. Dr. Wilke is an internationally known expert in religious inclusion, a minister in the United Church of Christ, a prolific author, and a sought-after speaker. He is particularly eloquent on the subject of his own disability. He was born without arms.

The afternoon before the conference was to begin, the leaders of the organization met to determine who would greet their keynote speaker. None of them felt comfortable doing so, and instead they decided to invite a junior member of the organization to represent them. The junior member had experience working with people who had various types of disabilities.

A board member called the young man. "How'd you like to have dinner tonight with our keynote speaker—on us?"

"I'd be delighted," he replied.

"Good. But I should tell you: he doesn't have any arms. I don't even know how you say 'hello' to someone without arms. But I know you can handle it. You can speak handicapped."

Later that evening the young man had the pleasure of meeting Rev. Dr. Harold Wilke (who bowed politely upon meeting his host, and the young man returned the gesture) and having dinner with him in the hotel's dining room.

Eating entirely with his feet, Wilke generated no small amount of interest in the dining room. During the meal he asked for his host's assistance only once. He apologized for not being able to use his toes to peel back the tinfoil on the butter patties.

The two diners had a lively conversation about mutual interests, and toward the end of the meal the host felt free enough to tell Wilke exactly what had happened that afternoon, what had been said, and why no one else was dining with them.

Wilke responded, "It doesn't surprise me. In fact it happens all the time. That's one of the reasons I'm here."

Should I Say "Handicapped"?

According to many national surveys, fear of dying is the second most common phobia. Taking first place is the fear of public speaking (Anderson 1997, 15).

It is easy to understand how this could be the case. Most people dread the possibility of making mistakes, revealing their ignorance, or incurring the disapproval of others in a public setting.

If this is true of public speaking in general, it is certainly true of speaking about disabilities. One of the most common comments that disability consultants hear from business executives goes something like this: "We notice that you use the term 'disabled' rather than 'handicapped.' Could you tell us something about 'acceptable terminology?'" Often, it becomes clear that some non-disabled individuals have been embarrassed by past "mistakes" they've made in addressing the issue, and many more are fearful of doing or saying something that would reveal their lack of "sensitivity"—they fear that they will be seen as "politically incorrect" on the subject of disability. The result is a pervasive sense of unease—certainly pertaining to *speaking* about disabilities, and sometimes about *anything* having to do with the subject.

In this chapter we will examine matters of language and behavior having to do with disabilities, what issues are important, why some issues are not as important as they are sometimes made out to be, and how businesspeople can effectively communicate and relate to individuals who have various disabling conditions.

Disability Terminology

With the exception of litigation, no other disability-related issue inspires greater anxiety among business leaders than "appropriate" disability language. Not only do many fear revealing their ignorance, they dread their fate at the hands of the "language police" whom they see as having unrealistic expectations and enforcing silly rules of political correctness. Conversely, people with disabilities know that they have long been the victims of dismissive treatment and even ridicule, and they feel strongly that they should be spoken to and about respectfully. Both sides are at least partly correct.

To understand the sensitivity of individuals with disabilities to the words that are used to describe them, one should probably start with the term "handicapped," long the most common one used to include all types of conditions.

The term has a twofold origin. The first is from horse racing, where wagers were customarily placed in a hat or *cap,* and favored horses were assigned additional weight to make the race more competitive (*OED*). The term first associated with the wager became associated with the additional burden, or *handicap.* Later, the term became associated with the custom of allowing disabled military veterans to beg for their sustenance by holding their uniform *cap* outstretched in their *hand.* Thus, the word *handicapped* has two negative associations: burden and begging. It is no wonder that people with disabilities disdain the term.

Other disability terms have equally objectionable origins and associations. For example, the words *cretin* and *mongoloid,* long used to refer to certain types of mental deficiency, came into being because some people thought that those with particular syndromes resembled certain ethnic groups—a racist and ethnically bigoted idea. Because of this, such terms have long been out of favor.

For different reasons, words like *epileptic, amputee, diabetic,* and *mute* have fallen into disuse. That is because they seem to equate the person with his or her disability as if no other personal characteristic had any significance. For decades, disability advocates have been making the point that people are much more than their disability, and their arguments have won wide endorsement.

Knowing disability word origins and objectionable terms can be helpful, but a speaker can run afoul of the language police without even knowing he or she has trespassed on sacred ground. Take for example the commonly used epithet *knucklehead.* This term was coined when individuals with hypothyroidism, a malady that can cause mental retardation in extreme cases, were noticed to have pronounced furrows on their foreheads—furrows resembling knuckles. Today few people are aware of the origin of the word, though it continues to mean what it meant originally—a person who is regarded as unintelligent.

The same might be said for two terms associated with mental illness—*ding-a-ling* and *dingbat.* In medieval England, mental illness was thought to be contagious, and people who had that condition were isolated from the rest of society and required to carry a bell that would warn others of their visits to town. In time, those unfortunate people became synonymous with the sound they were forced to make—*ding-a-lings*—and the sticks on which some of them carried their bells—*dingbats.* The fact that these terms continue to be used in ridicule, and continue to mean almost exactly what they meant centuries ago, underscores the important relationship between terminology and social standing.[1]

If flagrant errors were the only issue, it would be a fairly easy matter simply to list those noxious words and phrases that ought never be used, and be done with it. Sadly, things are not that simple. Even among people with disabilities, there are major disagreements about which terms are acceptable and which are not. Consider:

- Some members of the deaf community insist that people born without hearing should be described as *Deaf* with a capital *d;* those who lose their hearing later in life are *deaf* with a lowercase *d.* People with some hearing should be referred to as *hearing impaired.*
- Many people contend that *mental deficiency* should always be used in preference to *mental retardation,* partly because *retardation* is seen as an antiquated term, and one associated with centuries of mistreatment. Others say that even *mental deficiency* is too negative, and instead always use the term *developmental disability.*
- *Developmental disability?* That can't be synonymous with *mental retardation,* say some, because many other types of disabilities occur during the developmental period and don't necessarily involve mental deficiency (e.g., spina bifida).
- *All too negative!* contend the language extremists. Just say that someone has a *challenge*—a physical or mental *challenge.*
- *Rubbish!* reply some. We all face all sorts of *challenges.* What does that have to do with a *disability?*

Given the disagreements that even disabled individuals themselves have about the proper terminology to use, what is a businessperson to do? Is there *any* approach that is both reasonable and acceptable?

"People First" Language

The best-known of popular approaches to disability terminology is "people first language." This communication style had its origins in the self-advocacy movement of adults with mental retardation, which began in 1973 (Lehr and Taylor 1986). From its beginning, the "people first" movement stressed that people with disabilities were much more than the labels that others applied to them, and that such labels placed additional and unnecessary burdens on them. The primary tenet of this philosophy was that they were people first before any consideration of their disability status. As a remedy, they proposed that language used to describe them be modified so as to downplay their disability status and accentuate their personhood and their dignity.

During the next few years, many nonprofit disability service organizations developed various "people first" terminology rules and guidelines, and these were eventually adopted by many national organizations, including the Easter Seals (1980), Goodwill Industries (1992), and the American Association on Mental Retardation (1988, 1994).

Since "people first" standards were developed independently, there have never been uniform guidelines. Over time, however, a consensus has grown of the fundamental principles on which most adherents agree. The general guidelines offered by Goodwill Industries are typical:

- Put the person before the disability. For example, use 'people with disabilities' as opposed to 'disabled people' or 'the disabled.'
- Do not use phrases such as 'confined to a wheelchair,' 'crippled,' 'afflicted,' 'victim of,' or 'suffers from a disorder.' These references diminish the individual's dignity and magnify the disability. Instead, refer to 'the person who uses a wheelchair' or 'the person with an emotional disorder.'
- Avoid portraying people with disabilities as superhuman, courageous, poor or unfortunate. Remember, people with disabilities do not want to be, nor should they be, measured against a separate set of expectations.
- Avoid using trendy euphemisms to describe people with disabilities. Expressions such as 'physically challenged,' 'special,' and 'handi-capable' generally are regarded by the disability community [*sic*] as patronizing and inaccurate. Stick with simple language, such as 'people with disabilities' or 'the person who is deaf.' (Goodwill 1992)

Some of these principles were both cogent and helpful. For example, despite the fact that people who use wheelchairs are commonly referred to as "confined to a wheelchair," that phrase is literally untrue. Not using it makes a lot of sense. The same can be said for avoiding disability stereotypes.

The most problematic guideline is the one from which the practice takes its name: people first. Virtually all "people first" guidelines mandate that the word "disabled" and similar referents *never* be used before "person." This has come to be a "mandated metaphor" for disability advocates: our dignity and personhood must be respected, not just in the choice of words used, but also in the *order* in which they are used.

This principle is dogma to "people first" advocates. Adherents often not only use this approach, but insist that others do so. This can create problems for those unfamiliar with the practice and, less frequently, for those who disagree with the concept. Today, it is not unusual for someone speaking to a group of disabled individuals—or to one "people first" advocate—to be corrected, admonished, or even ridiculed if he or she does not always preface disability-related words with "person with," "people with," or other such approved phraseology.

Some people have objected to "people first" language requirements simply because they are awkward and wordy. Practical issues aside, there are two major problems with this approach. The first pertains to linguistic theory. In English, word order does not convey the relative importance of concepts. The most important word in a phrase might be first, last, or somewhere in between. For example, take the sentence "She was a beautiful, beguiling, conniving murderer." One would be hard pressed to argue that the emphasis was intended to be on the word *beautiful*. "People first" language proponents have never explained why, in regard to disability terminology, but nowhere else in the English language, putting the word "person" first in a sequence necessarily increases its importance.

Similarly, in the English language, nouns may be modified by attributive adjectives (e.g., *modern art*) or by an adjectival phrase or relative clause (*art of the modern period*) with no difference in meaning. Generally, in English the substitution of an adjectival phrase for an attributive adjective only makes the thought less concise. In fact, by multiplying the number of words needed to convey an idea, such a practice might call greater attention to the modifier, or cause the listener to infer that the speaker is unable to communicate succinctly.

The second major problem with "people first" language is strategic. If we assume that the overall intent of this practice is to promote the social status of people with disabilities, then its practical impact must be considered. Unfortunately, in the literature of the "people first" movement there is no evidence that such language strictures further the cause of disabled people. In fact, the theory that requiring people to communicate in non-normative ways will promote a more normal or positive image of those with disabilities is illogical. One of the primary tenets of the self-advocacy movement is that disabled people have endured more than enough "special" associations; therefore, the idea that one more "special" consideration will promote a more normal image is unreasonable.

On an even more practical level, people who are pressured into behaving in a certain way can become defensive, resistant, or even antagonistic. It is entirely possible that the "people first" language movement might cause similar reactions, to the detriment of those who are disabled. Sensing this, a vocal minority of advocates has begun to speak out against the practice.[2]

Perhaps advocates of "people first" word order are unaware that their mandates are based on incorrect and illogical assumptions. Many organizations have adopted "people first" policies with little or no debate and virtually no opposition. Perhaps some advocates are aware of fallacies inherent in the philosophy, but feel justified by the righteousness of their cause. At a minimum, advocates should assume the burden of proving that mandating non-normative language will promote more normal lives for disabled people. To date they have failed to do so.

Guidelines for Respectful Language

A man in his late sixties lay dying of colon cancer in an urban hospital. Late one night, he rang his call button to request assistance in urinating.

When an orderly responded to his request, the patient apologized for the inconvenience, saying that he was embarrassed to ask for help with something so personal he had always been able to do for himself. The orderly assured him that he was happy to be of service.

When the patient finished, he looked at the orderly and asked, "As you die, do you know what part of you goes last?"

"No, what?" the young man replied.

The patient looked him in the eye.

"Your pride," he said.

Anyone who is aware of some of the hurtful disability terminology practices of the past obviously wants to avoid causing further pain; but the most widely prescribed alternative—"people first" language—is at best awkward and illogical, and at worst counterproductive. Although there are many types of disabilities, and feelings concerning them can be very strong, communicating about the topic should not be made difficult or complicated.

Here are some general guidelines intended to promote effective communications in the area of disabilities. They incorporate some of the reasonable "people first" principles, while avoiding less useful restrictions. They are intended both for those new to the topic of disability and for those familiar with it.

- Keep in mind that nobody is perfect. Promote tolerance by modeling it.
- Practice speech that promotes both understanding and respect.
- Discuss disability only when the subject is germane. Disabled people have many other characteristics—passions, religions, interests, hobbies, ethnicities, occupations, and so on. Disability is not relevant to everything they are or everything they do.

  For example, a newspaper headline that reads, "Group home resident struck crossing street" implies a connection between an individual's disability and the event described. Would a reporter as likely have written, "Brunette struck crossing street," "Presbyterian struck crossing street," or "Cubs fan struck crossing street"?
- Avoid words and phrases that usually cause offense. These include:

afflicted	dumb	mongoloid
confined to a	feeble-minded	moron
wheelchair	handicap	mute
cretin	handicapped	retard
crippled	idiot	spastic
deaf and dumb	imbecile	sufferer
deaf mute	invalid	victim
deformed	lame	wheelchair bound

- Avoid terms that equate a person with his or her disability. Some examples:

asthmatic	epileptic	quadriplegic
diabetic	midget	retardate
dwarf	paraplegic	

- Never criticize anyone's communication methods in public. If you have a suggestion, make your comments privately and present them in a constructive way.
- Express your appreciation for, and otherwise reward, constructive attempts at communicating about disabilities.

(For a discussion of communication issues in supervising employees with disabilities, see chapter 9. Chapter 11 includes a discussion of communication issues in marketing.)

Disability Etiquette

> There were several categories people fell into when it came to Rhyme's [a police forensics expert who has quadriplegia] injury.
>
> Some took the joking, in-your-face approach. Crip humor, no prisoners taken.
>
> Some . . . ignored his condition completely.
>
> Most . . . tried to pretend that Rhyme didn't exist and prayed that they could escape at the earliest possible moment.
>
> It was this response that Rhyme hated the most—it was one of the most blatant reminders of how different he was.
>
> —Jeffery Deaver, *The Empty Chair*

Although most disabled people want no special treatment and greatly appreciate being treated the same as everyone else, there are occasions when it is helpful to know commonly accepted manners that promote inclusion.

The following suggestions are distilled from years of experience, many published treatments of the topic,[3] and the suggestions of many individuals who are disabled. Please keep in mind that there are no hard and fast rules of disability etiquette, and people frequently disagree on optimal practices. For example, one authority cautions those meeting someone with a disability: "A handshake is NOT a standard greeting for everyone." Another source lists as one of its first precepts of communicating with people who have disabilities: "Offer to shake hands when introduced." When dining, some people who are blind appreciate it when sighted companions describe the location of the food they are served ("The salmon is at 'six o'clock' on your plate; mashed potatoes are at nine.") Others consider such help to be a disability cliché. People can and do disagree on these practices. There are few hard and fast rules.

The following are some useful tips, by no means all one could know on the subject, but some helpful information with which to start.

General Considerations

- Begin by imagining how you would like to be treated if you were the person with whom you are interacting.
- Interact with a person, not a disability. Do not pay more attention to the disability than is warranted.
- Do not assume anything. If you do not know, ask.
- Always speak to a disabled person directly, even if he or she is using an interpreter.
- Be patient and willing to learn. Be prepared to take a little extra time or exert a little extra effort.
- Offer assistance if it seems to be needed, and wait for your offer to be accepted before acting.
- Make effective communication a priority. Studies repeatedly show that social acceptance is the single most important factor in job success and employee satisfaction.
- Relax. A sincere commitment to including people with disabilities will compensate for most mistakes. A sense of humor should cover the rest.

Interacting with People Who Have
Mental Health–Related Disabilities

Considerations

- There are many types of mental and emotional illnesses. Some are severe, and others are relatively mild and more easily controlled.
- Mental illness can be chronic or short-term. A majority of the population experiences some sort of mental illness at some time.
- Mental illness can be caused by biochemical, emotional, or environmental factors.
- There are many types of medication available to assist in the treatment of mental illness.
- The presence of mental illness or the fact that a person takes a psychoactive drug does not automatically preclude their being able to work.
- Some medications used to treat mental illness have side effects. It is important to consider that these are a result of the treatment and control of the illness, not the illness itself.
- Some individuals are uncomfortable talking about their illness.

• Mental illness is an example of an "invisible disability." For this reason, it is particularly important that the confidentiality of the individual involved be preserved.
• Mental illness is the disability most frequently encountered and dealt with in employment situations.

Suggestions for Interacting with People Who Have
Mental Health–Related Disabilities

• Always discuss issues related to mental illness in private. A quiet location with no distractions is generally best.
• The dignity and autonomy of people with mental illness are sometimes ignored. Treat the individual with respect, and involve him or her in problem solving.
• Do not attempt to counsel the individual or provide therapy.
• In the workplace, behavioral policies must always apply to all. If training on mental illness is provided to employees, it should be provided to all and without reference to any specific person or incident. Make sure both trainers and training participants understand the importance of confidentiality and respect for co-workers.

Interacting with People Who Have Physical Disabilities and Mobility Limitations

Considerations

• There are many reasons for a person to use a wheelchair, walker, crutches, brace, or other device. People with physical limitations have a wide range of capabilities, and may need assistance or assistive devices only at particular times, or not at all.
• Wheelchairs, walkers, canes, and other devices come in all shapes and sizes. Some wheelchairs are sleek and lightweight, others are quite heavy and cumbersome.
• Do not consider any space for which you are responsible (office, interview location, recreational area, etc.) to be physically accessible unless you know it to be the case. Although no building is totally accessible to everyone, there are minimum criteria that should be considered. (For a discussion of building accessibility issues, see chapters 8 and 10.)

Suggestions for Interacting with People Who Have
Physical Disabilities and Mobility Limitations

- If you are unsure whether a person would like to shake hands, ask.
- Regard a wheelchair, cane, walker, or similar device as an extension of the person's body. Never lean on a person's wheelchair, or touch it without permission.
- If you are conversing with someone in a wheelchair for more than a few moments, use a chair so your face will be at eye level. If a chair is not available, kneel or crouch facing the person.
- When expecting someone who uses a wheelchair, see that a reasonably wide path is clear. Move aside a chair, or otherwise prepare a place for him or her to sit.
- Many people find standing for extended periods uncomfortable. When possible, provide places to sit and rest.

Interacting with People Who Have Learning Disabilities

Considerations

- Learning problems are a common disability.
- Learning disabilities affect how people process information, and may influence how they think, speak, write, read, listen, spell, or perform mathematical computations.
- There are a great number of types of learning disabilities. The stereotype of someone with a learning disability "reversing" the letters in a word is accurate for only a small minority of people.
- By definition, a person with a learning disability has average or above average intelligence.

Suggestions for Interacting with People Who Have Learning Disabilities

- If you need to know how a person with a learning disability best learns or works, begin by asking him or her.
- Be prepared to communicate in multiple formats: notes, written instructions, tape recordings, verbal directions, etc.

- Be prepared to allow a person with a learning disability to practice a new skill, or otherwise physically experience an action, rather than assuming he or she will understand just by reading or hearing about it.
- Say literally what you mean. Using subtleties such as intonation, humor, irony, or suggestion to communicate your message may be counterproductive.
- Encourage someone with a learning disability to work creatively and to develop productive nontraditional methods of working.

Interacting with People Who Have Mental Retardation

Considerations

- There are many levels of intellectual deficiency, and intelligence is multifaceted. Be willing to take time to understand how a person learns and prefers to communicate.
- All too often, adults with intellectual deficiencies are treated condescendingly or as children.
- Many people with mental retardation are extremely reluctant to discuss their learning problems. Some go to great lengths to "pass" as a person without a disability. (This phenomenon is discussed in chapter 6.)
- Because of their previous experience, many people with intellectual limitations are particularly sensitive to signs of approval or disapproval. Your smile and undivided attention can pay great dividends.

Suggestions for Interacting with People Who Have Mental Retardation

- Avoid condescension and childish treatment.
- Keep your conversation simple.
- Avoid busy, noisy, or confusing environments in which to work and communicate.
- Do not hurry conversation or interactions.
- Be prepared to repeat or paraphrase, or to ask politely that a comment be repeated.
- When giving instructions, break them down into component steps.
- Encourage the use of aids that promote learning or remembering: charts, lists, colored folders, pictures, labels, etc.

Interacting with People Who Have Hearing Impairments

Considerations

- Some people, especially people born deaf, do not consider themselves to have a disability in the traditional sense. They regard deafness as a culture, and describe themselves as "Deaf" with a capital *D*.
- There are many different levels of hearing loss. Most people with hearing impairments have some hearing.
- Not all people who are deaf use sign language. Not all people who are deaf or hearing impaired can read lips or speak.
- Not all people with hearing impairments use hearing aids or augmentative devices. Those who do use them may not do so all the time.
- While many deaf and hearing-impaired people can read lips, the best lip readers can make out only about 35 percent of spoken words.
- Sign language has its own rules, customs, grammar, and idioms. It is not a simple translation of English.
- While a slight increase in volume may enhance your communication with some people who have hearing impairments, excessive volume is inappropriate and may cause feedback in hearing aids.

Suggestions for Interacting with People
Who Have Hearing Impairments

- Find out the way in which the person prefers to communicate.
- To get a person's attention, tap him or her politely on the shoulder.
- Be prepared to use notes, or to communicate through an interpreter.
- Always look at the person with whom you are speaking, not the interpreter.
- If a person uses a hearing aid, avoid conversations in noisy, open areas. Do not shout. Speak clearly in a normal tone of voice.
- If a person reads lips, keep obstructions (smoking materials, hands, food, etc.) away from your face. Speak deliberately in short, simple sentences. Some simple gestures (nodding, shrugging shoulders) and facial expressions (furrowed brow, surprised look) may be helpful.
- Be patient and willing to repeat your message.

Interacting with People Who Have Speech Impairments

Considerations

• Many things can cause speech impairments: hearing loss, stroke, cerebral palsy, traumatic head injury, etc.
• People with speech impairments are frequently misperceived as intoxicated or mentally retarded.
• A person with a speech impairment may be easier to understand at particular times, and his or her speech may deteriorate with fatigue or in stressful situations.
• Successful communication can be a function of time: allowing time for a person to express himself or herself, allowing yourself time to understand. Eventually, you may be able to improve your receptive ability, and the speaker may be able to adjust to your listening style.

Suggestions for Interacting with People
Who Have Speech Impairments

• If you do not understand what a person has said, ask politely for a repetition. Do not pretend you have understood when you haven't.
• An area with background noise or distractions may make communication more difficult. Consider moving to a quieter location.
• In meetings or group discussions, people with speech disabilities can have difficulty being heard. Help them by assuring that the group allows them an opportunity to speak.
• Do not attempt to speak for another person or finish his or her sentences.
• When necessary, ask short, simple questions to confirm your understanding.
• If necessary, consider using written or some other form of communication.

Interacting with People Who Have Visual Disabilities

Considerations

• There are infinite levels of severity of visual impairments, from mild myopia to total blindness.
• Legal blindness is defined as 20/200 vision to the best correction.

- Many people who are considered blind do have some sight.
- Many people who are blind consider it to be more of an inconvenience than a disability.
- Although many blind people use Braille, most do not. Many use adaptive equipment such as text magnifiers and computers equipped with voice synthesis.

Suggestions for Interacting with People Who Have Visual Disabilities

- When you encounter a person with a visual impairment, introduce yourself or announce your presence and the names of those with you. Excuse yourself before you leave.
- Offer to describe the physical layout of a room, the position of food on a plate, and the names of other people present in a room.
- When guiding someone with a visual disability, do not grab him or her. Offer to be a "sighted guide." Let them take your arm; they will probably allow you to walk half a step ahead of them. Point out doors, curbs, stairs, and possible obstructions as you approach them.
- Don't pet or interact with a guide dog. The dog is working, and a vital part of its owner's safety and independence.
- Be aware that changing a physical environment (moving furniture, adding or deleting items, painting) can cause problems for someone with a visual disability. Inform the person of any alterations about which they should know.

Interacting with People Who Have Disabilities Relating to Stature

Considerations

- Adults under 4' 10" tall are generally considered to have a stature-related disability.
- Most people of short stature prefer to be called "little people" rather than "dwarfs" or "midgets."
- Many little people do not consider themselves to be disabled (although they are covered under the Americans with Disabilities Act). Many consider their primary challenges to be (1) adapting to physical environments that are not designed to meet their needs, and (2) receiving

treatment based on their size rather than their age, that is, adults being treated as children.

- People who are exceptionally large or tall may also qualify as having a disability.

Suggestions for Interacting with People Who Have
Disabilities Relating to Stature

- Try to establish eye contact at a mutually comfortable level. A seated position may be best, or stepping back to reduce the angle of sight may suffice.
- If a person appears to be having problems using furniture or other physical features, ask if there is something else he or she would prefer.
- Treat the person according to his or her age and status. Do not condescend or pat him or her on the head.

Getting Started

Anyone who has ever traveled in a foreign country knows that the natives tend to appreciate any effort by a visitor to understand their culture and speak their language. People who have disabilities also appreciate those who sincerely try to understand and communicate with them. That might involve something as simple as offering someone who is tired a place to sit down, or it could be as complex as taking lessons in sign language. The important thing is to make the effort.

The last word on this issue goes to a lady who lived for more than thirty years in a state institution for adults with mental retardation. For fifteen years thereafter she lived in a community-based family home until finally marrying, as she put it, the "man of my dreams." When asked for her thoughts about all the ways people refer to others who have disabilities, she thought for a moment and then said: "I think it's not so much *what* you say as *how* you say it."

Resources

American Friends Service Committee Affirmative Action Office
(Producers of the *Guide to Etiquette and Behavior for Relating to Persons with Disabilities*)
http://www.afsc.org/etiquette.htm/
1501 Cherry St.
Philadelphia, Pa. 19102
(215) 241-7000 Voice
(215) 241-7275 Fax

The California Governor's Committee for Employment of Disabled Persons
(Producers of the Windmills Training Program)
http://www.edd.ca.gov/gcedpind.htm/
P.O. Box 826880
Sacramento, Calif. 94280-0001
(916) 654-8055 Voice
(916) 654-9820 TTY
(916) 654-9821 Fax

Memphis Center for Independent Living
(Developers of the *Disability Etiquette Guide*)
http://www.mcil.org/
163 North Angelus
Memphis, Tenn. 38104
(901) 726-6404 Voice/TTY
(901) 726-6521 Fax

National Braille Press
(Braille publications and transcription)
http://www.nbp.org/
88 St. Stephen St.
Boston, Mass. 02115
(888) 965-8965 Voice
(617) 437-0456 Fax

National Business & Disability Council (NBDC)
http://www.business-disability.com/
201 I.U. Willets Rd.
Albertson, N.Y. 11507
(516) 465-1515 Voice
(516) 465-3730 Fax

The National Organization on Disability (NOD)
http://www.nod.org/
910 Sixteenth St. N.W.
Suite 600
Washington, D.C. 20006
(202) 293-5960 Voice
(202) 293-5968 TTY
(202) 293-7999 Fax

Program Development Associates (PDA)
http://www.pdassoc.com/
P.O. Box 2038
Syracuse, N.Y. 13220-2038
(800) 543-2119 Voice
(315) 452-0643 Fax
info@pdassoc.com

Reedy, Joel. 1993. *Marketing to Consumers with Disabilities.* **Chicago: Probus.**

Registry of Interpreters for the Deaf
http://www.rid.org/
8630 Fenton St., Suite 324
Silver Spring, Md. 20910
(301) 608-0050 Voice/TTY
(301) 608-0508 Fax

The City of San Antonio, Texas, Planning Department
Disability Access
(Developers of the *Disability Etiquette Handbook*)
http://www.sanantonio.gov/planning/disability_access.asp/
P.O. Box 839966
San Antonio, Tex. 78283-3966
(210) 207-7873 Voice
(210) 207-7957 TTY
(210) 207-7897 Fax

6

Disability and Innovation

Some Famous People with Disabilities

Alexander the Great
Muhammad Ali
Hans Christian Andersen
Ludwig van Beethoven
Werner von Braun
Lord Byron
Julius Caesar
Ray Charles
Agatha Christie
Winston Churchill
Charles Darwin
Charles Dickens
Emily Dickinson
Robert Dole
Fyodor Dostoevsky
Albert Einstein
King George III
Evelyn Glennie
Goya
Juan Gris

George Frideric Handel
Stephen Hawking
Homer
Stephen Hopkins
James Earl Jones
Barbara Jordan
Franz Kafka
Helen Keller
Charles Krauthammer
George Lucas
Henri Matisse
John McCain
Michelangelo
John Milton
Sir Isaac Newton
Friedrich Nietzsche
Niccolò Paganini
George Patton
Itzhak Perlman
William Pitt

Pierre Auguste Renoir
August Rodin
Franklin D. Roosevelt
Babe Ruth
Sir Walter Scott
George Bernard Shaw
Robert Louis Stevenson
Peter Ilyich Tchaikovsky
Mel Tillis
Leo Tolstoy
Henri de Toulouse-Lautrec
Harriet Tubman
Vincent Van Gogh
Leonardo da Vinci
George Washington
Heather Whitestone
Robin Williams
Woodrow Wilson
Virginia Woolf

Many people think of disabilities as deficits, losses, or burdens, and of those who have them as limited or diminished. Yet there is ample evidence that disabilities might be beneficial, both to people who have them and to others—abundant indications that disabilities themselves and the experience of having them are linked in many ways to human innovation and advancement.

It might at first seem absurd to suggest such a connection. The modern scientific mind is inclined in the opposite direction, to connect human progress with strength and intelligence. When Charles Darwin published *On the Origin of Species* in 1859, his theory of "natural selection" held that, over time, the weakest members of each species had the least chance of surviving to procreate, while stronger members tended to fare better and reproduce more successfully, a principle commonly referred to as "survival of the fittest." Darwin wrote, "The theory of natural selection is grounded on the belief that each new variety, and ultimately each new species, is produced and maintained by having some advantage over those with which it comes into competition; and the consequent extinction of less-favoured forms almost inevitably follows" (170).

Darwin was a naturalist, and he developed his theories from his observations of the animal kingdom. As a scientist, however, he knew that humans were also members of that kingdom, and therefore he saw a connection between his theories and the social sciences. Darwin observed that in the animal world, nature works with cold indifference to root out the weaker members of each species. He and other social theorists began to speculate that perhaps a system comparable to the one governing lower animal life might apply in human societies. As a result of his work, a theory known as "social Darwinism" soon became popular among the scientific community.

According to social Darwinism, people with physical or mental disabilities represent human weakness, and, as such, pose a threat to the continuity of the human species. By definition, they are weaker than others and, therefore, less adaptable. In the philosophy of social Darwinism, disabilities were considered human weaknesses that could be, and ought to be, eliminated from the human species.

In the United States, the growing acceptance of social Darwinism eventually led to widespread support for the "science" of eugenics. The eugenics movement attempted to give nature a helping hand in improving the human species by eliminating the possibility that the weakest members of society would reproduce. In 1907, Indiana became the first state to mandate the forced sterilization of disabled people who lived in its institutions (Leaming 1977).

Many states soon followed. In Europe, Germany was quick to follow the American lead. Social Darwinism and eugenics appealed immensely to the leaders of the Third Reich in their quest to develop a "master race." Disabled people became their early targets, even before the pogrom against Jews began on Kristallnacht. An estimated 275,000 Germans with disabilities died in the Nazi "Aktion T-4" killing program, which developed techniques that would later be used on Jews. Many more men, women, and children with disabilities later died in concentration camps, and more than 400,000 were sterilized (Disability Rights Advocates 1999, 3).

Darwin, one of the most influential scientists of the past millennium, strongly championed the belief that human progress was, and would be, a result of the inevitable domination of the strong over the weak. It was, to his thinking, the way of nature, and the fate of humankind. His theory of "natural selection" was considered revolutionary because it contradicted theories that had dominated human understanding for many centuries. The primary conflict was with religious traditions known as "creationism"; but Darwin's theories also contradicted then popular notions of human disability, in particular the idea that disabled people might represent some good to humankind.

Appreciation of Unbalanced Minds

Psychosis

In contrast to the modern scientific thinkers, the ancients often posited a connection between human advancement and disabilities, especially mental illness. Aristotle once observed, "There never was a genius without a tincture of madness." In the *Phaedrus,* Socrates said that "the greatest blessings come to us through madness, when it is sent as a gift of the gods." He believed that poets and prophets who exhibited signs of mental illness were, in fact, possessed and inspired by the gods. The durability of this theory is shown by the fact that Shakespeare often used inspired "fools" in his dramas, written almost twenty-one centuries after the death of Socrates.

Conventional wisdom on the subject of disability has been influenced greatly by disabled individuals, both famous and infamous. History provides prominent examples of well-known people whose extreme intelligence and accomplishment have been combined with insanity, or what psychiatrists refer to as "psychosis"—people such as Caligula, Sir Isaac Newton, Vincent Van Gogh,

Fig. 6.1. *King Lear and the Fool in the Storm* by William Dyce (1851). *(National Gallery of Scotland—used with permission)*

Friedrich Nietzsche, Virginia Woolf, Sylvia Plath, and Ezra Pound. At some time during their lives, all of these distinguished individuals truly suffered from the "madness" to which Aristotle referred—and not just a "tincture" of it.

But most psychologists conclude that, while Aristotle might have been correct in his observation of a trace of "madness" in the highly gifted, the theory that insanity and genius are intertwined must be rejected for at least two reasons.

First, the relatively high incidence of severe mental illness could account for many, if not all, of the geniuses with psychoses that we could mention. An estimated 10 percent of the population lives with the condition, and most people experience some form of mental illness at least once during their lives. Second, while although psychosis and creativity may characterize a person at some point in life, they rarely coexist simultaneously. Psychological biographer Anthony Storr writes: "The apparent incompatibility of insanity and creativity is . . . supported by the fact that creative people, when they do become insane, generally show a decline in the quality and quantity of their productions.

> He [Dr. Gachet, Van Gogh's physician and friend] said to me besides, that if the depression or anything else became too great for me to bear, he could quite well do something to diminish its intensity, and that I must not find it awkward to be frank with him. Well, the moment when I shall need him may certainly come, however up to now all is well. And things may yet get better . . .
>
> > Vincent Van Gogh, from a letter to his brother Theo and sister-in-law Jo, Auvers-sur-Oise, May 25, 1890
>
> ❖
>
> I began to frequent the offices and couches of the local psychiatrists, who were all running back and forth on summer vacations. I became unable to sleep. I became immune to increased doses of sleeping pills. I underwent a rather brief and traumatic experience of badly given shock treatments on an outpatient basis. Pretty soon, the only doubt in my mind was the precise time and method of committing suicide.
>
> > Sylvia Plath, from a letter dated December 28, 1953, while she was a patient at McLean Psychiatric Hospital, Belmont, Massachusetts

Schizophrenic painters, for example, often show a shift in their paintings toward subjects reflecting their own personal disturbance which have little relevance to the perceptions of the normal person" (1988, 252).

Neurosis

While psychoses invariably stifle creativity, neuroses often seem to have the opposite effect. Conditions such as depression, anxiety, and mania are found disproportionately among those of great talent. Such people are often referred to as "temperamental" geniuses, a euphemism for their often-unorthodox behavior. Once again, history has provided many instructive examples. In literature there are Goethe, Balzac, Shelley, Poe, Tolstoy, Thoreau, Brendan Behan, Norman Mailer, Ernest Hemingway, and many more. In political affairs there are Jefferson, Lincoln, Churchill, Richard Nixon, and scores of others. In art, da Vinci, Michelangelo, Picasso, Rodin, and Pollack come immediately to mind. Many, if not most, of these individuals were neurotic throughout the most productive periods of their lives, perhaps an indication that their neuroses actually bolstered their ingenuity. Beethoven, who had a bipolar disorder, composed some of his finest music during periods of manic energy. Samuel

Historians, psychologists, and hagiographers have long debated whether St. Francis of Assisi was holy, mentally ill, or both. There is no dispute that he claimed to hear the voice of God, or that his behavior was often very unconventional.

The following selection from *Butler's Lives of the Saints* recounts an incident that occurred after St. Francis took some of his father's goods, sold them, and gave the proceeds to a parish priest for the repair of his church.

> After some days spent in prayer and fasting, he appeared again, though so disfigured and ill-clad that people pelted him and called him mad. Bernardone [his father], more annoyed than ever, carried him home, beat him unmercifully (Francis was about twenty-five), put fetters on his feet, and locked him up, till his mother set him at liberty while his father was out. Francis returned to St. Damian's. His father, following him thither, hit him about the head and insisted that he should either return home or renounce all his share in his inheritance and return the purchase-price of the goods he had taken. Francis had no objection to being disinherited, but said that the other money now belonged to God and the poor. He was therefore summoned before Guido, Bishop of Assisi, who told him to return it and have trust in God. Francis did as he was told and, with his usual literalness, added, "The clothes I wear are also his. I'll give them back." He suited the action to the word, stripped himself of his clothes, and gave them to his father. (Walsh 1991, 315)

Johnson, who had chronic anxiety and insomnia, harnessed his enormous intellectual powers to produce the first dictionary in English.

Unconventional Learning

Some types of disability are not noticed immediately, but become more obvious over time. This is particularly true of learning disabilities, which are frequently not diagnosed until children enter school. The diagnostic process is complicated by the fact that unique learning patterns are often difficult, or impossible, to distinguish from disabilities.

Because, by definition, those with great gifts are different from others, their families, friends, and especially teachers often misunderstand them. Thomas Alva Edison, perhaps the greatest inventor in American history, had a severe learning disability, and could not read until he was twelve. As a result, he had trouble in school, and was regarded as a "problem" child. In reality, of course, he was so gifted that school lessons often bored him. In honor of the inventor, some educational researchers have used the term "the Edison effect" to describe the phenomenon of mistaking great energy, creativity, and atypical learning styles for intellectual "problems." Sir Isaac Newton, Gregor Mendel, Albert Einstein, Alexander Graham Bell—all had educational experiences similar to Edison's in their youth.

Today, children with great capabilities that accompany learning peculiarities are still frequently misunderstood and likely to be labeled as "hyperactive" or having an "attention deficit disorder." Like Edison, they may be given a disability-related label when, in reality, they have unique abilities. It is others who lack the ability to understand *them*. So often are such problems encountered by technically gifted students that at the Massachusetts Institute of Technology dyslexia is often referred to as "the M.I.T. disease."[1]

At the end of the spectrum of "unbalanced minds" where behavioral abnormalities are likely to be viewed as weaknesses, quirks, and eccentricities, there are also connections to creative genius. So common are such traits that conventional wisdom has come to expect them among all the greatly gifted. This conclusion is reflected in two currently popular stereotypes: the "absent-minded professor" and the "computer nerd."

The first stereotype is of an academic so absorbed in contemplation of the abstract that he or she constantly botches simple practical tasks. Fred McMurray played such a character in the movie entitled, appropriately enough, *The Absent-Minded Professor,* as did Jimmy Stewart in *No Highway in the Sky.* Both portrayed brilliant but bumbling intellectuals so wrapped up in their work that they proved incompetent in handling the ordinary affairs of life and needed others to take care of such matters for them.

The "computer nerd" is a relatively new stereotype, usually characterized by technological preoccupation, unkempt appearance (disheveled hair; outdated, ill-fitting clothes; and a pocket protector), and minimal social skills. The computer nerd is often presented as a humorous, idiosyncratic character, but in a few cases the stereotype is associated with some types of mental illness. Some scholars and researchers believe that some highly technologically oriented individuals, while not truly mentally ill, exhibit behaviors associated with disorders such as schizophrenia and autism. (See a discussion of this issue in the portrait of Dr. Temple Grandin in chapter 7.)

All of the examples given above may be viewed as proof of the obvious: those with great minds are not like the rest of us. The experience of being spe-

Fig. 6.2. Alonzo Clemons with his Dolphin Rainbow sculpture. *(Photo courtesy of Driscoll Gallery, Aspen, Colorado)*

cially gifted likely involves a preoccupation with a particular interest, and relatively less concern about unrelated matters. Like the ancient philosophers, modern generations have come to accept that intelligence so dominates the personalities of the highly gifted that other aspects of their lives are likely to be distorted.

That is not to say that all people who have a disability are likely to be gifted. Unfortunately, that is not the case. Some people—very few, admittedly—seem to have great talents that are inextricably linked to their disabilities. These people are commonly referred to as "savants." A few examples have become well known in the public mind. Alonzo Clemons is a renowned sculptor of animal subjects. He has brain damage and an IQ in the severely mentally disabled range, yet he can glimpse an animal and quickly sculpt an astoundingly accurate image of it.[2] Dustin Hoffman portrayed Raymond Babbitt, a savant with incredible counting and memorization skills, in the film *Rain Man;* screenwriter Barry Morrow based Babbitt on a real-life savant, Kim Peek.[2] In the movie *Shine,* Geoffrey Rush portrayed a gifted pianist, David Helfgott, who has schizophrenia.

From psychosis through idiosyncrasy, nature seems to have established multiple connections between human genius and human disabilities. But if nature has created links between these two forces, what about *nurture?* Is there anything about the experience of living with a disability that influences an individual's creative ability?

The Experience of Having a Disability

At the Forefront of Human Experience

Disabilities frequently present challenges in the extreme, but they may at times also provide singular opportunities. Mention a connection between disability and human invention, and many people will think first, and perhaps solely, of Alexander Graham Bell. Bell's research in audiological equipment for the deaf (his wife had a severe hearing impairment) led directly to the invention of the telephone. So important was this connection to Bell that on the occasion of his seventieth birthday he said that he much preferred being remembered for his work with the deaf than for his invention of the telephone.[3]

There are many other examples of innovations that owe their existence, at least in part, to disabilities. The typewriter was invented in Italy in 1808 by Pellegrino Turri, who wanted to develop a "writing machine" for his friend Countess Carolina Fantoni da Fivizzono, who was blind.[4] Carbon paper was originally developed for scriveners with visual disabilities because they often were unaware when their quills had run out of ink (Microsoft 2000). The "talking book" made its appearance in 1934, intended to help meet the information needs of people who were blind (Jacobs 1999). In 1950, the Sony Corporation paid Western Electric $25,000 to purchase the patent rights to the transistor. Western Electric had been producing transistors for hearing aids, but Sony developed many new applications for it, a move that eventually made the company a corporate giant, and transformed the Japanese economy (*Playboy* 1982). Most recently, inventor Dean Kamen introduced the Segway HT (for *human transporter*), a high-tech scooter-like device. Previously, Kamen had been known for a series of revolutionary medical and disability-related inventions, including heart stents and the first portable insulin pump. The Segway HT grew out of Kamen's work with the iBot, a wheelchair capable of climbing stairs and putting its occupant in a standing position. *Time* magazine wrote: "As Kamen and his team were working on the iBot, it dawned on them that they were onto something bigger. 'We

Despite its horrors, the eugenics movement had one positive effect. Shortly after the sterilization of adults with mental retardation began in the early part of the twentieth century, medical personnel at state institutions began to notice an unusual phenomenon. The castrations they were performing influenced the incidence of baldness, and the effects appeared to depend on the age of the individual "patient." In some cases, castrated men who had previously been bald regrew a thick, full head of hair. The physicians passed on their observations to the larger medical community, leading to a better understanding of the connection between the hormone *testosterone* and baldness.

realized we could build a device using very similar technology that could impact how *everybody* gets around,' he [Kamen] says" (Heilemann 2001, 81).

Innovations inspired by disability have also influenced the world of sports. The football "huddle" was introduced in 1894 at Gallaudet University, a school for deaf students. The players wanted to avoid having their opponents "steal" the signals for their next play. The hand signs used by baseball umpires were first used to accommodate a deaf outfielder named William Hoy, who was unable to hear the umpires' calls.

And then there's the Internet. The development of the early computer protocols that led to what is now called the Internet should be credited to Dr. Vinton Cerf. Dr. Cerf, who was hearing impaired, was married to a woman who was deaf, and frequently corresponded with her using text messaging. His familiarity with this format was key to his work with ARPANET, the precursor of the World Wide Web (Jacobs 1999).

Imagine for a moment Dr. Cerf, a person with a hearing impairment, pounding away on a computer keyboard (a descendant of typewriter technology) on a text messaging machine, sending data over telephone lines, as he develops the precursor of the Internet, and you will begin to realize that the link between human innovation and human disability could not possibly be merely a matter of chance.

In addition to inspiring such momentous breakthroughs, disabilities provide people who have them with unique perspectives on everyday life. For example, people who are paralyzed perceive walking differently from others. Out of necessity, they view it as one, but not the only, means of personal mobility. While individuals capable of ambulation might not think twice about it, a person with paralysis is more likely to think about mobility frequently, considering every alternative *but* walking. People unable to hear or speak likewise perceive communication in a different way. With typical conversation denied them, they must consider other alternatives (e.g., signing, lip reading, written language). Their perspective is similarly unique.

Since, by definition, disabilities involve a disruption of a major life activity, adaptations to disabilities also relate to important practical matters. At times, such adaptations can be particularly valuable, even uniquely useful. Consider the following examples:

- A person with a hearing impairment trying to use a telephone experiences difficulties similar to those of a person trying to use a phone located in a noisy area.
- A person who has paralysis of one hand confronts the same problem as cellular phone users who also may have only one hand available to grasp the phone.
- A person with a motor impairment faces problems similar to those encountered by astronauts in a weightless environment. Both may have to use unconventional procedures to move from one location to another.
- A blind traveler and a sighted person who are in a burning, smoke-filled airplane are both unable to see; but the person who is blind can call upon a lifetime of experience in adapting without sight.

All of these examples have obvious relevance to the world of business, and help to explain why a growing number of corporations are seeking out disabled individuals as consultants, product testers, and researchers. Some businesses today view people with disabilities as being at the forefront of human experience, with a particularly valuable perspective. This is a major shift. Disabilities are no longer seen only as a scourge or a burden; they can be appreciated for the important point of view they provide.

Adaptation Becomes a Necessity

It's not that I'm so smart. It's just that I stay with problems longer.
−Albert Einstein

Some whom others consider to be disabled—such as people who are born Deaf—argue that they have lost nothing, that their functioning only represents a different "lifestyle" or culture. For the vast majority of others, however, disability presents real challenges that require adaptations. Disabled individuals are faced with a choice: go on living with an ability impaired, or somehow compensate.

"Necessity is the mother of invention," the saying goes, and people with physical or mental limitations tend to be intimately familiar with the benefits of creative adaptations. Many are surprisingly resourceful in how they deal with their challenges.

The following example illustrates that adaptive responses to disabilities are not uncommon. They can be observed even in people some would not expect to be highly creative and resourceful.

The Former Residents of Pacific State Hospital

In 1927 the state of California opened the Pacific State Hospital, a residential institution for people with mental retardation. The institution was originally merely custodial in design, but over the decades medical, educational, and even occupational services were initiated. In its heyday the institution housed more than 3,000 individuals, who were cared for by 1,500 employees.

Between the years 1949 and 1958, 110 individuals "graduated" from the institution's "vocational" program and were discharged into the community. These individuals, all of whom were mildly or moderately mentally retarded, were sent back to the area where they had been born, in most cases after many years of institutionalization. The state of California gave them very little support and no supervision. They were on their own.

During the following decade, Robert Edgerton, a young anthropologist, began an intense study of 53 of these former residents—those who had settled in the greater Los Angeles area and were willing to participate in his research. Edgerton sought to study this group and its ways of adapting to "life on the outs" (Edgerton 1967).

The result of Edgerton's and his assistants' efforts was one of the most important studies in the history of disability. After careful research, the anthropologists found astounding adaptive abilities among these 53 very limited individuals. Virtually all of them struggled to deal with their mental retardation and to adapt to the multiple challenges of living in the community after many years in the state institution. The number and the sophistication of their survival tactics, and the fact that such otherwise limited individuals had such capabilities, had never before been known or documented.

Through extensive interviews and observations, Edgerton and his associates

determined that the vast majority of the former Pacific State residents carried on
great personal struggles to become assimilated into the outside world. Although
the researchers documented many adaptive strategies at work, two appeared to
be most critical. The first was the effort to obtain the protection of a benefactor
or benefactors who would assist the adults in "making it"—typically friends,
relatives, co-workers, even landlords. The former residents relied on these pro-
tectors to assist them with everything from getting a job and paying bills to

No poet ever composed in greater obscurity than William Black. Black
spent most of his adult life as a resident of a state institution for people with
mental retardation in Apple Creek, Ohio.

William Black was a "born" poet who could neither read nor write, and
in his older years he was both blind and deaf. The poem below is one of only
four published during his lifetime. It appeared in the institution's newsletter,
Apple Sauce, in October of 1978. Black's poem is remarkable for its humor,
structure, wit, and certainly its chauvinism. He must have delighted in teasing
the mostly female employees of the institution as he recited his work.

Willie's Sweetheart

Badmen want their women to be like
    cigarettes.
There are so many, all slender and
    dressed just alike.
When you know how to be selected
    cellophaned, and wrapped
When the fire's out, discarded.

More fashionable men prefer women like
    cigars
These are more special, work better and
    last longer.
Then if the brand is real good
    they aren't given away to other suckers.

Wise men treat women like pipes
They become attached to them the older
    they get.
And when the flame has burned out
They still look after them,
Knock them gently, care for them
    always.

No man in this world shares his pipes.

—William Black

using the telephone, things they never had to do in the institution. The anthropologists found that success in obtaining such a benefactor was a critical determinant of an individual's chances of survival in society.

Another skill was at least equally important, and highly valued by the adults themselves—the ability to develop ways to deny, obscure, and cover up their mental retardation. Edgerton found this quest almost universal among his subjects, and called their attempts to hide their previous institutional lives "donning a cloak of competence."

The anthropologists observed that, despite their years of institutionalization and relative isolation, the former residents were highly sensitive to the social "cues" that convey an individual's status in the community. They worked ceaselessly to hide their intellectual deficits, to explain away or deny their institutionalized past when confronted with it, and to exhibit contradictory "status" symbols that would tend to lead others away from the idea that they were, or ever had been, mentally retarded.

One frequently used survival strategy was to describe their institutionalization as a mistake. Some former residents told interviewers that they had been sent to the institution because of a betrayal by their families; others claimed they

As he approached the age of eighty, author James A. Michener experienced a period of prolific accomplishment. His output increased almost immediately following a quintuple heart by-pass, hip replacement, dental reconstruction, and what he describes as "an attack of permanent vertigo." In his preface to *The Eagle and the Raven,* one of ten books he wrote during this time, he related the following story to explain how such adversity can serve to inspire:

> The farmer at the end of our lane had an aging apple tree which had once produced good fruit but had now lost its energy and ability to give us apples. The farmer, on an early spring day I still remember, found eight nails, long and rusty, which he hammered into the trunk of the reluctant tree. Four were knocked in close to the ground, on four different sides of the trunk, four higher up and again well dispersed about the circumference.
>
> That autumn a miracle happened. The tired old tree, having been goaded back to life, produced a bumper crop of red, juicy apples, bigger and better than we had seen before. When I asked how this had happened, the farmer explained: "Hammerin' in the rusty nails gave it a shock to remind it that its job is to produce apples."

had been at the hospital only for medical procedures; many claimed they had been at Pacific State only temporarily and for educational reasons. Some of the subjects even appeared to believe their own rationalizations.

Others hid, or blatantly lied about, their past. Several people admitted falsifying job applications, and several lost jobs when the truth was discovered. In most cases, only a few family members, or very close friends, knew the real story of the adults' past. Some of the subjects intentionally adopted shyness as a way to hide their intellectual deficits, and avoided conversations that might have forced them to reveal information about themselves, much like the survival tactics of soldiers trapped behind enemy lines. One explained: "The best way to get by when you're with outsiders is just to keep your mouth shut. You know if you just keep your mouth shut you won't say nothing foolish" (163).

While hiding the stigmatized aspects of their past, the former residents also sought out status symbols that might mislead others about their past fortunes and present capabilities. Some collected souvenirs, photos, and other memorabilia they could display in their apartments or homes in an attempt to impress visitors. In many cases the items were entirely bogus—borrowed, stolen, or purchased in junk shops. Edgerton reported that one woman "had over forty china cups, saucers, and dishes, for each one of which there was a history involving travels, good friends, fine memories, and the happy exchange of gifts. All of these tales were false" (157).

One man kept an inoperable automobile parked in front of his living quarters. He would customarily say to those he wanted to "impress": "I'd like to take you for a ride in my car but I've got to get that generator tuned up" (161). Others hoarded mail they couldn't read, prizing any correspondence that came to them, or even stole others' discarded junk mail.[22] Several people who were unable to tell time wore no watch, but found people who would alert them when they had to go to work or leave for home. One man customarily wore a broken wristwatch: "I say that my old watch stopped, and somebody always tells me how close it is to the time when I got to be someplace" (166).

Edgerton's portraits of the former institutional residents showed that the experience of having a disability could inspire even relatively less gifted individuals to highly creative adaptations. A consideration of Edgerton's work leads inevitably to another question: If the experience of having a disability can foster creativity among people with very limited abilities, what might it engender in those with much greater gifts?

Benefiting from Adversity

Sweet are the uses of adversity,
Which like the toad, ugly and venomous,
Wears yet a precious jewel in his head;
And this our life, exempt from public haunt,
Finds tongues in trees, books in the running brooks,
Sermons in stones, and good in every thing.
—As You Like It, act 2, scene 1

Not all challenges entail suffering, but a disability frequently does. The suffering may be physical, mental, or even spiritual. It may be directly related to the impairment, or it could have a secondary cause. Suffering directly related to disability could include the physical pain resulting from an accident or injury, the discomfort of enduring paralysis, or the trauma of medical treatment or rehabilitation—all obvious examples. Secondary sources of disability-related suffering tend to be less well understood. One of the most painful, and most frequently encountered, is the experience of separation from others, commonly called "distancing." Distancing may be simply the result of physical or sensory barriers to participation or communication, but it can also result from the perceived shame or embarrassment of being disabled, or the misunderstanding of others. In some cases, the consequences of distancing—such as loneliness, segregation, or unemployment—create barriers that are more problematic than the disability itself.

In some segments of our frequently hedonistic society, the idea that suffering can have beneficial consequences is anathema; some observers, however, would grant that experiencing some adversity can help a person to grow and learn. Most parents believe a child raised without some hardship or challenge would be "spoiled." In hiring and promotion, many employers look for job candidates who have faced significant challenges in previous positions and developed effective solutions to them. Weightlifters have a saying: "No pain, no gain," meaning that before muscles grow they must first be subjected to stress. In a similar way, by experiencing the suffering accompanying a disability, an individual may have the opportunity to develop some important strengths, such as tolerance, patience, endurance, determination, and adaptability. These strengths may then be applied to other aspects of life.

The following example will lend support to this theory.

Roosevelt and Churchill

According to many historians, June 6, 1944, was the most important day of the twentieth century. Early that morning, Allied armies landed on the beaches of Normandy to begin the decisive assault on the forces of the German army. The landing forces knew that on their shoulders rested the future of the free world. If they succeeded, the tyranny that had plagued much of Europe for almost a decade would come to an end. If they failed, all free people would be mortally imperiled, and the hopes of those oppressed by Nazism would be dashed.

On the day of the Normandy invasion, the two greatest free nations in the world were led by men of incomparable skill and determination. Both were seasoned politicians, although little in their political experience could have prepared them for such a test. Both were from families well known in their respective countries, although their connections and "blue blood" could not help them with the crisis at hand. But the two men had one more characteristic in common, one that neither ever wanted to acknowledge publicly, but one that might have been more important than any other. Both leaders were disabled.

Franklin Delano Roosevelt contracted polio at the age of thirty-nine. At first he had almost total paralysis of his lower extremities, and was not even able to sit up in bed. He described himself as being at first "in utter despair" at his loss (Miller 1983, 184). Soon, however, he forced himself to pursue various treatments and therapies for his condition. Although he gained skills to compensate for his loss of the ability to walk, he never became able to stand without assistance, nor was he ever reconciled to his paralysis. Roosevelt never wanted his picture to be taken in a wheelchair or while receiving assistance, and the national press politely complied with his request.

Prime Minister Winston Spencer Churchill of Great Britain struggled with manic depression (now referred to as "bipolar disorder") throughout his adult life. He would settle into deep, dark moods for days, weeks, or months, to the chagrin of his friends and family. At other times he would appear to be just the opposite: energetic, optimistic, and ebullient. After observing his friend Churchill, Lord Beaverbrook wrote: "What a creature of strange moods he is, always at the top of the wheel of confidence or at the bottom of an intense depression" (Manchester 1983, 24). In Churchill's era, medicine offered little relief for his condition, and so he often had to endure his "spells" until they left him as mysteriously as they had come.

Because of their disabilities, both Roosevelt and Churchill were well acquainted with pain, fear, and adversity. Their experiences no doubt had a pro-

Fig. 6.3. Roosevelt and Churchill in Casablanca. *(The Franklin Delano Roosevelt Library)*

found effect on their character. Nathan Miller, one of Roosevelt's biographers, describes some of the inner strengths that F.D.R. had due to his paralysis, one of them being the ability to go about his business while defiantly "laughing" at his problem:

> When a firm that was making special arch supports for his shoes wrote to ask if he walked with "a cain," he scrawled a note along the side of the letter: "I cannot walk without a *Cain* because I'm not *Abel.*" To another correspondent, he wrote, "I have renewed my youth in a rather unpleasant manner by contracting . . . infantile paralysis." Something comic might be described as "funny as a crutch," and when finishing a conversation, he would often say, "Goodbye, I've got to run." (1983, 190–91)

Churchill's strength was sheer endurance. His biographer, Anthony Storr, observes:

> In 1940 any political leader might have tried to rally Britain with brave words, although his heart was full of despair. But only a man who had known and faced such despair within himself could carry conviction at such a moment. Only a man who knew what it was to discern a gleam of hope in a hopeless situation, whose courage was beyond reason, and whose aggressive spirit burned at its fiercest when he was hemmed in and surrounded by enemies,

> **Sonnet**
>
> When I consider how my light is spent
>   Ere half my days in this dark world and wide,
>   And that one talent which is death to hide
>   Lodg'd with me useless, though my soul more bent
> To serve therewith my Maker, and present
>   My true account, lest he returning chide,
>   "Doth God exact day-labour, light denied?"
>   I fondly ask. But Patience, to prevent
> That murmur, soon replies: "God doth not need
>   Either man's work or his own gifts: who best
>   Bear his mild yoke, they serve him best. His state
> Is kingly; thousands at his bidding speed
>   And post o'er land and ocean without rest:
>   They also serve who only stand and wait."
>
> —John Milton

could have given emotional reality to the words of defiance which rallied and sustained us in the menacing summer of 1940. (1988, 4)

Could it be that Roosevelt's struggle with polio endowed him with the strengths required to contend with an even more pernicious foe? Could Churchill's experience of mental illness have prepared him for the dark days of the Blitz and all that he and England had to endure before eventual victory?

How much of the great leadership qualities of Churchill and Roosevelt were owed to their experience with disability is impossible to say. But it is worth considering that the freedom we enjoy today was made possible in no small part by the talents of two great leaders who suffered the effects—for both good and ill—of significant disabilities. It is also wonderfully fitting that the atrocities of the Third Reich, which began with a pogrom against people with disabilities, were ended by free nations led by two great disabled men.

People with Disabilities Prize Liberating Technology and Services

Although people with disabilities can benefit from their experiences with adversity, they also work diligently to make their lives as comfortable and enjoyable as possible. Of course, almost everyone does this, but for individuals with disabilities extra efforts may be required to achieve what others obtain with ease. For this reason, many disabled people are eager to try new technology and services developed for the enjoyment of the masses. They are early, enthusiastic, and loyal users of innovative products and services, especially those that enhance their capabilities—a fact not always appreciated by the businesses that make and market those products.

George is Exhibit A in support of this theory. George has a Ph.D., a good job, a lovely family, and a severe case of dyslexia. One thing that George doesn't have is a sense of direction, a problem related to his disability. For that reason, George was among the first consumers to buy an advanced Global Positioning Device, or GPD. GPDs use satellite technology to provide consumers with exact coordinates of their location or destination. Sophisticated GPDs, like the one George has, can present the information in the form of highly detailed maps.

After connecting the GPD to his laptop computer, George is able to navigate the local downtown area where he works, consulting a map of his current location and ultimate destination displayed on the computer's screen. He can quickly tell if he is getting closer, if he has made the correct turn, and so on. His computer and GPD guide him until he arrives at his desired location, or the area begins to look familiar to him.

GPD technology has gone a long way toward compensating for George's lack of directional sense. He is not otherwise a technology wonk, but like most people, George takes a great interest in anything that allows him to live more independently or with greater dignity. And so he has eagerly embraced a rather sophisticated technology, and now walks around his downtown area looking a bit like James Bond—but happy.

No technological item has provided greater benefit to people with disabilities than the computer. So limited are the physical skills required, and so flexible is the machine itself, that almost anyone can use one. Equipped with a joystick or head-pointing device, even someone with extensive physical paralysis can communicate. People with gross motor paralysis, but normal speech, quickly learn to use speech recognition software, dictating to their computer faster than many people can type. Users with visual disabilities equip their personal computers with voice synthesizer programs that read the text on the screen to them; many deaf users find the computer and the Internet as easy to use as the TTY (teletypewriter) they have relied on for so long. Such is the enthusiasm that disabled people have for the enabling effect of computers that, despite the fact that they are greatly economically disadvantaged relative to the rest of society, they are almost as likely to be computer owners (Microsoft 2000).

There are many other examples of technology with great appeal to disabled consumers. Vibrating pagers were originally developed to allow hearing users to receive silent notification of messages awaiting them, thus avoiding embarrassing moments during religious services, concerts, plays, or meetings. Very quickly, however, people with hearing impairments discovered that the pagers also met their information needs, and the technology found a new and very receptive market (Frost 2000). The same can be said for remote control devices, sound-activated switches, and "touch" lamps—lamps that go on and off with a simple touch of the base. These products were originally developed for consumer convenience, to assist those who were too lazy to operate a light switch, or too lethargic to get out of bed to turn a television on or off. But people who *can't* turn a light switch, and people who *can't* get out of bed immediately saw what these things would mean to them, and they now constitute a new and very loyal "submarket." A typical consumer might tire of the novelty of a touch lamp, but one with osteoarthritis never will.

Just as enabling products appeal to people with disabilities, so do services that make independent living easier. People with disabilities are heavy users of taxis, lawn care, housecleaning, catering, pick-up and delivery, 800 numbers, television shopping, and countless other services usually associated with convenience. For someone with a disability, however, such services can mean the difference between access and exclusion, between independent living and dependency.

The Internet is a great example of an enabling service. The World Wide Web connects people who have the necessary technology and the ability to operate a computer. It is oblivious to other personal characteristics. Many people with impairments of all sorts who have been socially isolated have found that the Internet provides them virtually unlimited access to others. It has even created job opportunities for many previously unemployed people with disabilities. Because the Internet is so valuable to them, people with disabilities spend, on average, twice as much time online as typical consumers.

Writer Lou Ann Walker describes how the Internet has transformed the lives of people who are deaf:

> I've seen it firsthand in my own family. My mother and father are deaf, as were my aunt and uncle, and I signed even before I spoke. Not long ago, I went to a senior citizens' luncheon for deaf people in Indianapolis. As hands flew, I noticed something quite surprising about the conversations I was seeing among my parents' friends. These older people were wired! "Did you get my e-mail" "When I was surfing the Web, I found a great new site . . ." This was not the deaf world I knew growing up. (2001, 5)

Businesses that pay attention to this important market segment can reap great rewards. When the developers of an Internet-based grocery delivery service constructed their business plan, they thought they would appeal mostly to urban workers who were short on time but could well afford the small extra expense involved. While this proved to be true, they discovered that many people with mobility limitations also quickly became customers. One provider, Kozmo, now displays on the first page of its employee training manual a letter of appreciation from Cameo C. Massey, a customer who has Epstein-Barr, a viral condition that can be associated with chronic fatigue in extreme cases. Massey wrote: "Your service has helped make my life filled with more quality time. By being able to order books, magazines, movies, games and food from Kozmo, I find that I am able to feel more in touch and up to date with normal people" (Blair 2000).

All of these examples demonstrate that people with disabilities find great value in products and services that can help them lead more independent, productive, and fulfilling lives. The lesson for businesses is clear: *technology and services that make some things easier for many tend to make them possible for others.* Those others quickly become loyal, core customers.

Disability-Inspired Innovations Expand to Benefit Many

Because of the aging of the population, the civil rights movement, and the passage of the Americans with Disabilities Act, U.S. society has recently initiated many significant changes aimed at making living with a disability easier. As these improvements have been provided, time and time again they have come to benefit many more people than their designers originally intended and expected.

So-called "wheelchair" ramps have become so popular that many buildings now provide them instead of, rather than in addition to, steps. Everybody wants them, and everybody uses them. Automatic doors, previously found only in grocery stores and luxury hotels, are now used in many types of public buildings. Although they are not required by the ADA or by most local architectural standards, they are more popular than ever. Mechanized doors obviously facilitate entering and exiting by people with mobility and grasping impairments, but they also aid delivery personnel, parents with strollers, customers carrying packages—anyone and everyone.

Audio cues on elevators and at crossing points have become ubiquitous, and many forget they were originally intended to help people with visual impairments. Now they also aid the distracted or forgetful. Before the ADA, very few offices or restaurants offered oversized restroom stalls, but after they were required to do so to accommodate people who use wheelchairs, business owners found oversized stalls so popular with the general public that many now offer more than building codes require. Designers credit the ADA with a "renaissance" of large and gracious restrooms in New York's finer restaurants, each one trying to outdo the last in size, luxury, and ease of use (Marin 2000).

The most famous example of the popular use of disability-related innovations is, of course, the curb cut. Originally required on public sidewalks to allow people using wheelchairs, crutches, and walkers to cross the street with greater ease, curb cuts are now also used by cyclists, skate boarders, pedestrians, delivery personnel, and parents with carriages. As noted in chapter 1, so many people have benefited from curb cuts that engineers have termed the phenomenon of many people benefiting from accommodations intended for the disabled the "curb-cut effect."

A corollary to this phenomenon is the "electronic curb-cut effect." This term refers to the fact that many technological enhancements created to help disabled people end up being embraced by the masses. There are countless examples.

On August 5, 1972, Julia Child's *The French Chef* became the first nationally broadcast television program with "closed captioning for the hearing impaired." Today, most primetime television programs offer closed captioning, even for live events. Broadcasters have learned that many people other than deaf and hearing-impaired viewers make use of captions—people who want to watch television with the sound turned down (perhaps while a spouse is sleeping), viewers in noisy sports bars, students learning a foreign language, even television editors and researchers. (It's much easier to perform a word search through captioned text than to roll through reams of videotape.)

A few years ago retail locations began using cash registers with picture-based keyboards instead of, or in addition to, numerals and letters. The machines were intended to help people with learning or reading disorders, but employers soon found out they also made immigrants and slow readers more employable, and they often came to be preferred over the old-style cash registers by all employees. They were simply easier for *anyone* to use (Jacobs 1999).

The list of popularized accommodations is endless: talking alarm clocks and calculators, telephones with oversized buttons and hearing "loopsets"—all were developed with the "disability" market in mind, but all quickly found a larger following. Again and again businesses have learned the lesson of the curb-cut and the electronic curb-cut effects: *innovations that make actions*

On July 26, 1990, when the Americans with Disabilities Act was signed in the White House Rose Garden, the Rev. Dr. Harold Wilke was standing right beside President George Bush. Wilke is an eminent figure in the field of disability rights, especially as they relate to religious inclusion.

A brilliant man with an impressive record of achievements, Wilke's talents would be the envy of many—as minister, author, lecturer, husband, and father. Most, people, however, are most impressed by the fact that he was born without arms. In their place, Wilke uses his feet just as most people use their hands.

Wilke nonchalantly describes the proper way to change a diaper—using only your feet:

> We have five sons, all of whom I have helped to take care of and several of whom I alone took care of for several days. Two of them came to us when there were no modern diapers, so I used the cloth ones with safety pins; when the child squirmed a good deal, it wasn't easy! I would hold him on the floor, half lying, supported by my thigh, fastening it. I would then lie on the floor, grasp him under the arms with my two feet, then lift him into his playpen or feeding table. (1984, 6)

Wilke's brilliance in adaptation has allowed him to live independently throughout his life. When he decided to give up driving—well into his seventies—he had the lowest "safe driver" rates offered by his insurance company. He knew, however, that his eyesight was failing him.

possible for some tend to make them easier for many others. Disability access tends to generalize into user friendliness. It is a lesson that every manufacturer, product designer, and marketer should understand.

Adaptation Becomes a Habit

Companies spend thousands of dollars training their employees to "think out of the box," to perceive and respond to challenges in unconventional and innovative ways. For disabled people conventional responses are frequently not an option. Their status demands—and rewards—creative responses to typical problems. When you meet someone with a disability, chances are you are with someone who quite frequently "thinks out of the box."

Examples of daily adaptations are well known to anyone who has a disability. Here are a few:

- A business executive who has had a stroke learns to tie his necktie with one hand.
- A person with mental retardation learns social skills (e.g., feigned shyness) that help her hide some of her intellectual deficits.
- A person with a severe hearing impairment learns to watch body language intently to gain clues that will confirm the meaning of the words he is lip reading.
- An executive who is blind develops her memorization skills so she can recall hundreds of phone numbers and know her appointment calendar three months into the future.
- A person who uses a wheelchair redesigns her home to make things more easily accessible to her.
- A child with a learning disability develops his capacity to listen intently during class lectures to compensate for his reading difficulties.

Conventional wisdom pays homage to the adaptive skills of disabled people in the popular assumption that disabilities often carry with them special talents—that people with mental retardation are gentle, that blind people have heightened senses of hearing, that those who use wheelchairs are indomitable, and so on. The element of truth in these myths is that adapting to disabilities can indeed produce some benefits, but they are the result of hard work, not mysterious influences. It is often much easier to note the things a person *cannot* do than to credit them for what they have *learned* to do well.

The overall impact of habitual adaptation, constantly responding creatively to life's challenges, is a little-understood aspect of disabilities. It is certainly deserving of greater study. The habit of adaptation might account, at least in part, for many examples throughout history of highly creative and productive individuals who have had disabilities. It might also mean that many less well-known disabled people also have hard-won skills that are under-appreciated.

Business executives who pay great sums for consultants to teach them to "think out of the box" would do well to observe the habitually creative thinkers in their midst—their co-workers with disabilities. The necessity of addressing mundane problems with creative solutions has likely prepared them to be innovative in more complex areas, including the challenges faced by business.

The Risks of Underestimation

The Germans built a four-gun battery on the cliff just west of Port-en-Bessin. Big fortifications, big guns—155mm. Beautifully camouflaged with nets and dirt embankments, they could not be seen from the air.

The farmer on whose land they were built was furious because he could not graze his cattle or grow crops on the field. He paced off the distances between the bunkers, from the bunkers to the observation post on the very edge of the cliff, from the cliff to the bunkers, and so on. He had a blind son, eight or nine years old. Like many blind people, the boy had a fabulous memory. Because he was blind, the Germans paid little attention to him.

One day in early 1944, the boy hitched a ride to Bayeux. There he managed to get in touch with André Heintz, an eighteen-year-old in the Resistance. The boy gave Heintz his information; Heintz sent it on to England via his little homemade radio transmitter (hidden in a Campbell Soup can; today on display in the Battle of Normandy Museum in Caen); thus the British Navy, on D-Day, had the exact coordinates of the bunkers.

–Stephen E. Ambrose, *D-Day*

As the preceding story indicates, underestimating the capabilities of disabled people can be dangerous. Not the least of these dangers is the waste of talent. It is impossible to imagine a world deprived of the gifts of all the talented individuals who have lived their lives with disabilities. Yet the longstanding 67 percent unemployment rate for those with significant disabilities proves that many capable and talented people are being overlooked and underutilized.

In the twenty-first century, every business will have to be able to survive in a highly competitive marketplace. Competition will dictate that businesses take every advantage of the markets and talents available to them. The intelligent exploitation of nontraditional resources will be rewarded. In the future, business cannot afford to overlook the valuable resource people with disabilities represent.

The paradox that presents itself here is almost an inversion of Darwin's "survival of the fittest" theory. If there are multiple connections between disability and human innovation, then a business's survival can be promoted by paying attention to people with impairments as well as those without them—their talents, their energy, and their genius for adaptation. In this context, the mandate to "adapt or die" takes on a new meaning. Adaptation is an outcome not just of strength, but also of learning to live and thrive despite deficiencies.

Although he never said so explicitly, Darwin eventually may have had a similar realization. He had ample opportunity to do so, not just because of his observations as a naturalist, but also because of his own experience with ill health. For the latter half of his life, after returning from his voyage on the *Beagle,* Darwin incurred the debilitating effects of what was likely chagas disease, which he contracted from an insect bite he received in South America.

Darwin's illness had a profound influence on his work from then on. While his condition frequently robbed him of his strength, it also gave him a sense of determination and urgency, a fact he remarked upon at the beginning of *Origin of Species*: "My work is now nearly finished; but as it will take me two or three more years to complete it, and as my health is far from strong, I have been urged to publish this Abstract" (6).

Perhaps at the end of his life Darwin's personal experience of debilitation had taught him a deeper lesson about the progress of the species: It is not only the survival of the strongest that benefits future generations. People who adapt to their weaknesses or imperfections can also make great contributions.

Resources

Disability Social History Project
http://www.disabilityhistory.org/
255 3rd St., #202
Oakland, Calif. 94607
sdias@disabilityhistory.org

VSA Arts
http://www.vsarts.org/
1300 Connecticut Ave. N.W., Suite 700
Washington, D.C. 20036
(800) 933-8721 Voice
(202) 737-0645 TTY
(202) 737-0725 Fax
info@vsarts.org

7

Profiles of Four Business Leaders

This chapter presents profiles of four unique individuals. The first is a leader in the telecommunications industry; the second a renowned academician and business consultant; the third a "new economy" Internet entrepreneur; and the fourth a human resources professional in a major high-tech firm. All four have significant impairments: respectively, a learning problem, a form of mental illness, a physical disability, and a sensory impairment.

None of these profiles is from the familiar "inspiration" or "triumph over adversity" genres of disability literature. Each presents a personal story that raises fundamental issues about what disabilities are and aren't, and how businesses might respond to disabled employees in ways that both respect and utilize their unique talents.

Craig McCaw: "Dyslexic Visionary"

Although highly creative learning styles are frequently mischaracterized as disabilities, it is also true that many accomplished individuals have overcome real and severe learning problems. Examples include Alexander Graham Bell, Dwight D. Eisenhower, Werner von Braun, Leonardo da Vinci, and Edgar Allan Poe. In the business world, those who have

struggled with learning disabilities include Ted Turner, Thomas Watson Jr., William Hewlett, Fred Friendly, Paul J. Orfalea, Charles Schwab, and many others.

No example of a business leader who overcame a learning disability is more compelling than that of Craig McCaw, the billionaire founder of McCaw Cellular. McCaw's story shows that learning disabilities can not only be overcome, but sometimes even used to great advantage.

Getting Started in Business

Craig McCaw was born in Centralia, Washington, in 1949, the second of four boys. His father, J. Elroy McCaw, was a highly regarded pioneer in the television and cable industries, but he was also a "seat of his pants" businessman, famous for the informal style he used in conducting his affairs. The elder McCaw owned a broadcast and cable operation, Twin City Cablevision, and Craig began working in the family business at the age of sixteen.

In 1969, when Craig McCaw was nineteen and a sophomore at Stanford University, his father died suddenly, leaving the business in a difficult, almost chaotic situation. Only at the death of the senior McCaw was the extent of his disorganization known, and the McCaw family was soon forced to liquidate many of its holdings in order to satisfy creditors (Corr 2000, 28). They managed to retain control of the cable television provider, however, and Craig McCaw began managing the small company while still at Stanford. After graduation he turned his attention to the company full time.

During the 1970s the cable industry was still in its infancy, but McCaw grasped its potential and devoted all of his energy to expanding Twin City by acquisition. By amassing large amounts of debt, and using newly purchased properties as collateral, he quickly expanded the business from a tiny family-run operation to a major regional provider. When McCaw finally sold the business in 1987 for $755 million, he had expanded the operation from four thousand subscribers to nearly half a million. This pattern—seeing and seizing major opportunities before competitors could react—would characterize McCaw's operational style throughout his career.

McCaw sold Twin City Cablevision not just to make a profit—although he certainly did that—but to enable him to focus all his attention on another fledgling industry, an industry he was convinced would offer much greater opportunity than cable television: cellular communications. At a time when the feasibility of cellular was still being debated, and the market for it was unknown, McCaw moved quickly to grab market share. Proceeding much as he had with cable television, he borrowed heavily to purchase franchises and licenses, and then used his new acquisitions to obtain more financing. By the end of the 1980s, McCaw Cellular was a major national player. But for McCaw, the main thrill of business was creating companies, not operating them. By 1994 McCaw had guided McCaw Cellular through an explosive period of borrowing and growth, and the company had become a leading national provider of cellular telephone services. That year he sold the business to one of his major competitors, AT&T, for $11.5 billion.

Not one to rest on his accomplishments, McCaw quickly moved in a new direction. Through the holding company he directs, Eagle River, Inc., he made major investments in several communications companies, including Nextel, which provides radio dispatch and other wireless services, and Nextlink, a fiber-optic provider to businesses. Currently, McCaw is developing a broadband satellite company, Teledesic LLC, which he co-founded with Microsoft CEO Bill Gates. The goal of Teledesic is to establish a network of 288 satellites that will enable broadband wireless communications anywhere on earth, what McCaw has termed "an Internet in the sky," by 2005 (Feder 2000). Teledesic is by far his most ambitious undertaking.

Management Style

Craig McCaw's success is especially noteworthy for the extraordinary way in which it was achieved. Throughout his career, Craig McCaw has focused his attention on enormous challenges—establishing a large cable television system, becoming a national cellular telephone provider, launching a worldwide wireless communication network. In meeting these challenges, McCaw faces complex financial, technical, and market issues—all while dealing with a learning disability that makes it extremely difficult for him to understand detailed information, especially in written form. Time and again he has proven himself more than equal to the task, able to comprehend complex issues others cannot. According to his closest associates, McCaw's working habits are highly unusual—perhaps unique.

Some observers—including McCaw himself—attribute both his operational style and his success to his learning disability. Since childhood, McCaw has experienced enormous problems with reading, and has exhibited characteristics associated with hyperactivity disorder. To compensate, McCaw has developed his own management style. He carefully avoids the customary practices and procedures of most executives. For example, he goes into his Seattle office as seldom as possible, by some accounts spending as little as 25 percent of his time there (Hardy 2000). He stays away from almost all company meetings and is often regarded, even by his own employees, as something of a recluse. McCaw disdains lengthy written documents, leaving them to be handled by his assistants, and he carefully controls the information that does make it to his desk. Of his early work in the cable business, an associate noted: "he understood the mechanisms of how to grow his business as well as anybody in the cable business . . . but the details of the loan agreement that we put together? He never saw to that" (Corr 2000, 78).

But he is far from being a Howard Hughes type of business eccentric. McCaw long ago defined himself as a "big-picture" thinker, whose primary value to his business lies in planning, rather than in attention to detail. His absence from the daily affairs of his company is intentional and strategic. Although McCaw eschews the ordinary office routines, he is constantly in touch from his home, his yacht, or his aircraft. And McCaw behaves not at all like a pampered executive playing with his oversized toys. He is fully qualified to captain both his yachts and pilot his Gulfstream jet, seaplane, and personal helicopter.

Such technical expertise, and McCaw's eagerness to use it, is illuminating. While mindful of his limitations, he is not hesitant to exploit his strengths to their fullest potential. For example, he understands he lacks a gift for organization, so he leaves that to others. He has hired some of the best organizational minds in business. McCaw devotes most of his time to thinking creatively and analytically about his business challenges, areas in which he knows he excels. He avoids everything that would distract him from his role, no matter how unusual his habits may seem to others.

And others are frequently baffled by his behavior. *Business Week* noted: "McCaw has the playfulness of a kid. With friends, he disguises his voice almost every time he calls them—Daffy Duck one time, British royalty another. He loves to do spontaneous things, like fly his helicopter down to Oregon for seafood dinners" (Elstrom 1998, 6). Like a Rogerian psychotherapist, he will often punctuate conversations with long silences. Says Tom Hull, a former co-worker: "You'd go in to talk to him and sometimes he wouldn't say anything for a while, and you'd have to say something because it was too uncomfortable. I don't know if it was a trick or something, but he was just a really mellow guy" (Corr 2000, 78). In meetings, McCaw will customarily challenge his executives to consider all of the possible consequences of a move, from the most likely to the truly wacky (77). He once brought together a group of his top executives and challenged them with the question: "What business are we in?" (171).

While sometimes baffling and befuddling his co-workers and competitors, McCaw continues to earn their respect. Ed Tuck, a longtime associate, marvels

---

"The greatest ideas you will ever have are the ones that other people don't understand."

---

at his ability to comprehend and take on enormous challenges, successfully tackling problems few can even understand. "Craig manages to be involved in things that are closer to the optimum level of instability," he says (Corr 2000, 268). Samuel Glinn, a competitor, observes: "He has the talent to see things that other people don't see" (Elsrom 1998, 5). Another competitor stated simply: "He's one of the people I've met in my life whose IQ starts with a 3" (Hiltzik 1999, 3).

McCaw on His Dyslexia

Craig McCaw is candid about his learning disability. In his childhood, he found that dyslexia created great problems for him in completing his schoolwork, and he frequently required the help of tutors to master his studies. After learning to cope with his own learning problems, he spent considerable time studying dyslexia itself.

McCaw explains: "You see the world differently because of [dyslexia]. I have no idea as to why, but I understand that, and I've seen a certain number of dyslexics who are that way. So maybe it's a strategic asset, though it makes detail and organization more difficult" (Corr 2000, 29). He acknowledges that his management style is highly dependent on others: "I can't go to a piece of paper and organize things as most people would. I have to explain conceptually what we want to accomplish, and then somebody else has to translate that into a concise, organized plan."[1]

Of course, not all people with "learning disabilities" are as talented as McCaw. The phrase itself is a catchall, and, like all such terms, can be misleading. For years psychologists have included under "learning disabilities" many neurological complexities that do not correspond to the norm, including every-thing from the classic "letter reversal" to much more severe perceptual deficits. Many people with learning disabilities have no counterbalancing strength, but some others have extraordinary capabilities.

One researcher, Thomas G. West, has summarized this phenomenon as follows: "perhaps not all dyslexics can be shown to be highly gifted in some way, but those who are highly gifted may have gifts that are unusual and some-how distinctive—since theory would suggest that in this population distinctive neurological mechanisms may produce distinctive talents as well as distinctive difficulties" (1998, 3).

McCaw seems to have harnessed intellectual abilities so profound as to be truly abnormal. Like many gifted people, he has learned to use his personal abilities to the maximum. He understands his learning style often creates prob-lems for his co-workers as well as himself: "people have trouble understanding what I'm saying. The more literally they listen to me, the more trouble they have understanding. I'm a conceptual thinker. I speak in conceptual rather than literal terms. Figuratively rather than literally" (Corr 2000, 114).

The limitations imposed by his learning problem, McCaw believes, have required him to rely on his real strengths—a hidden blessing. He is regarded by his associates as an astute listener, and is reportedly able to remember conver-sations verbatim months after they occur. He is also uniquely talented in his ability to comprehend complex, abstract problems. Says McCaw: "Dyslexia forced me to be quite conceptual, because I'm not very good at details. And be-cause I'm not good at details, I tend to be rather spatial in my thinking—ori-ented to things in general terms, rather than the specific. That allows you to step back and take in the big picture. I feel blessed about that."[2]

McCaw's foresight and ability to discern major opportunities in the com-plex world of communications have earned him the title of "the prophet of tele-com" by *Business Week* (Elstrom 1998, 2) and "dyslexic visionary" by *Fortune* (Kupfer 1996). Through it all, he shows a disdain for the limelight and mini-mizes his own genius, saying, "I'm the master of the obvious. So whenever I have an idea that I think is obvious, I pursue it" (Corr 2000, 234).

His struggles with learning have taught him much more than a coping style. In addition to his reputation for idiosyncratic behavior, McCaw is also known for his kindness and tolerance. Unlike some executives known for their exacting standards, he does not engage in or allow meanness in his business dealings: "You need to respect other people, and one of the most destructive things in an organization is sarcasm and making fun of other people" (Corr 2000, 173). As a result of his personal struggle, McCaw has become involved in helping others with learning problems, donating a total of $2.7 million in support of Seattle Public Schools' "Team Read" project.[3]

Global Perspective

Although he has achieved great success in the past with cable television and cellular communications, those challenges pale in comparison with his current goal: to establish a global wireless broadband communication system, based on a grid of satellites circling the earth. Communications experts have estimated the cost of a worldwide satellite system at $10 billion, minimum (Feder 2000). This is a "high stakes" business venture in every sense. As in the past, many skeptics believe McCaw has drastically misjudged both the feasibility of the project and the value of the market. This time, however, most agree that if Teledesic is successful, its profitability could be unlimited. John Pike, a satellite expert at the Federation of American Scientists, comments: "I think it is extremely unlikely that Teledesic is going to happen or make any money. On the other hand, if it does happen and does make money, it will make a preposterous amount of money" (Kupfer 1996, 71). Samuel A. Farrer Jr., another satellite specialist, comments: "He's thinking of tens of millions of customers for satellites. . . . No one else is talking those numbers" (Feder 2000).

The scope of the Teledesic plan is unprecedented, but it plays right into what McCaw perceives as his primary strength—the ability to decipher extraordinary new opportunities long before others do. McCaw's career is a work in progress, and it remains to be seen just how far his visionary abilities can take him, especially whether or not he is "reading" the opportunity for a worldwide "Internet in the sky" correctly. Preliminary results are not encouraging. One other major attempt by others to establish a satellite-based communications network—ICO Global Communications—ran out of financing and was bailed out by McCaw and his partners in May 2000 at a cost of $1.2 billion.

Yet McCaw perseveres, unfazed by the skeptics: "It's necessary that you insulate yourself from what others think. The greatest ideas you will ever have are the ones that other people don't understand. And if you're in that position, and you care too much what they think, you will not do the right thing. . . . I don't mind if they don't agree with me. In fact, it's a lot of fun when they don't, because life is a long time, and the more they criticize you, the more they compliment you later if you're right" (Corr 2000, 146).

Dr. Temple Grandin: Uneven Talent

On paper, Dr. Temple Grandin would seem to be just one more accomplished academic with a lucrative sideline as a consultant to businesses. She is an assistant professor of animal science at Colorado State University, the author of three books and numerous professional papers, the recipient of many professional awards and honors, and the sole proprietor of Grandin Livestock Handling Systems, Inc. Her consulting firm specializes in designing equipment and  facilities for the meat-packing industry, and her work can be found all over the United States, and in Canada, Mexico, Europe, Australia, and elsewhere. Over half of all the cattle processed in the United States pass through a system designed by Temple Grandin.

But what makes her career all the more remarkable is the fact that she has succeeded as a person with the psychological disorder known as *autism*. First identified by Leo Kanner in the 1940s, autism is a severe psychological syndrome characterized by social withdrawal. It usually has an onset around the age of two or three, and it lasts a lifetime.

Features of Autism

Early researchers into autism noticed delayed or absent speech development in afflicted children, and certain other "soft" signs, including thematic fixations, ritualistic gestures, rocking, finger flicking, and other forms of self-stimulation. Many children with autism were found to have perceptive disorders, and many had extreme sensitivity to sensory stimulation. Although early researchers focused on the suspected role of abusive parenting in precipitating the condition, most now believe autism is caused by genetics. Neurological abnormalities in autistic individuals have been confirmed by autopsy.

People who have autism exhibit a wide range of characteristics, and the severity of the condition varies greatly. About one person in one thousand has autism, and although mental retardation is often associated with it, many people with an autistic diagnosis have normal or above normal intelligence. A small percentage are known to be "savants"; that is, they exhibit extraordinary mental abilities, such as unexplainable computational skills, complete recall of numbers and written passages, and the ability to determine instantly what day of the week any date in history occurred, or on what day any future date will fall. To the public, the best-known example of an autistic savant is the character Raymond Babbitt, portrayed by Dustin Hoffman in the movie *Rain Man.* Temple Grandin coached Hoffman for his role.

While the behaviors of people with autism are frequently puzzling, it is not just those with savant capabilities who can amaze. For example, many children with autism have a habit of moving, or "flicking," their fingers in an extremely fast and peculiar manner. Anyone else who attempts to perform the same action finds it impossible to do with equal speed and accuracy. The child, however, will perform the movement with lightning quickness, precisely the same way every time, his or her "muscle memory" duplicating the action perfectly. Canadian golf professional Moe Norman, a man with autistic behaviors, is renowned as the most consistent ball striker in the history of the game, a trait that has earned him the nickname "Pipeline Moe." Norman once gave an exhibition in which he drove 1,540 golf balls over a period of about seven hours. All of his drives went more than 225 yards, and all landed inside a thirty-yard-wide landing target. Every golfer strives to develop a consistent swing, but none has surpassed Norman.[4]

Obsessions and fixations are frequent characteristics of people with autism, and many have an ability to concentrate intently like a subject under hypnosis. Frequently, however, the fixation may seem peculiar or incomprehensible to others, creating social distance and isolation. For example, a young man with a fixation on mathematics went with a friend to a football game. During the game the young man spoke endlessly about the exact distance between various U.S. cities, the difference between temperatures Fahrenheit and Centigrade, and other numerical issues irrelevant to football. At half time, his friend asked the young man if he knew the score of the game. He replied: "Yes, I do. It's seven to ten," which was correct. Then he went on, "Or seven over ten, or point seven, or seven dimes, or fourteen nickels, or two quarters and two dimes, or . . ."

Growing Up Autistic

Temple Grandin was diagnosed with autism at the age of two and a half. Unlike many at the time, her parents never considered placing her in an institution. Instead, they initiated a rigorous schedule of activities and therapies that amounted to "early intervention." Grandin credits her parents' decision with making a critical difference in her life, although she acknowledges that autism has remained a major problem for her. "Social interactions that come naturally to most people can be daunting for people with autism. As a child, I was like an animal that had no instincts to guide me: I just had to learn by trial and error. I was always observing, trying to work out the best way to behave, but I never fit in" (1995, 32).

In addition to social difficulties, Grandin recalls she suffered greatly from oversensitivity to both touch and sound. "When I was little sound hurt my ears. I didn't realize there was something biologically different about me that made the sounds more difficult. I just thought that other people were somehow stronger. I didn't realize my sensory capacity was somehow different" (Blume 1997).

Grandin attended a neighborhood elementary school, but switched to a high school designed for students with "emotional problems." "High school was very bad. The other kids teased me constantly. I just didn't fit in" (Lifescape 2000). However, it was during this time that Grandin experienced two influences that would change her life and inspire her career.

The first was a visit to her aunt's cattle ranch when she was fifteen. At the ranch, Grandin noticed the cattle tended to become calm when confined in a chute. As a person who suffered from anxiety and was overstimulated by touch, she wondered whether a similar experience could serve to calm her. As a result of her observations, she designed what she called a "squeeze machine," a simple contraption she could control, placing herself between two large padded wooden plates. Grandin found the experience both enjoyable and calming. She became fascinated by her creation, and experimented with it endlessly.

The second influence Grandin credits for spurring her on to her career was an understanding high school science teacher. The teacher saw Grandin's fascination with animals as a sign of her potential. He encouraged her to pursue her interest in the "squeeze machine," and to explore why it seemed to be a calming influence on livestock.[5]

Although she exhibited many of the characteristics typical of children with autism, Grandin believes her case was mitigated by the effective intervention of her parents and teachers. "People are always looking for the single magic bullet that will totally change everything. There is no single magic bullet. I was very lucky to receive very good early intervention with very good teachers, starting at age 2½ years. I cannot emphasize enough the importance of a good teacher. A good teacher is worth his or her weight in gold" (Edelson 1996, 4).

Because of that intervention, Grandin believes the effects of her autism were limited: "I was the type of child where they could just jerk me out of autism by saying 'Now come on, pay attention'" (Edelson 1996, 2). Fascinated by animals and encouraged by her family and teachers, Grandin graduated from high school with high expectations.

She graduated from Franklin Pierce College in 1970. Admission into graduate school posed a problem. Grandin found the mathematics section of the entrance examination very difficult, but she persisted and was eventually accepted into Arizona State University, where she earned a master's degree. By 1978, she was beginning to design cattle feedlots and handling systems in Arizona. In 1989 she was awarded a doctorate in animal science from the University of Illinois. She was on her way.

Career Success

As she entered into the profession of animal science, Grandin had to struggle with her autism, and develop coping strategies to deal with the social customs of business. She explains: "When I started my career, I often made initial contacts on the telephone, which was easier because I did not have to deal with complex social signals. This helped me get my foot in the front door. After the initial call, I would send the client a project proposal and a brochure showing pictures of previous jobs" (1995, 135).

In a recent interview, she elaborated on her "telephone" strategy: "A lot of times I've called up a prospective client and said 'engineering, please' to bypass management and speak directly to the technical people. I've gotten a lot of jobs that way." Grandin believes this approach not only minimized her need for social skills, but tended to put her in touch with people who, like her, were more technically than socially oriented.

Grandin has great respect for technically talented people (she calls them "techies") like herself, and she is adamant about the need for employers to appreciate and develop their talents. Grandin sees her ability to understand animals and design systems for them as a by-product of her "disability." "As a result of my autism, I have heightened sensory perceptions that help me work out how an animal will feel moving through the system" (1995, 64). She maintains that as a person with autism she is a highly visual thinker, that she in fact thinks "in pictures." Of course everyone thinks visually at times, but Grandin describes her thinking process as exclusively visual. This, she believes, allows her to envision clearly just how animals experience their surroundings because they too, she contends, "think in pictures."

The handling systems Grandin has designed move livestock from their transport vehicles or holding areas to the slaughterhouse through curving chutes that minimize the animals' restlessness and anxiety. Sounds, shadows, speed—all aspects of the livestock's experience are carefully controlled until the very second of a quick and relatively painless execution. *Forbes* magazine has called Grandin's design "the most humane—as well as the most efficient—system for slaughtering animals yet devised" (Marsh 1998). Her systems are now so ubiquitous that not many remember how revolutionary they were when they first appeared.

As Oliver Sacks explained in his portrait of Grandin in *An Anthropologist on Mars* (the title of the book was taken from her self-description to the author), she is capable of constructing highly complex visual images and then "running" them:

> She designs the most elaborate facilities in her mind, visualizing every component of the system, juxtaposing them in different ways, viewing them from different angles, from near and far. Once the design is complete she will "run a simulation" in her mind—that is, imagine the entire plant in operation. This simulation may show an unexpected problem, and when this happens she will pinpoint the problem, modify the design, do another simulation. (1995, 283)

Once she has developed her complete mental "picture" and tested the design, she creates a blueprint. For her, that's the easy part.

Grandin's personal success has convinced her that people with autism often have considerable abilities—the counterparts to the neurological deficits that characterize their condition. To individuals with the condition who would seek to succeed as she has, she offers this advice: "You have to pick something and be really good at it. Then just learn the social survival skills."[6]

Dealing with Stereotypes

Although animal-related stereotypes are often applied in hurtful ways to people with disabilities, Grandin views them positively, and uses them herself. For example, Grandin recently told a reporter from *Forbes* magazine, "I think in pictures, and I assume the cow does too," and elaborated on the way this shared thinking process influenced the unique way she worked: "You've got to get down and look right up the chute to see what the animal is seeing" (Marsh 1998, 3).

Comparisons to animals, however, are not the only metaphors Grandin has used to explain the way she thinks, and many of her metaphors relate to popular disability stereotypes. For example, in her book *Thinking in Pictures* she writes, "In many ways I have remained a child. Even today I do not feel like a grownup in the realm of interpersonal relationships" (180). Elsewhere in the book she says, "I store information in my head as if it were on a CD-ROM disc" (24). On many occasions she has said her thinking process is similar to a computer or the Internet. As she did in talking to Oliver Sacks, Grandin has often compared herself to an extraterrestrial, particularly in regard to her socialization abilities: "I was like a visitor from another planet who has to learn the strange ways of the aliens."[7]

When asked about the dangers of using analogies that are close to popular stereotypes of people with disabilities, Grandin seems unconcerned. She maintains that obtaining respect for individuals with autism and other disabilities is primarily a matter of getting people to appreciate those who have "uneven talents."

But others have picked up on the disability analogies Grandin has used, and have taken them farther than some people would prefer to go. Roger Caras, president of the Society for the Prevention of Cruelty to Animals, has described her as "an alien from a different kind of place."[8] In a book on Asperger's syndrome, a mild form of autism, Francesca Happé criticized Grandin's "evident lack of interest in her own and others' emotions."[9] Grandin took great offense at this criticism, and responded at some length to Happé's characterization. She pointed out the many times she had expressed how difficult her childhood had been, how excited and enthusiastic she felt about her career, and other topics on which she had felt and expressed her emotions. Near the end of her self-defense she concluded painfully: "my emotional life is simple and I have put most of my energies into my career."[10]

Concern for Techies

Paradoxically, the topic of misunderstanding people with autism is one that gets Grandin quite emotional. When asked about Happé's description of her, she says emphatically: "I don't think she gets it. I'm intellectually more complex than most people with more developed emotions. There's a whole lot of social stuff that I'm just not good at; but I get a real satisfaction out of being a good person."

For Grandin, being a "good person" has meant becoming an authority on autism as well as her chosen field of animal science. Much of her recent writing has dealt with the unique characteristics of people with autistic tendencies. Grandin believes many autistic individuals have significant strengths that correspond with deficiencies they might have in other areas, especially social skills. "All geniuses have uneven talents," she says. "It can be shown in a brain scan. Logical areas of the brain have increased activity during a period of concentrated thought while other sections are much less active." Grandin is confident that many more than one in one thousand people have characteristics of autism. (A cover story in the May 6, 2002, issue of *Time* estimated that "1 in 150 kids age 10 and younger may be affected by autism or a related disorder.") Grandin estimates that in the computer industry alone about 25 percent of all employees have behaviors in the autistic spectrum. She points to the archetype of the technical professional, what many call a "computer nerd." Characteristics of that type include technical ability, limited social skills, and an unkempt appearance—all characteristics associated with autism.

During a discussion of her ability to conduct a mental simulation of the

"Where would Einstein be today? He'd probably be driving a truck. He would get frustrated and drop out of school."

systems she has designed, Grandin becomes animated about the importance of businesses understanding and utilizing technical talents like her own. She mentions that the designers of automobile air bags originally didn't consider the damage such devices could cause to babies in car seats. Grandin contends she would have performed mental simulations with all sorts of passengers—tall, short, skinny, obese, old, young, and infant—and, she believes, her abilities would have prevented a loss of life.

"That's the kind of design mistake I never would have made. It's a very, very serious design mistake." She is adamant and emotional in making her point, not at all like the stereotype of the disengaged autistic individual.

According to Grandin, technical fields such as computer programming, product design, illustration, and architectural drawing all hold great promise for people with autistic characteristics. To optimize the chances for them to succeed, however, major changes both in education and business are needed.

Educators, she believes, should be more understanding of less verbal "visual thinkers." "We've got to work on a person's talents, not their weaknesses," she says. Grandin contends that much of the quality design work being done today is produced by high school graduates who never made it through college—not because of their own shortcomings, but because schools weren't able to understand their capabilities.

"The education world is becoming increasingly verbalized," putting students with technical, rather than verbal, skills at a distinct disadvantage, she argues. The consequent loss of talent, Grandin believes, is enormous. Using Einstein as an example—one of her favorites because of his many autistic traits—she says: "Where would Einstein be today? He'd probably be driving a truck. He would get frustrated and drop out of school."

Grandin believes that unstable individuals who attack technical companies are often people with autistic characteristics who have been mistreated by their employers. "A lot of computer hackers have been abused. They're fighting back. A lot of people who are flunking out of school or on SSI [Supplemental Security Insurance, a benefit provided by the federal government for people with disabilities] should be in a talented and gifted program, or they should be working for a computer company."

Grandin offers business managers who want to utilize the skills of technically talented employees the following advice:

- Give "techies" a well-defined goal.
- Don't ruin them with management responsibilities.
- Pay them properly and don't exploit them.
- Minimize requirements for using social skills. "Avoid the personnel department. Take them right to tech."

In Grandin's experience, people like her rarely find a good and lasting employment "fit." "A lot of people with autism get into positions as draftsmen or lab technicians and do a good job. But when they get promoted to management they don't have the skills for it and they end up getting fired."

A Sense of Satisfaction

One of Grandin's most notable characteristics is her ability to understand and accept herself, and to withstand the criticism she receives, both personally and professionally. She has stated, "If I could snap my fingers and be nonautistic, I would not—because then I wouldn't be me. Autism is part of who I am" (Sacks 1995, 291). While struggling with autism, she has also often had to defend her work against attacks from vegetarians and animal rights activists. Grandin makes it clear she abhors any perspective that she calls "radical." She stresses she has great concern for the animals with which she works, and considers her designs an important contribution to their welfare. "Some people can't get it through their heads that force *isn't* the way to DO things," she says (Marsh 1998, 3). In acknowledging the ultimate fate of the livestock, she is pragmatic: "If we hadn't bred them, they wouldn't have lived at all. I feel very strongly that all these animals should have a decent life." Indeed, if there is one theme that runs through all of Grandin's work, it is the importance of a life decently lived.

Grandin says the quality of her own life has been much improved recently by the antidepressant medication she now takes. She finds it reduces the level of her anxiety, much as her "squeeze box" did in the past. This allows her an even greater ability to concentrate on her work. "I use my mind to solve problems and invent things. I get a tremendous satisfaction from inventing things and doing innovative research" (Edelson 1996, 6).

John Harris: Taking Chances

In 1996, John Harris decided to pursue his dreams. He already had an excellent job with an advertising agency, and he had won awards for his design work. He enjoyed what he was doing, and got along well with everyone at his workplace, but he wasn't satisfied.

"I knew as a kid that I wanted to have my own business," Harris says. "As a senior in high school, I knew I wanted it to have something to do with advertising. In college my goal was to work for others for ten years to get experience—to learn everything I could. When I worked for an advertising agency I was observing all aspects of the business. Then as I got older the desire to be on my own became more intense—something that was a goal deep within me. But I still worried: Do I have the skills? Am I ready?"

By 1996, Harris was thirty-one, and right on schedule. He had experience, and understood the advertising industry. The Internet was beginning to take off, and people with his skills were at a premium. "I felt that this was the time. It was 'now or never.'" Despite feeling "terrified," he decided to make his move.

In retrospect, it seems Harris was indeed ready. His company, ViewSource

Media, a marketing and design firm in the Cincinnati suburbs, did $100,000 worth of business in its first year. Harris began by running the company out of his bedroom, but within sixteen months he was leasing office space. By 1999, the company had hit the $1 million mark in sales and had a dozen employees (Eckberg 2000). The "new economy" was soaring like a rocket, and ViewSource Media was soaring right along with it. In 2000, ViewSource's growth slowed to a mere doubling of revenues, but major clients were coming on board every month—companies like Nationwide Insurance, Xtel, and Champion Windows.

"It's a bigger challenge than I ever imagined, but I'm a firm believer in following your dreams," Harris says.

It's just the type of success story you read about in business magazines, but it's a story with a twist. If John Harris had a familiar goal, he was an unusual person. Born with osteogenesis imperfecta, a congenital disorder that makes his bones as breakable as fine china, he is only three feet tall and weighs all of forty pounds. Harris has never been able to walk, and spends almost all his waking hours in a wheelchair. At birth, many of his bones were broken, and the breakage has continued. Despite his physical limitations, Harris has succeeded by anyone's standards in one of America's most competitive industries.

Family Support

John Harris attributes his success to two influences: his strong religious faith and the support of his family. Harris is reserved about his religion—he's active in his local church, and designed its Internet website, although he rarely speaks about his faith—but he's quick to credit his parents for all he has achieved.

During his childhood, Nancy and Wilbur Harris encouraged their son to lead as normal a life as possible, and to "reach for the stars."

"My mother would always say, 'John, your body isn't going to do it for you; your mind is going to have to carry you through life,'" Harris recalls. "She'd say, 'You're not going to play football, but that doesn't mean you can't own the team'" (Gregg 2001, 48).

Harris's mother and father felt their son would have to learn to live with others, and they made it their business to see he did. After sending Harris to a special education pre-school, they registered him at the neighborhood elementary school. Because the school building was inaccessible, Nancy Harris went along with her son, pushing or carrying him from class to class. She did that throughout his school years, and even carried him across the stage to receive his high school diploma.

Harris' mother was committed to the idea her son would be allowed a full life, despite the risks that inclusion entailed.

"I knew his bones were going to break," she said. "It was just a matter of where."

"That attitude shaped me," Harris believes. "She took chances with me" (McCrabb 2000).

Throughout his career, Harris has taken his own chances, and has had more than his share of successes. He has managed whatever challenges he has faced, doing whatever he needed to do to succeed. At his first job in advertising, Harris would climb on top of his design board because he was too short to reach it. Clients and co-workers would come into his office and see Harris climbing all over his work.

He laughs at the memory: "I took some kidding, but no one really minded, as long as I got the work done."

Harris's greatest challenge has been his fragility. Fractures remain a constant danger, only slightly less so than in his childhood. A person shaking his hand too aggressively can shatter his metacarpals. A jarring impact in an automobile that leaves others uninjured could be catastrophic to him. Even routine movements can cause a fracture. He once broke an arm while attempting to scratch his back.

Harris long ago learned to accept the pain he has had to endure. "I've broken each of my arms and legs at least thirty times. I've lost count. It's just something that I have to deal with."

Although not one to dwell on his disability, Harris is happy to talk about it with anyone interested, and he's an active disability advocate, especially in supporting groups concerned with osteogenesis imperfecta. But what really interests him these days is his business. ViewSource Media is his obsession.

ViewSource Media

At a recent Monday morning staff meeting, John Harris gathered with a dozen of his staff members to get caught up on current and potential projects. Each project manager had a long list of items to be accomplished during the week, and the sales staff reported on client prospects. Spirits were high, since the company had recently been selected over much larger competitors for several key accounts.

Toward the end of the meeting, Harris congratulated his staff, but urged them to be careful: "Being proud is one thing; being arrogant is another." During the meeting Harris had received no special treatment, either because of his position or his condition. The subject of disability came up only once—as a project manager described a client's desire that its new website be fully accessible to visually impaired customers with computer text readers.

In his business life, Harris makes few concessions to his fragile constitution. He keeps a normal schedule, travels frequently to client offices to discuss contracts, and once even flew coast to coast to make a presentation to a prospective client. He almost never asks for special consideration. Even when making a new acquaintance, he won't warn them that a tight handshake could shatter the bones in his hand.

But Harris's osteogenesis imperfecta does present him with limitations. He can't drive, and many activities most other people in wheelchairs can do—such

> *"I realize that some people may have preconceptions and stereotypes, so I'm always careful to convey an image of competence. That's very important to me. I'm looking to prove the stereotypes wrong. I like to win."*

as wheelchair sports—could be lethal for him. He relies on his mother and father for assistance, and lives with them in their home. He must be assisted getting into and out of his bed, into and out of his chair, and so on. His father is his chauffeur and traveling companion. His mother is his office receptionist, bookkeeper, and assistant. To accommodate his immobility, he uses several wheelchairs: a motorized chair takes him around his office suite; a smaller, lighter version travels with him; another stays at home.

Harris is a true technophile, and he counts as one of the most important events in his life the day his father brought home an Apple IIe computer. He brought the computer into his bedroom, and his life hasn't been the same since.

"I always felt that I had a good brain," Harris comments, "but the physical act of drawing and designing was a real challenge. That computer changed everything. I knew I could use that mouse as well as anyone."

Now Harris's office is filled with the latest technology, and he loves it.

One of his favorite items is an ultra-lightweight Sony Vaio laptop computer. Showing it off to a friend shortly after getting it out of the box, he joked: "I found one I can lift!" Harris takes the Vaio with him everywhere, using it to pitch ViewSource's website development services to prospective clients.

Those who come to the ViewSource offices are occasionally not quite prepared for a three-foot-tall, forty-pound CEO in a wheelchair. Harris understands many people in the business world aren't comfortable around disabled people, and he admits there have been a few awkward moments. On one occasion, when ViewSource was a finalist for a major contract, one of the executives interviewing Harris asked him, "How do you go to the bathroom?"

He just laughs it off. Harris has been dealing with gaffes like that all his life, and he acts as if it just comes with the territory. Over the years, he has developed an understanding of his disability, and even an appreciation of it.

"I think that, in some ways, my disability is an advantage. First of all, there's the 'visual thing.' When I meet somebody at a meeting, they're not going to forget me. That cuts both ways, though. I realize some people may have preconceptions and stereotypes, so I'm always careful to convey an image of competence. That's very important to me. I'm looking to prove the stereotypes wrong. I like to win."

He believes dealing with osteogenesis imperfecta helped to get him ready for the challenges he faces today. "Without knowing it, really, it prepared me for the adverse situations in the cycle of business," he recently told a reporter from the *Wall Street Journal.* "For instance, growing up, everything is going along fine, and you break a bone, and you're immobile for three weeks and you have to change the whole way you operate. In business, you have changing market conditions, you lose a big client, and you have to change the way you think at a moment's notice. You have to adapt very quickly" (Crowley 2000).

Harris sees other benefits: "There are a lot of things I can't do because of my disability. I can't play football or tennis; I can't drive a car. But in some ways it's an advantage. I never waste time. When I'm not working, I'm browsing the web to learn about a competitor. Other people may be out playing golf—not me."

Harris believes another motivator for people with special needs is the "urgency" of accumulating wealth. What would represent luxuries for some are necessities for people with disabilities. They may have extraordinary medical expenses, or need to purchase special services or equipment merely to live an independent life. This issue is particularly important to him as he sees his parents aging.

"I've thought about all of the things I'll need to live independently, but especially designing my own house. I'm really looking forward to doing that, and I'll do it right—not something extravagant, but comfortable with the accessibility amenities I need."

Heightening the importance of building wealth is the issue of time, he says. "Another reason people like myself can be highly motivated is that we might not have the longevity expected by other workers. We might be forced to retire early."

Thoughts on Employment

Harris is convinced others with disabilities represent an important untapped resource for business.

"The key is to focus on strengths, not on weaknesses. That goes for the employer and the worker. The employer shouldn't be quick to make the assumption that disability equates to incompetence. People may be using [their disability] as a strength. And the employee shouldn't try to be something he's not. You can't be a 'jack of all trades.'"

Delegation has become an important issue since ViewSource began its meteoric growth. Harris realizes he'll soon have to relinquish some of the duties he has always handled. "I don't have the background to do all of the things this business needs—things like accounting and personnel."

Most potential employees with disabilities, Harris believes, are people who have learned how to manage their strengths and weaknesses. Unfortunately, he admits laughingly, he's not a good example. "That's what you *should* do. I tend to take over more than I should be doing. I have to learn how to delegate."

Harris has encountered many of the other problems business owners typically face. "The greatest challenge has been what some people call the 'entrepreneur myth.' It's the myth that you will be your own boss. You end up working for your employees and your clients. The work you love, that you're really passionate about, you do very little of. Ninety percent of my time is spent managing employees and resources. I'm doing very little design work now. My employees are doing what I love to do."

Consequently, Harris plans to make changes that will enable his business to manage—and survive—its torrid rate of growth, while allowing him more time to reap the benefits of his work. "As each year passes, I'm looking forward to doing more of what I want to do."

On March 31, 2001, a few weeks after completing his last interview for this profile, John Harris died from the complications of pneumonia. Several of his employees subsequently purchased a majority interest in ViewSource Media, and the company continues.

Jenny Hwang: Capability and Dedication

Employment of People with Visual Impairments

Photo courtesy of Jenny Hwang

For people who have a significant visual disability, the road to employment can be long, frustrating, and—for too many—endless. According to the U.S. Bureau of the Census, only 30 percent of legally blind adults of working age are employed in the United States,[11] and this includes part-time workers and others who are underemployed or who work in "sheltered" employment situations.

According to the National Federation of the Blind, "the real problems of blindness arise not from the inability to see but from the inability of many people to believe that the blind can compete on the basis of equality."[12] That problem is undoubtedly due, in turn, to a lack of familiarity with blindness on the part of most employers. Most adults have imperfect sight, and an estimated 10 million Americans have a visual impairment. But legal blindness (defined as 20/200 vision in the better eye with correction, or a visual field of 20 degrees or less) is a "low incidence" disability, affecting only about 1.3 million Americans. In some cases, medical conditions such as diabetes, glaucoma, and macular degeneration produce visual deficiencies later in life, when issues other than employment may take precedence. In fact, elderly individuals account for over half of all those legally blind or visually impaired.[13] The combination of a low-incidence disability and even lower incidence of employment combine to make most potential employers unfamiliar with the capabilities of job candidates with visual disabilities.

On the positive side, recent developments have greatly expanded what is available in assistive technology—everything from audio narration to text magnifiers. The advent of personal computers alone has provided enormous benefits to people with visual impairments. Most computers come with standard accessibility provisions and can be outfitted easily with additional features such as screen-reading voice synthesizers, optical scanners, text enlargers, voice recognition software, and Braille output devices. In addition, the cost of most assistive technology is modest (e.g., voice recognition software can be purchased for about $100; voice synthesis costs about $1,000), making the "reasonable accommodations" required by the American with Disabilities Act within the reach of most employers.

Such developments have greatly expanded the work potential of adults with all levels of visual impairments, but employment capabilities remain largely potential rather than realized. Despite these daunting barriers, there is a new generation of people with significant visual impairments who are well educated, technologically savvy, and highly motivated to succeed. One of these is Jenny Hwang, a human resources professional with Computer Associates in Islandia, New York.

Professional Employment

Jenny Hwang (pronounced *WONG*) would be the last person to consider herself an exemplary or exceptional professional. She doesn't particularly enjoy talking about her accomplishments, and says that her most important goal "is just doing my job day by day." That job entails a host of human resources responsibilities, ranging from benefits management to accounts payable for the largest eBusiness software developer in the world.

Although Hwang is quite capable of handling her professional responsibilities, she realizes that her accomplishments are the result of a great deal of effort, and not just her own. Most of all, she credits her success to her family. "My family has always been very supportive. When I was a student they would take me to the library, provide me with a text magnifier and help me with my research projects." Her family believed strongly in the importance of a good education, and saw that she received one.

Ms. Hwang is a member of the "new generation" of individuals educated after 1975, when the "Education for All Handicapped Children Act" first mandated a "free and appropriate education" for all, regardless of type or degree of disability. For those fortunate enough to benefit from the provisions of the federal legislation, educational alternatives both improved and expanded. Previous generations of children with disabilities were routinely denied educational services, but people of Jenny Hwang's age could often choose from several alternatives. After grade school and a parochial high school education, Hwang attended the College of New Rochelle. "I had a great college experience. At school, I was on scholarship, resided for four years in the dormitory, and basically took care of myself. I was, however, provided with a reader and was able to take extra time to complete my exams" (Schneider 1998/99, 24).

In college, Hwang took full advantage of the opportunities presented to her. "I worked hard and studied hard, but I also made a lot of friends and looked for opportunities beyond the classroom." Her coursework allowed her to expand her perspective without limitation, and she eventually majored in international studies. "I thought it was very interesting to learn more about the world in general." Since college, Hwang has supplemented her education with vocational training from agencies including the Helen Keller Center and the New York State Commission for the Blind.

Computer Associates

At work Hwang appears to be a typical professional, although her skills are complemented by an array of assistive technology, including a tape recorder, text scanner, and Braille computer equipped with speech synthesis. Other "assists" that Hwang receives are decidedly low- or no-tech, ranging from Braille signage on elevators to occasional rides provided to company meetings by fellow employees. Within her department which includes thirty professionals,

"The highlight of my work is dealing with employees and finding ways to meet their needs."

Hwang will occasionally job share and work on team projects. Of all her experiences in the workplace, Hwang is perhaps most pleased by the acceptance she has received from her fellow employees. She describes them as "very friendly," and frequently socializes with them outside of work.

Social skills are important in meeting all of the challenges usually faced by a human resources professional. Relishing such challenges, Hwang finds particular satisfaction in interacting with the many fellow employees with whom she comes in contact. She describes those experiences as "the highlight of my work . . . dealing with employees and finding ways to meet their needs."

Although she is not one to consider herself an expert on employment, Ms. Hwang does have some advice for other job candidates who have visual disabilities: "Keep looking, keep trying. Master new skills, and learn how to use new technologies. Learn to communicate well." For those who have jobs and want to succeed further, she recommends paying particular attention to socializing. "In the work environment it helps to have a lot of contacts. Networking is critical."

It is interesting to note that Computer Associates is one of many high-technology companies that have the reputation of being leaders in inclusive employment (I.B.M., Microsoft, Apple Computer, and Intel are other examples). Such companies appear to approach issues of adaptation and accommodation from an "insider's" point of view, seeing employment barriers facing people with disabilities as not very different from those encountered by everyone else, and relishing the opportunity to address and overcome them.

Personal Perspective

In her spare time, Hwang pursues hobbies that include reading, music, and exercise. She currently has little time for, or interest in, activities relating to disability advocacy, explaining simply, "I like to stay in the background." However, she often attends meetings at the local Council for the Blind where participants discuss practical problems of employment, socialization, and independent living.

Hwang has been with Computer Associates for more than four years, and looks forward to a long career with her employer. In a work environment where job turnover and mobility are usually taken for granted, Hwang's attitude toward her work and her employer may seem quaint and outmoded. When asked about her long-term career goals, she replies: "I just want to be successful in accomplishing the day-to-day responsibilities of my job."

As Hwang talks about her professional career and personal life she is always careful to emphasize the positive—her supportive family, her excellent education, all of the support she receives from fellow employees at Computer Associates. Notably absent is anything even resembling frustration, let alone a complaint. Instead, she comes across as a competent and engaged professional who enjoys her work and is very good at it. Her attitude seems genuine.

Just as they are well educated and technologically capable, the new generation of employees with disabilities is well aware of the obstacles that their predecessors have faced for generations. That awareness, more than any amount of vocational preparation, might account for the tendency of these individuals to be hard-working, dedicated, and loyal employees. Though disabilities and vulnerabilities may often be more easy to notice, this strength is a characteristic well worth considering. In work environments often plagued by societal problems and individual failings, competence and professionalism like Jenny Hwang's are a refreshing change.

8

A Plan for Inclusive Employment

Part I: Pre-employment Issues

As technology continues to transform the economy of the United States, it creates an abundance of new employment opportunities. At the same time, adults with disabilities increasingly are being recognized as the greatest source of untapped talent available to business. Disabled individuals are not only the nation's largest minority, they are the most chronically underutilized segment of the labor force. With recent advancements in education, technology, transportation, and architecture, the employment possibilities for this population have increased dramatically. This is a golden opportunity, both for qualified individuals with disabilities who want to work and for employers who realize their potential.

Businesses that decide to increase the number of disabled people they employ face several barriers. First, with some exceptions, most businesses have not previously employed significant numbers of such workers. For most, this is new territory. Second, the Americans with Disabilities Act, while attempting to eliminate barriers to work, has also raised the anxiety level among some employers. They fear the law is simply another way for them to become embroiled in expensive litigation. While a vast majority of businesses want to obey the law, they want to do so in a way that is least costly and most productive for them. Third, many businesses consider the topic of employing disabled workers to be an area traditionally overseen by nonprofit organizations. Some businesses find nonprofit procedures cumbersome, their interrelationships confusing, and their programs of questionable value to employers. They want, but can't always find, nonprofit organizations that can speak their language and help them find good, qualified employees.

Employing people with disabilities is unquestionably good business. Doing so, however, requires careful preparation. Previous chapters in this book have presented information businesses need to know in order to understand inclusion thoroughly. This chapter is the first of two that together outline an inclusive employment plan. Each subsection starts with a discussion of the major considerations pertaining to the topic covered, followed by a checklist of procedures to be followed, and resources that can assist employers along the way. The information presented is detailed, but readers who want more comprehensive data, such as architectural standards or up-to-date information on laws and regulations, should consult the resources listed.

Management Commitment

Since the passage of the Americans with Disabilities Act, employees, stockholders, and the public have come to expect companies to pursue inclusive employment, much as they expect them to pursue "diversity."

And, as with diversity, a company's expression of commitment to inclusion doesn't make it a reality. Many businesses claim to value inclusive employment, but do very little to include more disabled people as employees. They may work diligently to comply with legal requirements—especially if doing so will help them avoid litigation—but increasing employment opportunities for people with disabilities is another matter. The continued high unemployment rate for disabled adults leaves no doubt how little progress has been made.

If a company is to become truly committed to inclusive employment, and not just give it lip service, top management must demonstrate its personal commitment. In promoting inclusion, there is no substitute for business leaders who are personally and deeply dedicated to the issue. They can make all the difference.

How can managers use their influence to promote inclusive employment? Here are some suggestions:

- If a manager has a personal reason for being interested in this issue, he or she should consider saying so. It isn't necessary to give a great deal of personal information, but a simple explanation—about a past injury, or a family member with a disability, for example—can be very persuasive. Sharing a personal perspective accomplishes three things: it transforms the subject of disability from the abstract to a concrete, human reality with which employees can identify; it makes the point that disabilities can happen to anyone—even employees themselves or someone close to them; and it demonstrates a persuasive reason why inclusive employment is a priority with management.

- Managers should educate employees about the practical benefits of being an inclusive employer—the size of the population, the available talent pool, performance statistics, and so on. Employees who understand why inclusion benefits their employer tend to work harder to achieve it.
- Managers should provide necessary resources—employee training, reference materials, local governmental and nonprofit contacts, etc.
- Managers should establish concrete goals for implementation, just as they would any other initiative.
- Managers should appeal to the altruistic values of employees. Many research studies have shown that employees appreciate being affiliated with companies that have strong corporate values. Employees, like customers, appreciate the "cause-related" activities of corporations. Inclusion is a cause with strong popular appeal.
- Most importantly, managers should prove their company's dedication to inclusion by recognizing and rewarding those who promote it. Effective

Corporations strongly committed to promoting inclusion can frequently have an impact well beyond their own employees. When a major consumer products manufacturer committed to employing a greater number of disabled individuals, it implemented most of the expected steps—instituted newly designed recruitment procedures and established specific annual goals for increased hiring, for example.

Then it went beyond the usual. First, in partnership with a state rehabilitation agency it hosted a symposium on inclusive employment to which it invited most of the major employers in the region of its home office.

Secondly, it gathered its major suppliers and contractors—everyone from chemical manufacturers to the operators of the company cafeteria—and told them: "We are committing this corporation to inclusive employment practices; we encourage you to do the same, and we will be happy to work with you if you choose to do so."

recruitment, productive accommodations, good mentoring—all can be considered in matters of compensation, promotion, and recognition. A company that rewards inclusion will have more of it.
- In these and many other ways, managers can both tell and show employees they are truly committed to inclusive employment.

Management Commitment Checklist

☐ Management has carefully examined its legal and ethical obligations pertaining to people with disabilities, and the potential benefits of becoming an inclusive corporation.
☐ Management has clearly and convincingly communicated to employees a commitment to inclusive employment beyond mere legal compliance.
☐ Management has provided the necessary resources and established goals for implementation.
☐ Management has begun to implement practical steps to reinforce this commitment, such as tying progress in inclusion to compensation and promotion.
☐ If appropriate, the company's commitment has been communicated to affiliates, customers, contractors, suppliers, and the public.

Legal Review

When a corporation has committed to becoming an inclusive employer, it is still necessary to conduct a thorough review of the company's obligations under the Americans with Disabilities Act, the Rehabilitation Act of 1973, and similar legislation. At a minimum, this will involve a careful review of Title I of the ADA—the employment-related provisions of the law. Corporations, governmental bureaus, nonprofit organizations and others involved in public services, public accommodations, transportation, or communications will, of course, have to examine other relevant sections of the Act as well.

It would be a major mistake to assume that a dedication to going beyond the requirements of the law reduces the importance of legal compliance. Disability-related legislation is sufficiently complex to require careful study, and the courts continue to develop their interpretation of crucial concepts like "reasonable accommodation" and "undue hardship." All companies need to stay up-to-date on legal requirements, no matter how involved in inclusion they may be.

Most medium-sized and large corporations have their procedures, policies, and obligations reviewed by legal counsel. Since this is a new and rapidly developing area of the law, it is advisable to use the services of an attorney who is familiar with this subspecialty of labor law. Although a legal review will likely begin with the expertise of an attorney, it should not end there. An architect thoroughly familiar with accessibility standards should review the status of physical facilities. Key personnel who must implement ADA-related policies, such as human resources personnel and building managers, should also be involved. Issues related to health, disability, and life insurance should be reviewed with policy carriers. Finally, ADA-related policy and procedure reviews should be conducted on a regular basis.

Small businesses often do not have the resources for such careful analysis. To help meet their needs, the government has created Disability and Business Technical Assistance Centers (DBTAC). A call to (800) 949-4232 will be routed automatically to the DBTAC in the caller's region. The DBTACs are a free service of the National Institute on Disability and Rehabilitation Research (NIDRR). They can answer most questions, or refer callers to other resources.

Legal Review Checklist

☐ Management has reviewed the requirements of Title I of the ADA, and any other pertinent legislation.

☐ Legal counsel has reviewed policies and procedures for compliance.

☐ Management has reviewed the company's policies and procedures for compliance.

☐ Management has evaluated the status of physical facilities for compliance, and has sought professional review where appropriate.

☐ Management has reviewed disability-related insurance coverage with carriers.

☐ Management has reviewed the company's record of accommodation requests, disability-related complaints, injuries and illnesses, and so on.

☐ Policies, procedures, and experience are reviewed on a regular basis.

Accessibility Issues

The term "accessibility" refers to the characteristics of a place or activity that permit the full participation of people with disabilities.

As it relates to employment, accessibility can be considered according to the *context* in which issues arise:

- the application, testing, and evaluation process
- the job site or potential job site
- benefits and privileges

In each of these contexts, employers must consider issues of both *physical* and *communication* accessibility.

Before considering all of the issues that might arise under these three broad categories, managers should know that most accessibility issues can be dealt with simply and inexpensively. Although accessibility problems can seem daunting in the abstract, in the real world they are generally easily handled. Recent innovations in building design, transportation, assistive technology, and communications now provide employers with "built in" or easily available solutions to most problems. People with disabilities often bring with them, or can suggest, appropriate accommodations. Should matters occasionally get more complex, plenty of assistance is available.

The Application, Testing, and Evaluation Process

Employers often fail to understand that the right of individuals to access their business begins even *before* employment. This means that any place a company uses to interview, screen, or test applicants must be as physically accessible as the job site. A person with a disability who cannot get into a business just to *apply* for employment has sufficient grounds for filing a complaint against that employer under the Americans with Disabilities Act. Therefore, a review of the accessibility specifications of each site involved in the hiring process should be conducted by a knowledgeable architect, with the participation of the building manager or maintenance supervisor.

In addition, recruitment, application, and testing materials—any information involved in communicating with job applicants—must be available in alternative formats to accommodate the needs of employment candidates with various types of disabilities. This does not mean all materials must be immediately available in any conceivable format, but that "reasonable" accommodations can be provided if requested.

For example, to make job applications accessible to people with reading-related disabilities, human resources personnel should be available to assist in

One of the employer's greatest "accommodation resources" can be the job candidate him- or herself.

An engineer with a severe hearing loss was applying for a position with a regional communications company. The individual was a qualified and capable candidate, and a capable lip-reader, but most people found his speech difficult to understand.

To ease the process of communication, the individual brought to his job interview a PalmPilot on which he had written several questions. The interviewer happily answered his questions, and the interview proceeded with ease.

the completion of required forms, reading and writing for the applicant, if necessary. A similar service could be provided to an applicant with a visual impairment, if a large-type version of the application is not easily available, or does not meet the needs of the applicant. Making all information always available in every conceivable format is not only unnecessary, it is impossible. No place or process is ever totally accessible to everyone. An informed capability, and eagerness to meet the individual accessibility requirements of job candidates, are the most important components of an accessible job application process.

Keep in mind this general principle: companies must maintain the same standards of both physical and communication accessibility with job candidates as they do with employees.

The Job Site or Potential Job Site

All too often, companies assume that buildings designed, built, or renovated after 1990 (the year the ADA was passed) are completely physically accessible. While it is true that ADA accessibility standards are now routinely incorporated into building designs, the actual implementation often leaves much to be desired.

As an example, a state-of-the-art large office building opened in 1997 with what management thought were all the required, and quite a few optional, accessibility provisions. The building had automatic doors, ramps, audio-cue elevators, Braille signage, and a host of other features.

But problems became apparent the first day the building was open to the public. An office tenant parked his lift-equipped van in one of the convenient oversized parking spaces designated for such vehicles, and headed in his wheelchair toward one of the shiny new garage elevators. As he approached, however, he noticed a small curb entirely surrounding the elevator entrance.

That was as far as he could go. For want of a simple curb cut, he was unable to access the state-of-the-art elevator without assistance.

This example demonstrates an important point: while it is important to begin with a design done according to approved accessibility standards, there is no substitute for consumer involvement. Beginning with the design or renovation stage of any building project, companies should encourage their disabled employees to evaluate accessibility provisions or should employ the services of qualified consumer consultants to ensure they have provided complete physical accessibility.

Accessibility must include all communication formats used on the job. More and more companies are communicating, training, and conducting business via the Internet. While many Internet sites already incorporate standards that make them accessible to people with disabilities (offering text-only versions, large type, Universal Design features, and so on), some are unnecessarily problematic, especially for those with significant visual impairments. Fortunately, resources such as those listed at the end of this section can assist businesses in designing an accessible website or obtaining special equipment to assist individual employees and applicants with disabilities in accessing the World Wide Web.

One additional issue: with increasing numbers of disabled employees entering employment situations where those with special needs may not have been before, it is crucial to ensure their safety under all—not just ordinary—circumstances. This includes disasters, such as fires, floods, and earthquakes. A company's ability to notify and evacuate all job candidates, employees, customers, and visitors is one of the most frequently neglected issues of accessibility. Fortunately, substantial assistance is easily available through organizations like the Federal Emergency Management Agency (see FEMA resource listed below).

Benefits and Privileges

A small real estate development firm had the tradition of hosting an annual year-end party. When employees decided to hold the event on a chartered yacht, the company's party planner called the yacht operator to assure the boat was accessible, since one employee used a power wheelchair. The yacht operator said the boat was indeed accessible, although the gangplank posed a problem for large, heavy wheelchairs.

The employee involved was consulted, and after a brief discussion with the yacht operator, agreed that a dockside transfer to a lighter, standard wheelchair (provided by the boat owner) would meet his needs.

> By means of this simple accommodation, the employee was able to enjoy the company's social event of the year along with his fellow employees.

Just as accessibility needs to be provided even before employment, it also must be considered beyond the job site—involving anything in which the employer is directly involved.

Some issues are obvious: if health insurance and other benefits are provided to other employees similarly situated, they must be provided to workers who have disabilities. Other issues are less apparent. For example, an employer that provides a discounted health club membership for its employees must ensure that the health club is accessible to employees with disabilities. Similarly, if employees have meetings, conventions, or company-sponsored social events away from the job site, those activities should be conducted in accessible locations as well.

The same principle applies to issues of communication. Communication about benefits and privileges, and communication that occurs in the course of their dispensation and enjoyment, should be appropriately accessible. For example, an employer that presents or produces a training or promotional video should make it available with closed (available on a special track) or open (seen by all viewers) captioning. This is another example of many people benefiting from accommodations intended originally for people with disabilities, since many with perfectly good hearing learn more effectively if they also read what they are hearing.

Although accessibility issues relating to "benefits and privileges" are sometimes viewed as of marginal importance, they can be critical for disabled employees. Access to activities outside the ordinary work site is a good example. Study after study has shown that the employment success of people with disabilities is highly dependent on social contacts and networking. Of course, this is also true for almost all employees, but for people with disabilities, who may be coming to the job with fewer social connections and networking experiences, it can be even more important.

Additional Considerations

> A corporate foundation announced it was convening a meeting to discuss community needs and help determine foundation priorities for the coming year. Past grant recipients, community leaders, nonprofit executives, and board members were invited.
>
> The meeting was held at an exclusive downtown business club. Unfortunately, the only meeting room large enough to accommodate the

group was the only inaccessible location in the facility–down one flight of stairs at either entrance. Two invitees who arrived at the meeting in wheelchairs took one look at the steps, turned around, and left. A nonprofit board member who used crutches eventually negotiated the stairs with great difficulty.

The foundation quickly received several "suggestions" that it hold future meetings in accessible locations. Since then, all similar meetings have been held in accessible facilities, and the corporation has also adopted the practice of offering other accommodations, such as dietetic lunches and the services of a sign language interpreter.

Even though the legal requirements for accessibility can seem thorough and exhaustive, it is nonetheless important for a company or organization to maintain a commitment to the "spirit" of accessibility. This means that a company is willing to go beyond legal mandates in pursuit of real inclusion.

In the preceding example, the organization might not have been *legally* required to ensure that its meeting location was accessible (unless it had an employee with a mobility impairment who wanted to attend), but public expectations demanded it. A phone call to the business club's building manager, or a preview visit to the club by someone from the foundation, could have averted the problem. The foundation's failure to take simple measures to assure accessibility for its guests cost it some goodwill and caused some embarrassment.

Accessibility Checklist

Application, Testing, and Evaluation Location

Physical

☐ Architects/property managers have reviewed all facilities for ADA compliance.
☐ Accessible and appropriately designated parking spaces are available close to entrance.
☐ At least one lift-equipped van (oversized) space is available.
☐ Accessible pathway from parking to entrance is available.
☐ External ramps are appropriately graded (slope no greater than 1:12) and have handrails if appropriate.
☐ All access doors are at least 36 inches wide.
☐ Doors are automatic or easily opened.
☐ Doors have easy-to-grasp handles.

☐ Elevators have control panels lower than 54 inches from floor.

☐ Restrooms are accessible.

   ○ Automatic or easily opened door is available.

   ○ Door opens easily for both entrance and egress.

   ○ At least one oversized stall is available.

   ○ Oversized stall is equipped with handrails.

   ○ Commode is raised.

   ○ Accessible sink is available.

   ○ Accessible towel dispenser is available.

☐ Public telephone is accessible (installed at lower level).

☐ Accessible water fountain or dispenser is available.

☐ Pathways to all facilities are clear and accessible.

☐ Interview/testing room is accessible.

☐ Appropriate room lighting is provided.

☐ Background noise is eliminated or minimized.

☐ Appropriate desk/testing station lighting is provided.

☐ Physical accessibility features have been evaluated by consumers.

Communication

☐ Human resources staff has received training in ADA requirements, particularly in regard to interviewing and hiring procedures.

☐ Recruitment materials indicate that reasonable accommodations are available, and suggest applicants notify human resources office of any needs.

☐ Driving directions indicate location of accessible parking.

☐ Signage clearly indicates location of accessible parking.

☐ Raised symbols/Braille signage is provided on elevator.

☐ All facility signage is appropriate and accessible to individuals with visual and cognitive disabilities.

   ○ Large lettering is used.

   ○ Graphics and symbols are used.

☐ TTD or similar device is available.

☐ Sign language interpreter is available if requested.

☐ Reading service is available if requested.

☐ Written, large-type, audio, or Braille instructions are available.

☐ Application and testing materials are written in clear and uncomplicated language.

☐ Large-type, audio, or Braille application and testing materials are available.

☐ Computer testing procedures have large-print capabilities.
☐ Assistance in completing application or testing materials is available if requested.
☐ Flexible test timing is available.
☐ Notepads and writing instruments are available.
☐ Emergency procedures consider needs of people with disabilities.
   ○ Emergency warning system includes both audio and visual alarms.
   ○ Evacuation procedures are established.
   ○ Emergency notification procedures are established.
   ○ At least one evacuation chair is provided if required.

The Job Site or Potential Job Site

Physical

☐ Architects/property managers have reviewed all facilities for ADA compliance.
☐ Accessible and appropriately designated parking spaces are available close to entrance.
☐ At least one lift-equipped van (oversized) parking space is available.
☐ Accessible pathway from parking to entrance is available.
☐ External ramps are appropriately graded (slope no greater than 1:12) and have handrails if appropriate.
☐ All access doors are at least 36 inches wide.
☐ Doors are automatic or easily opened.
☐ Doors have easy-to-grasp handles.
☐ Elevators have control panels lower than 54 inches from floor.
☐ Restrooms are accessible.
   ○ Automatic or easily opened door is available.
   ○ Door opens easily for entrance and egress.
   ○ At least one oversized stall is available.
   ○ Oversized stall is equipped with handrails.
   ○ Commode is raised.
   ○ Accessible sink is available.
   ○ Accessible towel dispenser is available.
☐ Public telephone is accessible (installed at lower level).
☐ Accessible water fountain or dispenser is available.
☐ Pathways to all facilities are clear and accessible.
☐ Work areas are accessible.

☐ Pathways to and around work areas are clear and accessible.

☐ All equipment used in job performance is appropriate and accessible.

☐ All off-site training and work are conducted in accessible facilities.

☐ Appropriate room and lighting are provided.

☐ Appropriate work station lighting is provided.

☐ Background noise is eliminated or minimized.

☐ Physical accessibility features have been evaluated by consumers.

☐ Emergency procedures consider needs of people with disabilities.

    ○ Emergency warning system includes both audio and visual alarms.

    ○ Evacuation procedures are established.

    ○ Emergency notification procedures are established.

    ○ At least one evacuation chair is provided if required.

Communication

☐ Signage clearly indicates location of accessible parking.

☐ Raised symbols/Braille signage is provided on elevator.

☐ All facility signage is appropriate and accessible to individuals with visual and cognitive disabilities.

    ○ Large lettering is used.

    ○ Graphics and symbols are used.

☐ TTD or similar device is available.

☐ Sign language interpreter is available if requested.

☐ Reading service is available if requested.

☐ Written, large-type, audio, or Braille instructions are available.

☐ Internet use is accessible.

    ○ Company Internet site is accessible.

    ○ Internet access accommodations are available.

☐ Emergency warning system includes both audio and visual alarms.

Benefits and Privileges

Physical

☐ All employee benefits and privileges are provided equally to people with disabilities.

☐ All training, meeting, convention, and official socializing sites are accessible.

☐ Physical sites associated with job benefits and privileges are accessible.

Communication

☐ Information pertaining to employee benefits, corporate activities, and related events is available in appropriate formats.
☐ Reasonable accommodations are available if requested (e.g., readers, audio description, large-type materials, transportation).
☐ Videos and audio-visual materials are available with captioning.

Recruiting

Although the Americans with Disabilities Act goes well beyond simply prohibiting discrimination, it does not require employment quotas. Nothing in the law requires employers to seek out qualified employees who are disabled.

To companies that have no experience in employing people with disabilities, the idea of recruiting members of this minority group might at first seem ridiculous. As the co-owner of an employment placement firm said, "I have never had a client who wanted to hire anyone because of what they *couldn't* do."

Companies interested in attracting job candidates with disabilities, however, see things a different way. They realize that disabled people represent an enormous, relatively underutilized portion of the employment population. Research indicates such workers tend to perform as well as, or even better than, typical employees.

Recruiting workers with disabilities is not difficult, but it is often done poorly. Many companies go about recruitment backwards—trying to match a job to a "type" of person, instead of trying to find qualified candidates with the skills needed for a particular position. For example, a fulfillment house will say: "We employ dozens of people in customer service. They sit at a phone all day. Wouldn't this be a great job for someone in a wheelchair? Where can we find some?" Or a printer will say: "Our press operators work in an extremely noisy environment. Wouldn't this be a great job for a deaf person? The noise wouldn't bother them at all!" This approach not only typecasts job candidates with disabilities, it places the emphasis on what they *cannot* do. Remember: *effective employee recruitment is about skills, not deficiencies.*

Talented adults with disabilities are available in abundance. According to The 1998 National Organization on Disability/Louis Harris Survey, among adults with disabilities only one in ten is currently employed full time (compared with eight out of ten in the general population), and out of this group

Functional Limitation	Number
Going up a flight of stairs	17.5 million
Lifting a bag of groceries	16.2 million
Hearing what is said in a normal conversation	10.9 million
Seeing words or letters in ordinary newsprint, even when wearing glasses	9.7 million
Having one's speech understood	2.3 million
Walking a quarter of a mile	17.3 million

Fig. 8.1. American adults with physical limitations. (Some people have more than one limitation. Actual total is 34.2 million.)
Source: NIDRR 1996, 6

almost 80 percent are willing and able to work.[1] Their presence in a population of any size is a certainty (as the chart in fig. 8.1 indicates).

Employers who realize the potential of this enormous group of "nontraditional" job candidates are eager to consider them for employment. But where can they locate them?

In the past, some employers have had less than satisfying experiences with nonprofit employment service programs. In fact, so many disability-related employment programs were available that their numbers sometimes seemed overwhelming to the business community. In addition, many such services—both governmental entities and nonprofit organizations—had a reputation for operating with their own bureaucratic procedures and jargon. Some found it difficult to understand the culture of competitive business.

That is rarely the case today. In recent years, politicians have come to realize that effective vocational rehabilitation services are a great deal for all concerned— businesses, workers, and taxpayers. Each hiring of a person with a disability turns someone who is dependent on others into a productive employee and taxpayer, so the state is highly motivated to help business become more inclusive in its employment practices. As a result, nonprofit employment services have been improved. Employers who have not dealt with vocational programs recently will find them streamlined, loaded with resources, and highly focused on employer needs.

Inclusive employment is worth the effort it requires. With only a small investment of time, employers can reap great rewards: they can access a relatively underutilized pool of talented, trained, and motivated workers who have the skills their business needs. The process is not complicated:

- Start with a job description, as detailed as possible. This is the most important information you will need to provide. Employers do not need to identify jobs that would "fit" or "be perfect for" someone with a disability. Leave job matching (pairing the skills of an individual with the requirements of a particular position) to vocational professionals who know the skills of the job candidates they represent. They will closely study the skills required to succeed in the position you have available.
- Contact the state agency with the overall responsibility for assisting employers in finding qualified job candidates who have disabilities. Such agencies are usually listed in the telephone book under "vocational rehabilitation agencies." They can help you find qualified job candidates among their clients, or put you in touch with one or more of their non-profit contract agencies that represent many more available candidates.
- Be prepared to meet with one or more vocational professionals (sometimes called "job coaches" or "trainers") who will want to get to know your business, the skill requirements of particular jobs, transportation services available, and so on.
- The vocational professionals will present you with one or more qualified job candidates. Evaluate them for employment the same way you would any other candidate.
- Should you require assistance with issues such as communication, training, or accommodations, the vocational professional will be able to help you. Don't underestimate what he or she might be able to offer. Assistance can involve anything from providing a trainer to work with the job candidate right at the work site, to providing expensive accommodations required to make employment possible.

In addition to the large state rehabilitation agencies, many other sources of assistance are available. The Office of Disability Employment Policy (ODEP) recommends the following:

- *State Governors' Committees and ODEP Committee Liaison*
  Provide employment information and referral services as well as training on ADA and employment issues.
  Listed under state government agencies in your local phone directory.
- *Veterans Affairs local and regional offices*
  Provide employment preparation and job placement services to veterans

with disabilities under the Vocational Rehabilitation and Counseling Service.

Listed under federal government agencies, Department of Veterans Affairs, in your local phone directory.

• *Independent Living Centers*

Provide a variety of services to a broad spectrum of individuals with disabilities.

Contact the National Council on Independent Living (703)525-3406 or local vocational rehabilitation office.

• *Organizations serving people with disabilities*

Examples include local agencies connected with the Epilepsy Foundation of America, National Multiple Sclerosis Society, United Cerebral Palsy Foundation, and the American Red Cross.

Listed in your local phone directory, or contact the local office of the state vocational rehabilitation agency.

• *Local colleges and universities*

Provide access to students with specific professional and technical skills.

Contact the campus coordinator of services for students with disabilities.

• *Job Training Partnership Act (JTPA)*

Provides customized training or retraining to meet local employer needs. *Contact state or local Private Industry Council or office of the chief elected official in your jurisdiction.*

• *Projects with Industry*

Provide employment preparation and job placement services under guidance of employers.

Contact local office of the state vocational rehabilitation agency.

• *Rehabilitation facilities and transitional sheltered workshops*

Provide training and job placement services to persons with a variety of disabilities.

Contact the local office of the state vocational rehabilitation agency.

• *Special Education Transition and Vocational Education Training Programs*

Provide training, placement, and on-the-job supervision for youth with disabilities. Training can be geared to local employment needs.

Contact local secondary school authorities.

- *State employment service*
  Provides an array of employment referral services and is a good source
  for recruiting veterans with disabilities.
  Listed under state government agencies in your local phone directory.

  In addition, many national organizations offer various types of assistance.
Some of these include:

- *Job Opportunities for the Blind*
  (800) 638-7518
- *National Rehabilitation Information*
  (800) 34-NARIC
- *Association on Higher Education and Disability (AHEAD)*
  (614) 488-4972 Voice/TDD
- *National Information Center on Deafness*
  (202) 651-5051 TDD
  (202) 651-5052 Voice
- *Disabled American Veterans*
  (202) 554-3501

One caution: in dealing with disability-related vocational programs and
the people they refer, employers must remember that discussion of disability
issues must wait until after an offer of employment is made, when determining
necessary accommodations is appropriate, or until the job candidate initiates

A major corporation routinely recruited management candidates from
major universities throughout the United States. After reviewing its record of
hiring college graduates with disabilities, it noticed not one person with a severe visual impairment had been recruited for many years.

Seeking to solve this problem, it sought out the services of a disabilities
consultant. One of the first questions the consultant asked was "How do you
currently advertise that your recruiters will be coming to each campus?"

"In campus newspapers and through postings on placement office bulletin boards," came the reply.

Since people with visual impairments generally do not get their information this way, the consultant suggested that announcements on campus
radio stations also be part of the advertising mix.

Once adopted, this strategy provided the corporation with the candidates it was seeking.

the discussion. (See the section on "Interviewing and Pre-Employment Inquiries," later in this chapter.) Employers often have to be more conscious of this than rehabilitation personnel. Failure to keep this in mind could lead to misunderstandings or even legal jeopardy.

Companies need not always rely on third parties for recruitment assistance. By providing training, guidelines, and incentives to human resources personnel, and generally stressing their eagerness to employ qualified workers with disabilities, companies can generate many "word of mouth" referrals. Many workers with disabilities are well connected to the "disability community." Word gets around.

Employers will be surprised to find how easy it is to hire qualified workers with disabilities. With the many supports and incentives available, it can sometimes be easier than employing those not disabled.

Recruiting Checklist

☐ Corporation has clearly communicated intent to hire qualified workers with disabilities
  ○ within the corporation
  ○ to appropriate disability-related vocational agencies
  ○ to affiliates, suppliers, contractors
  ○ to the public
☐ Detailed job descriptions have been developed for all positions.
☐ Human resources staff has received appropriate training in recruiting qualified workers with disabilities.
☐ Human resources staff has established working relationships with appropriate state vocational rehabilitation agency and other referral sources.
☐ Procedures for narrowcasting employment openings to appropriate state vocational rehabilitation agency and other referral sources have been established.
☐ Current disabled employees are involved in, or consulted concerning, recruitment procedures.

Interviewing and Pre-employment Inquiries

As employers perform routine inquiries into the qualifications, employment history, and suitability of job candidates, they enter an area that presents some legal dangers. Whether the matter involves completion of an application form, a job interview, check of references, or other form of verification, it is critical for employers—and all employees involved in the process—to understand clearly what is and is not permitted under the ADA. Failure to do so—simple ignorance of the law, relying on the "old" procedures, or just using "common sense"—can lead to ill will and significant legal liability.

The Equal Opportunity Employment Commission provides the following guidelines for pre-employment enquiries:[2]

It is unlawful to:

- ask an applicant whether she is disabled or about the nature or severity of a disability, or
- to require the applicant to take a medical examination before making a job offer.

> You can ask an applicant questions about ability to perform job-related functions, as long as the questions are not phrased in terms of a disability. You can also ask an applicant to describe or to demonstrate how, with or without reasonable accommodation, the applicant will perform job-related functions.
>
> After a job offer is made and prior to the commencement of employment duties, you may require that an applicant take a medical examination if everyone who will be working in the job category must also take the examination. You may condition the job offer on the results of the medical examination. However, if an individual is not hired because a medical examination reveals the existence of a disability, you must be able to show that the reasons for exclusion are job related and necessary for conduct of your business. You also must be able to show that there was no reasonable accommodation that would have made it possible for the individual to perform the essential job functions.
>
> Once you have hired an applicant, you cannot require a medical examination or ask an employee questions about disability unless you can show that these requirements are job related and necessary for the conduct of your business. You may conduct voluntary medical examinations that are part of an employee health program.
>
> The results of all medical examinations or information from inquiries about a disability must be kept confidential, and maintained in separate medical files. You may provide medical information required by state workers' compensation laws to the agencies that administer such laws.

Some additional cautions are warranted:

- Not only may you not ask an applicant any questions about a possible disability, you may not inquire if anyone in his or her family has a disability.
- You are not permitted to ask if the applicant has a history of emotional illness.
- You are not permitted to ask if the applicant has ever seen a psychiatrist.
- You are not permitted to ask if the applicant has ever had an injury or disease.
- You are not permitted to ask about the applicant's previous experience with illness (e.g., "How many sick days did you take last year?").
- You are not permitted to ask if the applicant has ever had a drug or drinking problem.
- Companies must have, and adhere to, strict policies of confidentiality during this process.

According to the EEOC, questions you *are* permitted to ask during an interview include the following:[3]

- Can you perform the essential functions of this job . . . with *or* without reasonable accommodations?
- Can you meet the attendance requirements of this job?
- Would you describe how you would perform the essential functions of this job?
- How many days of leave did you take last year?

During the pre-employment period an applicant may *elect* to initiate discussion of his or her disability, the relevance of the disability to the job, any need for accommodations, and so on. (This frequently happens when a candidate has an obvious disability, or requires an accommodation to complete the application process.) If the applicant chooses to do this, the interviewer, of course, can discuss the topic with him or her. However, the interviewer should carefully note in the applicant's record that the applicant initiated the discussion of disability-related issues.

Interviewing and Pre-employment Procedures Checklist

☐ Human resources personnel and all employees involved in employment interviewing have received training in ADA-related regulations and procedures.

☐ Human resources personnel and all employees involved in employment interviewing are familiar with accommodations that can be provided during the interview process.

☐ Confidentiality policy and procedures have been established.

☐ Standard interviewing forms and procedures have been developed for use with all applicants.

☐ Interviewing procedures, applications, and questionnaires do not include disability-related questions.

☐ Physical examinations, if required, are required of all candidates in a job category, and are performed only after a conditional offer of employment has been made.

☐ Medical information is maintained confidentially, in a file separate from personnel file.

☐ Rehabilitation professionals or other noncustomary personnel (e.g., sign language interpreter) are not involved in interview unless requested by applicant.

☐ Interviewer notes are kept for all job applicants.

☐ Interviewer notes specify whether applicant initiated discussion of disability or requested an accommodation, and subsequent actions taken.

Training Employees about Disabilities

Business management sometimes approaches disability-related training as if it will be, at best, a waste of time. This does not need to be the case. Although much material of questionable value has been offered on this topic, there are now many excellent resources designed to meet the needs of employers. These resources include ADA compliance manuals, packaged training programs, audio-visual materials, experienced consumer/consultants, and both local and national organizations dedicated to promoting the employment of disabled Americans.

To be effective, training should be a component of a comprehensive inclusion strategy, not a "disabilities day" one-time event. Disability education should begin with top management, proceed to supervisors, and eventually include all employees. The curriculum could include all of the subjects covered in this book and any additional material of interest to a particular employer.

It is essential for training opportunities to model what they are presenting (practice what they preach):

- They should be held in accessible locations.
- They should feature presentations and information in accessible formats.
- They should involve the participation of individuals with disabilities.

Businesses often want to utilize the expertise of current employees who have disabilities. Disabled employees should be invited, rather than required, to take prominent or leadership roles in training. Some may not be effective trainers, and others may be uncomfortable under such circumstances. Their preferences should be respected.

Management should assure that disability-related training is of the highest quality available, and is perceived by employees as relating to: (1) maximizing the effectiveness of employees, (2) legal compliance obligations, and (3) promoting appropriate behaviors in the workplace.

Training Checklist

☐ The employer has identified training needs as part of a complete inclusive employment strategy.

☐ Training personnel have received special instruction in inclusive employment, or qualified training consultants have been identified.

☐ Management has communicated the specific goals of training.

☐ Specific training modules have been identified and developed to deal with fundamental inclusion-related issues.

☐ Senior management personnel have received comprehensive training in inclusive employment practices.

☐ Supervisors have received comprehensive training in inclusive employment practices.

☐ Employees have received comprehensive training in inclusive employment practices.

☐ All training is conducted in accessible locations.

☐ Training formats and procedures are appropriate to needs of all employees.

☐ Employees with disabilities are involved in training, if they so desire.

Resources

Architectural and Transportation Barriers Compliance Board (Access Board)
http://www.access-board.gov/
1111 18th St. N.W.
Suite 501
Washington, D.C. 20036
(800) 872-2253 Voice
(800) 993-2622 TTY
(202) 272-5448 (Electronic Bulletin Board)
Telecommunications Act Accessibility Guidelines:
http://www.access-board.gov/telecomm/html/telfinal.htm/
Transportation Guidelines:
http://www.access-board.gov/transit/html/vguide.htm/

Business Leadership Network (BLN)
www.usbln.com/
1331 F St. N.W.
Washington, D.C. 20004-1107
(202) 376-6200, extension 35 Voice
(202) 376-6868 Fax
(202) 376-6205 TTY
dunlap-carol@dol.gov

The California Governor's Committee for Employment of Disabled Persons
(Producers of the Windmills Training Program)
http://www.edd.ca.gov/gcedpind.htm/
P.O. Box 826880
Sacramento, Calif. 94280-0001
(916) 654-8055 Voice
(916) 654-9820 TTY
(916) 654-9821 Fax

Center on Education and Work
http://www.cew.wisc.edu/
1025 W. Johnson St.
Rm. 964
Madison, Wisc. 53706-1796
(800) 466-0399 Voice
cewmail@education.wisc.edu

Disability and Business Technical Assistance Centers (DBTACs)
http://www.adata.org/dbtac.html/

(800) 949-4232 Voice/TTY

This number will automatically route your call to the DBTAC in your region.

Equal Employment Opportunity Commission (EEOC)

http://www.eeoc.gov/
For technical assistance:
(800) 669-4000 Voice
(800) 669-6820 TTY
To obtain documents:
(800) 669-3362 Voice
(800) 800-3302 TTY

Federal Emergency Management Agency (FEMA)

(Producers of "Disaster Preparedness for People with Disabilities")
http://www.fema.gov/
500 C St., S.W.
Washington, D.C. 20472
(202) 566-1600 Voice
(Also see "Emergency Evacuation Procedures for Employees with Disabilities" at http://www.jan.wvu.edu/media/emergency.html/)

Job Accommodation Network (JAN) of the Office of Disability Employment Policy (ODEP), U.S.

http://janweb.icdi.wvu.edu/
Department of Labor
West Virginia University
P.O. Box 6080
Morgantown, W.V. 26506-6080
(800) 526-7234 Voice/TTY

National Braille Press

(Braille publications and transcription)
http://www.nbp.org/
88 St. Stephen St.
Boston, Mass. 02115
(888) 965-8965 Voice
(617) 437-0456 Fax

National Business & Disability Council (NBDC)

http://www.business-disability.com/
201 I.U. Willets Rd.
Albertson, N.Y. 11507
(516) 465-1515 Voice
(516) 465-3730 Fax

National Center for Accessible Media
http://ncam.wgbh.org/
125 Western Ave.
Boston, Mass. 02134
(617) 300-3400 Voice
(617) 300-2489 TTY
(617) 300-1035 Fax
ncam@wgbh.org

National Library Service for the Blind and Physically Handicapped
http://www.loc.gov/nls/
Library of Congress
Washington, D.C. 20542
(202) 707-5100 Voice
(202) 707-0744 TTY
(202) 707-0712 Fax
nls@loc.gov

The National Organization on Disability (NOD)
http://www.nod.org/
910 Sixteenth St. N.W.
Suite 600
Washington, D.C. 20006
(202) 293-5960 Voice
(202) 293-5968 TTY
(202) 293-7999 Fax

Office of Disability Employment Policy (ODEP)
(formerly The President's Committee on Employment of People with Disabilities)
http://www.dol.gov/odep/
1331 F St. N.W., Suite 300
Washington, D.C. 20004
(202) 376 6200 Voice
(202) 376 6205 TTY
(202) 376 6219 Fax

Program Development Associates (PDA)
http://www.pdassoc.com/
P.O. Box 2038
Syracuse, N.Y. 13220-2038
(800) 543-2119 Voice
(315) 452-0643 Fax
info@pdassoc.com

Registry of Interpreters for the Deaf
http://www.rid.org/
8630 Fenton St., Suite 324
Silver Spring, Md. 20910
(301) 608-0050 Voice/TTY
(301) 608-0508 Fax

Society for Human Resource Management
http://www.shrm.org/
1800 Duke St.
Alexandria, Va. 22314
(703) 548-3440 Voice
(703) 535-6490 Fax
shrm@shrm.org

Terry, E., ed. 1997. *Pocket Guide to the ADA: Americans with Disabilities Act Guidelines for Buildings and Facilities.* **Rev. ed. New York: John Wiley and Sons.**

U.S. Dept. of Justice ADA Home Page
http://www.usdoj.gov/crt/ada/adahom1.htm/
U.S. Department of Justice
950 Pennsylvania Ave. N.W.
Civil Rights Division
Disability Rights Section-NYAVE
Washington, D.C. 20530
(800) 514-0301 Voice
(800) 514-0383 TTY
(202) 307-1198 Fax

Universal Designers and Consultants, Inc.
http://universaldesign.com/
6 Grant Ave.
Takoma Park, Md. 20912-4324
(301) 270-2470 Voice and TTY
(301) 270-8199 Fax
UDandC@UniversalDesign.com

World Wide Web Consortium's Web Accessibility Initiative
http://www.w3.org/WAI/
MIT/LCS Room NE43-355
200 Technology Square
Cambridge, Mass. 02139
(617) 253-2613 Voice

9

A Plan for
Inclusive Employment

Part II: On-the-Job Issues

Accommodating Employees

A shipping clerk employed by an electronics component manufacturer suffered a stroke that limited his ability to grasp with his right hand. Since one of his responsibilities was to place plastic pellets around the electronic parts, this created a problem.

His supervisor came up with a solution: a large plastic scoop with an "easy-grasp" handle. In fact, the supervisor quickly noticed that the employee had actually become more efficient than he had been before his stroke.

In a short time, the company provided scoops to all its shipping clerks.

Management sometimes views accommodating employees with disabilities strictly as a matter of legal compliance. While legalities are certainly important, another issue is at least equally compelling: maximizing the productivity of each and every worker. Accommodations are not mere legal constructs. In essence, an accommodation is an aid or procedure intended to maximize the effectiveness of a particular employee. Because they benefit both the employer and the worker, "reasonable" accommodations are unquestionably good business practice.

They are so sensible, in fact, that much of the "hype" about accommodations provided by disability advocates prior to the passage of the ADA has actually been proven accurate: most are either free or inexpensive (the average cost of an accommodation is about $300). Nor is the procedure for developing accommodations necessarily complicated or burdensome to employers. In many cases, the individual requesting the accommodation is able to recommend the best approach; in most others, solutions are easily determined. As a result of business's positive experience with job accommodations, that requirement of the ADA is now among the law's least controversial.

Before outlining a procedure to develop accommodations, it might be helpful to review some basic information. "Accommodation" means

- modification to the job application process
- modification to the work environment or the manner under which the position held is customarily performed
- modification that enables an employee with a disability to enjoy equal benefits and privileges of employment

An accommodation can include

- job restructuring
- equipment
- part-time or modified work schedules
- assistive technology
- reassignment to vacant positions
- adjustment or modifications of examinations, training materials, or policies
- providing qualified readers or interpreters

Business experience with accommodations is now extensive enough that ample data exists on countless accommodation solutions. The Job Accommodation Network (JAN), a service of the Office of Disability Employment Policy (ODEP), keeps a comprehensive database of specific accommodations issues it has dealt with for over a decade. Employers can call a toll-free number ([800] 526-7234) and present a specific problem. For example, a shoe salesperson with a physical disability is having difficulty grabbing stock from the storage area. Trained accommodations specialists can search for previous similar problems involving shoe stores, stock handling, reaching and grabbing, and so on. They can quickly report what accommodations have been tried, and which ones have been most successful. In cases where accessibility equipment might be required, they can provide contact information for manufacturers and approximate costs. They also offer a large selection of informational material. All of this is fast—and free. JAN has recently initiated a service called SOAR (for Searchable Online Accommodation Resource: http://www.jan.wvu.edu/soar/index.html). SOAR allows those seeking information on accommodations to search its extensive database by disability, limitation, industry, job function, product, and vendor.

One more important consideration: all information provided to JAN is strictly confidential. Employers can consult the staff of JAN in complete candor and without fear of incurring legal liability. JAN has never been subpoenaed to testify in an employment discrimination–related proceeding.

The following are examples of real accommodations (with their actual cost) provided by JAN:

❖

Problem: A person had an eye disorder. Glare on the computer screen caused fatigue.

Solution: An antiglare screen was purchased ($39.00).

❖

Problem: A person with a learning disability worked in the mailroom and had difficulty remembering which streets belonged to which zip codes.

Solution: A Rolodex card system was filed by street name alphabetically with the zip code. This helped him to increase his output ($150.00).

❖

Problem: A plant worker had difficulty using the telephone due to a hearing impairment that required use of hearing aids. It was suggested that he take a lower-paying job that did not require telephone use.

Solution: A telephone amplifier that worked in conjunction with his hearing aids was purchased. He kept the same job ($48.00).

❖

Problem: A clerk developed limited use of her hands and became unable to reach across the desk to her files.

Solution: A "lazy-susan" file holder was provided so she could access the files and keep her current job ($85.00).

❖

Problem: An individual lost the use of a hand and could no longer operate a camera. The company provided a tripod, but that was too cumbersome.

Solution: A waist pod, such as is used in carrying flags, enabled him to manipulate the camera and keep his job ($50.00).

❖

Problem: A receptionist, who was visually impaired, could not see the lights on her telephone that indicated whether the telephone lines at her company were ringing, on hold, or in use.

Solution: The company bought a light-probe, a pen-like product that detected a lighted button ($45.00).

❖

Problem: An insurance salesperson with cerebral palsy had difficulty taking notes while talking on the telephone.

Solution: Her employer purchased a headset for a phone ($49.95).

❖

Problem: A person applied for a job as a cook and was able to do everything required except opening cans, due to the loss of a hand.

Solution: The employer called the Job Accommodation Network, was given a list of one-handed can openers, and bought one ($35.00).

❖

Problem: A medical technician who was deaf could not hear the buzz of a timer, which was necessary for specific laboratory tests.

Solution: An indicator light was attached ($26.95).

❖

Problem: A person who used a wheelchair could not use a desk because it was too low and his knees would not go under it.

Solution: The desk was raised with wood blocks, allowing a proper amount of space for the wheelchair to fit under it ($∅).

❖

Problem: A person who worked outdoors had a medical condition that caused his hands to be unable to tolerate cold.

Solution: The individual used gloves with pocket hand warmers such as those used by hunters ($50.00).

❖

Problem: A person with an unusually soft voice was required to do extensive public speaking.

Solution: A hand-held voice amplifier did the trick ($150.00).

❖

Problem: An employer wanted to make the elevator accessible to a new employee who was blind and read Braille.

Solution: Raised-dot self-adhesive elevator symbols made the elevator accessible ($6.00 apiece).

❖

Problem: A company wanted to hire a clerk who could not access the vertical filing cabinets from her wheelchair.

Solution: The company moved the files into a lateral file and hired her ($450.00).

❖

Problem: A person had a condition that required two-hour rest periods during the day.

Solution: The company changed her schedule and allowed her longer breaks, although she worked the same number of hours ($0).

❖

Problem: An employer wanted an individual who was short statured to drive a heavy loading machine. His feet did not reach the brake pedals.

Solution: The machine was fitted with special seating ($1,200.00).

❖

Problem: A mail carrier with a back injury could no longer carry his mailbag.

Solution: A cart that could be pushed allowed him to keep his route ($150.00).

❖

Problem: A longtime employee in a factory developed allergic reactions to dust and aerosol sprays.

Solution: He was fitted with a portable air respirator ($200.00).

❖

Problem: A sales agent was paralyzed from the neck down and could not access his tape recorder.

Solution: A drafting table, page-turner, and pressure-sensitive tape recorder were purchased, enabling him to keep his job ($800.00).

The effectiveness of providing accommodations to employees with disabilities is now so clearly demonstrated that some employers have begun to invite requests from any and all employees—whether or not they have a disability. Why should the benefits of enabling technology be limited to a few?

As the following checklist indicates,[1] management must establish the necessary policies and procedures to assure that accommodations are provided in a fair and efficient manner. After that, accommodation requests should be handled strictly on an individual basis.

Accommodating Employees Checklist

Management Preparations

☐ Management has developed appropriate procedures for requesting, identifying, developing, providing, and evaluating accommodations.

☐ Procedures for appeals and revisions have been developed and approved.

☐ Procedures for maintaining confidentiality throughout the accommodations process have been developed and implemented.

☐ Accommodation policies and procedures have been communicated to all employees.

☐ Human resources personnel have received training in regulations and best practices relating to accommodating employees with disabilities.

☐ Job descriptions have been written to indicate the essential functions of each position.

Procedure for Specific Requests

☐ Essential functions of the position have been reviewed.

☐ Employee has been determined to be qualified to perform essential functions of the position with or without a reasonable accommodation.

☐ Relevant functional limitation/s of employee has/have been identified.

☐ Employee has been consulted about needs and preferences.

☐ Rehabilitation personnel have been consulted, if necessary.

☐ Potential accommodations have been identified.

☐ Potential accommodations have been evaluated for effectiveness and cost.

☐ Employee has participated in evaluation of potential accommodations.

☐ Selected accommodation/s has/have been monitored and evaluated for effectiveness and user friendliness.

☐ Accommodation/s has/have been modified, if necessary.

☐ Monitoring/evaluation of accommodation/s is ongoing, if appropriate.

Supervising and Supporting Employees

In 1994, a disability consultant "invented" a navigational device to aid people with visual disabilities. The device was a hand-held button that activated a sounding device at a predetermined location—a building entrance, corridor, emergency exit, etc. Using this device, a blind person could obtain a location "cue" sonically, just as most people do visually.

> The consultant carefully developed plans for the device and took
> them to a patent attorney to research the concept for possible patenting.
> Several weeks later the attorney delivered the bad news: a nearly identi-
> cal device had been patented in Japan several years earlier.
>
> Two months later a friend introduced the consultant to the "Abledata"
> database—a free service. He entered the terms "blind," "navigation," and
> "electronic," and in seconds Abledata provided detailed information
> about the Japanese invention. Had the consultant known about Abledata
> earlier, he could have saved himself some trouble—and a legal bill!

Supervising an individual with a disability can be a challenge; it can also be an incomparably rewarding experience.[2] At times, it can even be just like supervising anybody else.

The most critical issue in inclusive employment is *ability*. Supervisors should always keep that in mind. All employees are hired because of what they can do, not because of what they can't do. Although workers with disabilities may require accommodations, they should be held to the same standards as all other employees. Supervisors should especially avoid any temptation to treat workers with condescension or pity. Praise should not be awarded too easily, nor criticism withheld unreasonably. To "bend the rules" for a disabled employee out of sympathy, friendship, or low expectations is to do that worker a disservice.

Effective supervision begins with clear leadership from management, which provides clear expectations and goals. Management must also provide supervisors with the training and resources they need to work effectively with disabled workers. Occasionally, management unknowingly creates obstacles to the implementation of its own goals. For example, if substantial training or accommodation costs must be borne solely by the small unit in which a disabled individual is to be employed, this can act as a powerful disincentive for inclusion. Management must replace such obstacles with solutions, incentives, and rewards.

Supervisors have every reason to expect employees with disabilities to be able to perform the essential functions of their positions well. All of the available research indicates that disabled employees are equal to, or better than, their peers in attendance, safety, reliability, and productivity.

On the other hand, employees with disabilities also tend to exhibit two weaknesses: inadequate social skills and limited work experience. Given the fact that people with disabilities, until relatively recently, have tended to suffer from social isolation and continue to have extremely high rates of unemployment, this is quite understandable. However, this is *only* a tendency, *not* a universal characteristic. Without making any assumptions about a specific worker's likely weaknesses, supervisors should pay particular attention to the informal supports (peers, workgroups, networking) available in the work environments. Although formal supports (trainers, mentoring programs, accommodations) are critical, informal supports can often make the difference between employment success and failure. They can help the worker with a disability quickly adapt to the culture of employment, if such adaptation is required. Supervisors who take a supportive, enthusiastic attitude toward employees with disabilities demonstrate to co-workers the type of behaviors they expect them to demonstrate.

The following section presents some considerations and strategies that can be helpful in supervising employees with various disabilities. It is important to remember, however, that in supporting workers, more resources and procedures do not always mean a greater chance of success; in fact, "less" is often "more." Disabled employees often appreciate having as little attention as possible called to their needs, and the use of unobtrusive supports can often minimize the chance that fellow employees will be envious or resentful.

Supervisory Strategies

Even with the whole-hearted support of management, sufficient resources, and training, supervising employees with disabilities can sometimes be challenging. The following is a not uncommon scenario:

Sylvia had a medical condition that caused occasional drowsiness, and she occasionally had to take unscheduled rest breaks. She had spoken to her supervisor about her condition and need for accommodation, but she had requested that her fellow workers not be informed she had a disability.

One co-worker became annoyed with Sylvia's occasional rest periods, and asked for "equal treatment" from her supervisor. When she was denied this perk she demanded to know, "Why can Sylvia take extra breaks, and I can't?"

The supervisor was in a difficult position: in order to justify the action she had taken with Sylvia, she would have to reveal confidential information. How could she satisfy the other worker while meeting her obligation of confidentiality?

(In this case, the supervisor might have told the other worker she must respect issues of confidentiality, and asked her, "Do you have any particular needs that might necessitate additional breaks?")

Employees with Learning Disabilities

Learning disabilities involve disturbances in how individuals process information. People with learning disabilities have normal or above-normal intelligence, and learn in atypical ways that vary according to the type of learning disability.

Learning disabilities can be frustrating for the individual involved, and all of the available research indicates that past experiences with failure can play an important role in adult employment. Individuals with learning disabilities can have a deep-seated fear of failure, and may go out of their way to avoid disappointments and embarrassments. This "avoidance behavior" can be misunderstood as unfriendliness, noncooperation, or lack of ambition. For example, an individual may steer clear of new responsibilities not out of laziness or contrariness, but because of a lack of confidence. He or she may also be unusually sensitive to signs of approval or disapproval. Understanding such tendencies, and responding appropriately, presents a real supervisory challenge.

Consider the following suggestions for supervising employees with learning disabilities:

- Talk to the employee about the ways he or she prefers to communicate, receive information, and learn.
- Take time to understand, and to be understood.
- Control workspace noise, lighting, interruptions, and distractions.
- Determine ways to maximize the employee's effectiveness: maximize functions that play to his or her strengths, and avoid areas in which he or she is relatively weak.
- Supervise constructively: frame evaluations and suggestions positively, and demonstrate appreciation and approval overtly.

Employees with Mental Retardation

Individuals with mental retardation have subaverage intelligence and learn at a relatively slow rate that varies according to the severity of the disability.

Like learning disabilities, mental retardation can be frustrating for the individual involved, and employees with mental retardation may also have a significant fear of failure. In addition, employees with mental retardation are sometimes reluctant to discuss their disability, and may take offense if the phrase "mentally retarded" is used to refer to them. On the other hand, they may be very open to positive approaches to learning, such as discussions about how they can be an even better worker. Like people with learning disabilities, those with mental retardation may be particularly sensitive to signs of approval or disapproval, especially direct comments and criticism, of course, but also subtleties including voice tone, facial gestures, and body language.

Consider the following suggestions for supervising employees with mental retardation:

- Take time to understand, and to be understood.
- Use simple, concrete language.
- Break tasks into component steps, and guide the employee through the learning process at a pace appropriate to his or her capability.
- Reinforce instruction with repetition.
- Use prompts (color coding, tip sheets, checklists, pictures, samples) if needed.
- Use occasional nonverbal, concrete signs of approval (thumbs up, handshake, OK/check mark).
- Avoid subtleties and nuances when communicating important information.
- Control workspace noise, lighting, interruptions, and distractions.
- Reinforce informal supports and promote social integration.

Employees with Physical Disabilities

Given all the changes in technology, architecture, transportation, and education during the past two decades, employees with physical disabilities are now much less likely to need physical accommodations. In many cases, informal supports, such as personal assistance offered by co-workers, may be the only help required; in other instances, technological solutions may be readily available.

In arranging job accommodations, supervisors should make every effort to use the least obtrusive, least restrictive solution available. Usually, this is the solution favored by the employee who is disabled.

Whenever employees with physical disabilities are involved, physical accessibility is an issue. Supervisors should never assume a work site is fully accessible simply because it meets building codes. Often, people with physical disabilities can provide valuable data about physical changes that can provide greater accessibility.

Consider the following suggestions for supervising employees with physical disabilities:

- The employee's workspace may need to be reshaped to provide maximum efficiency.
- Technology can be particularly helpful—ergonomic furniture, automatic tools, assistive devices, etc.
- Stamina may be an issue requiring accommodation: some individuals with physical disabilities may experience significantly different energy levels at various times throughout the day, and from one day to another.
- Labor problems can be avoided if all accommodations are carefully documented, from initial request to periodic evaluation.

Employees with Psychiatric Disabilities

Psychiatric disabilities are among those most likely to be encountered by supervisors, and no disability is associated with more misinformation, mythology, and stereotyping. Because of this, effective employee education and training is of critical importance. In providing employees with essential information about psychiatric disabilities, great care must be taken to preserve the confidentiality of all employees. Training should provide general information, never focusing on specific problems or behaviors associated with particular individuals. The approach should be positive and supportive, with an emphasis on proactive behavioral strategies and the many recent improvements in the treatment of mental illness, especially the development of new medications.

Supervising an employee with a psychiatric disability can pose some difficult problems. For example, considerations of confidentiality might prevent a supervisor from explaining to a co-worker why "special provisions" (i.e., accommodations), such as a flexible schedule or medication breaks, are being given to one employee and not to others. At other times, supervisors may have to deal with the issue of whether an employee poses a direct threat to the health and safety of himself or others.

Supervisors must prepare carefully for the challenges they may face. At the same time, they should make sure they are able to relax in the company of the employee involved. The necessary confidence and ease can be promoted through adequate training and preparation. Supervisors should take time to establish effective communication with the employee, always treating him or her with appropriate respect.

Consider the following suggestions for supervising employees with psychiatric disabilities:

- Employees with psychiatric disabilities should be involved in their workplace accommodations just as other employees would be.
- People with psychiatric disabilities may be particularly sensitive to eye contact, voice level, body language—various signs of interest, attention, and approval.
- Some individuals may have significant problems dealing with change, even change involved in helping them, such as providing them with needed accommodations.
- Supervisors should keep in mind that what might appear to be simple or uncomplicated issues to others may not be perceived as such by an individual with a psychiatric disability. For example, the expectation to attend social functions may be problematic, and the employee may require an exemption as an accommodation.
- Supervisors should avoid inappropriate responses, such as overinvolvement in a worker's personal life, giving unsolicited advice, or coddling.
- Confidentiality is critical. Information pertaining to an individual's psychiatric disability must be controlled with great care and shared only on a "need to know" basis.
- Supervisors should never tolerate idle chatter about any person's disability.
- Although the employee still has the responsibility to request job accommodations, disability-related issues, such as fear or passivity, may present obstacles.
- Reassignment (of duties, work location, supervisor) may be required as a reasonable accommodation.
- Coordination should be maintained with existing resources (counseling, support groups, employee assistance programs).
- When issues of a potential threat to health and safety are involved, supervisors should seek additional professional assistance.

Employees with Visual Disabilities

Perhaps more than any other disability, visual impairments present supervisors with the issue of "diminished expectations." Because most people receive almost 90 percent of their information visually, many find it difficult to understand how an individual with a visual disability can be an effective employee. For this reason, many people with visual disabilities are never even considered for jobs they are quite capable of performing.

Any person responsibile for supervising a worker with a visual disability would do well to make a conscious effort to *forget* all, or at least most, of the conventional wisdom he or she has absorbed over the years about people with sight-related disabilities. Most of it is misleading, inaccurate, and counterproductive. Secondly, supervisors should *discard* all assumptions they might have about the capabilities of a particular individual who has a visual disability. Then, and only then, should they begin to discuss the job at hand with the worker at hand and begin to make decisions based on accurate information.

Perhaps more than most, employees with visual impairments appreciate an orderly and uncluttered work environment. Achieving this involves the cooperation of all employees. Sighted workers should make it a regular practice to inform fellow employees with visual impairments of any major physical change in the work site, such as repairs underway, equipment that has been added, or furniture that has been moved or removed.

In practice, supervising an individual with a visual disability can be most challenging in the area of information sharing. Many information sources most people take for granted—written memos, handbooks, web-based data, even bulletin board announcements—present problems for people with visual impairments. Supervisors may need to provide employees with readers or similar aids, or provide information in alternate formats. Many technological solutions—everything from ordinary tape recorders to text-reading computers—are available. Sometimes a solution can be as simple as making one large-print copy each time an employee memo is circulated.

A second important issue is transportation. In an economy dependent on the automobile, people with visual impairments can be at a significant disadvantage. Some assistance in meeting job-related transportation needs may be required. The supervisor should communicate clearly what the employee's responsibility is, and what the employer will provide.

An effective supervisor will pay close attention to issues of expectations, communication, and transportation, and develop practical solutions to any problem that might occur. Frequently, the employee will be the most valuable source of information on available accommodations.

Consider the following suggestions for supervising employees with visual disabilities:

- As a safety matter, keep the job site uncluttered, and inform the employee of any major changes in the work environment.
- Focus on information sharing—do not let barriers prevent the communication of necessary knowledge.
- Provide assistance for job-related transportation if required.
- Involve the employee in developing accommodations.

Employees with Hearing Impairments

Developments in technology hold great promise for people who have disabilities. This is particularly true for those with hearing impairments. If the following hasn't happened yet, it soon will:

A technology company convenes a meeting of division managers to discuss strategic planning. One person in attendance is Michael, a recently hired data analyst. He has a significant hearing impairment.

Michael is one of the first to arrive in the conference room. He opens his laptop computer, which is equipped with a highly sensitive microphone and voice recognition software.

During the meeting, Michael looks at the computer screen and sees a "live" transcript of what is being said. When only one person is speaking, his software picks up the conversation with over 90 percent accuracy. At appropriate times, the new employee offers his comments to the group. They, too, appear on his screen.

As the meeting comes to an end, the CEO comments: "Michael, that system of yours is really something. Does it give you a record of everything said at this meeting?"

"Just about," Michael replies. "It's pretty accurate, and I can usually decipher its mistakes by looking at the context of the comments."

"Could you give me a transcript?" the CEO asks.

"I'd be happy to," Michael responds.

A few minutes later, the CEO receives a transcript of the meeting by email.

Like people with visual impairments, employees with hearing-related disabilities often need assistance in the area of communication. Simple solutions, like eliminating background noise, writing notes, speaking clearly and directly at the employee, and conducting meetings around oval or round tables, can sometimes be the only accommodations necessary. In other cases, more sophisticated solutions, such as text-based communications, telephone volume controls, and light signals, may be required. Once again, the disabled employee will likely be an important resource for solutions. More complicated issues may require consultation with an audiology professional.

Effective communication must exist between the supervisor and the employee, but should also include fellow workers, customers, suppliers, contractors, and the public. Informal supports will be much more effective if the employee is socially integrated in the work group. The supervisor should make sure such integration is occurring.

At times, the supervisor may be required to represent the employee's essential interests to the larger company. In particular, he or she should see that company information is available in a format that is accessible to the employee. For example, a supervisor should ensure that employee training films are available with captioning.

In regard to safety, care should be taken that appropriate visual warning devices and other safety provisions are available on the work site and at alternate locations, such as conference and training facilities. Companies that make travel arrangements for their employees should request accommodations needed by employees. Most hotels now offer rooms accessible to guests with hearing impairments, or can provide accommodation "kits" containing visual door and telephone signals, flashing smoke detectors, and so on.

Consider the following suggestions for supervising employees with hearing disabilities:

- Assure effective communication between employee and supervisor, and between employee and fellow workers, customers, suppliers, and the public.
- Promote socialization and access to informal supports.
- Reduce or eliminate background noises.
- Use round meeting tables, plan the disabled employee's workspace to face others, use voice and phone amplification equipment as needed.
- Communications solutions may involve lip-reading, notes, personal digital assistants (PDAs), email, computer instant messenger, etc.

- Assistive technology is plentiful, but be sure to provide it in a way appropriate to individual needs.
- Ensure the accessibility of all pertinent employer information and communications.
- Always provide appropriate safety and warning devices.

Employees with Speech Impairments

Significant speech impairments affect less than 3 percent of adults and an even smaller portion of the working population. Because of the relative rarity of employees with speech impairments, supervisors may feel uneasy in communicating with them. This need not be the case. Although speech impairments can present real barriers to communication, many accommodations are available.

Supervisors should begin by expressing their eagerness to establish effective communication. Often, the employee already has well-established procedures—anything from simply slowing down his or her speech, to using notes, personal digital assistant devices, or talking computers.

Supervisors should do everything within their power to eliminate distractions, competing noise, and stress during interactions with employees who have speech disabilities. They should allow adequate time for interaction, with the understanding that less time will undoubtedly be required as each party comes to better understand the other's communication style.

Consider the following suggestions for supervising employees with speech impairments:

- Put the employee at ease. Assure him or her that you will take the time needed to establish effective communication.
- Eliminate background noise and other distractions.
- If necessary, ask the employee to repeat what he or she has said. Usually, the employee will slow his or her speaking and try to articulate with greater clarity.
- Technology can be helpful—e.g., speech synthesizer, speech amplifier, communication board, personal digital assistant, laptop computer.
- Time and practice will enhance communication effectiveness.

Employees with Diabetes

Approximately 13 million Americans have diabetes. Many control their condition through diet; others require insulin, diabetes pills, or similar treatments. Diabetes can have some significant side effects, including weight gain, coronary and kidney disease, and visual impairment.

Not all people who have diabetes will require accommodations. Some employees may choose not to notify their employer of their health status or request an accommodation. Those who do request accommodations may need additional breaks to check blood glucose levels, take medications, or eat a snack. Others may need rest periods or schedule flexibility.

Supervisors seeking additional information or training will find the national office ([800] 342-2383) or local affiliate of the American Diabetes Association very helpful.

Consider the following suggestions for supervising employees with diabetes:

- Begin by talking with the employee about his or her particular needs.
- The employee's physician may be able to provide useful suggestions. Obtain the employee's permission before contacting the physician.
- Secondary problems associated with diabetes (e.g., kidney disease, visual impairment) may also require accommodation.
- Many employees, not just people with diabetes, will welcome sugar-free snacks and beverages at company gatherings.
- Contact the American Diabetes Association for more information.

Employees with Histories of Drug and Alcohol Abuse

Although alcoholism is specifically protected as a disability under the Americans with Disabilities Act, the current use of illegal drugs is not. A history of abuse and dependency, not simple or occasional use, raises drug or alcohol use to the level of disability. The ADA also protects those who are *perceived* as having such a history—even if that perception is *erroneous.*

This area of the ADA is one of its most controversial, and it is also constantly under interpretation by the courts. For that reason, supervisors should seek legal assistance if they have any doubt as to whether a particular individual is protected under this legislation. Common sense is not always a reliable guide.

Confidentiality is always important in regard to the disability status of employees, but it is especially so in regard to drug and alcohol problems. All information must be carefully controlled, including the results of drug tests. Obviously, this information is highly sensitive. In addition, such tests can sometimes yield information irrelevant to drug abuse, but pertinent to other disability issues (such as indicating a medical condition or the use of prescription medication). The number of employees permitted to know or examine the results of drug tests should be kept to an absolute minimum.

Accommodations for an employee in this category might include flexible scheduling to permit controlled medication, or the temporary suspension of nonessential tasks that might place the employee in personal jeopardy during his or her treatment. (For example, a delivery person fighting alcoholism might ask not to be required to make deliveries to businesses that serve alcohol.) Employers are not required to retain any employee who poses a direct threat to the health or safety of others.

Consider the following suggestions for supervising employees with histories of drug and alcohol abuse:

- This area of the ADA is evolving—stay informed! Obtain legal advice if you are uncertain how to proceed.
- Remember: people with current alcohol problems who are able to perform their jobs *are* covered by the ADA.
- Drug tests may be required only after a conditional offer of employment.
- Drug testing sometimes provides information related to other disabilities. This information must be kept in strict confidence and *not* be considered in hiring, promotion, or any other type of management decision.
- If there is any question whether an individual poses a threat to the health or safety of others, get professional advice. This could include a lawyer, physician, rehabilitation counselor, etc.
- Employees may need flexible scheduling to obtain medication (e.g., methadone) or attend treatment sessions.
- Nonessential tasks that pose increased risks may need to be suspended during treatment or eliminated completely.

Employees Who Are HIV Positive

The ADA specifically protects employees with HIV, the virus that causes AIDS. Recent advances in treatment and medication have greatly increased the rate of workforce participation for individuals who are HIV positive.

As in the case of psychiatric disabilities and drug or alcohol abuse, confidentiality is of particular importance when supervising an individual who is HIV positive. And like psychiatric illnesses, HIV is a subject often characterized by misunderstanding, misinformation, and stereotyping. Training and information on HIV should be provided for all employees, and it should never refer to any particular individual. Accommodations for someone with HIV might include flexible scheduling that would allow the employee to receive treatments, rest periods, auxiliary aids for related physical ailments or needs, and additional unpaid leave.

This is another area of supervision in which the issue of a "threat" to health and safety can arise. A qualified person can be denied employment or terminated only if he or she poses a "direct threat" to health or safety, if accommodations are not available, or if accommodations would pose an "undue hardship" to the employer. The unfounded fears of those who have not been properly educated about HIV must not interfere with an employee's right to work.

Supervisors and employers can often obtain helpful assistance from local health authorities or nonprofit organizations that provide services to people who are HIV positive.

Consider the following suggestions for supervising employees who are HIV positive:

- Relevant information must be shared on a "need to know" basis only. Confidentiality is critical.
- Workplace education should include information about HIV as one component of disability-related training; it should not focus on individual cases.
- Employers may inquire about HIV status after a conditional offer of employment.
- An offer may be withdrawn, or employment terminated, only for one of the following reasons:
  - The candidate poses a "direct threat" to health or safety.
  - No reasonable accommodation is available that would enable the person to perform the essential functions of the job.
  - Accommodation would cause an undue hardship.

Supervising and Supporting Employees Checklist

☐ Management has clearly communicated priorities and goals.
☐ Management has established procedures to cover equitably the costs associated with inclusive employment.

☐ Supervisors have received training in disabilities, accommodations, support strategies, the ADA, and other issues relating to inclusive employment.

☐ Effective supervision and support of employees with disabilities is valued, promoted, and rewarded.

☐ Supervisors have been given all related information, including
  ○ specific information about the accommodation needs of employees they supervise
  ○ information pertaining to the disabilities of employees they supervise
  ○ contact information for counselors, rehabilitation personnel, interpreters, or other professional resources they might need

☐ Assistance of rehabilitation personnel or other professional resources is available, if necessary.

☐ Mentoring relationships are encouraged.

☐ Workgroup supports are encouraged.

☐ Supervisors and co-workers promote workplace enculturation, networking, and socialization.

☐ Employees have been given clear instructions and goals.

☐ Employee performance feedback is frequent and constructively communicated.

☐ Employees with disabilities know how to obtain necessary assistance and support.

☐ Employee training is appropriate, accessible, and ongoing.

Disability Management

Comprehensive disability management and return-to-work programs should incorporate both effective treatment and prevention. The major components of a comprehensive disability management program should be identification, intervention, outcome reporting, process improvement, and prevention. (See fig. 9.1.)

1. Identification
   • Rapid response—The first line of defense against all on-the-job accidents and injuries is the prompt identification of the person ill or injured, and of the workplace hazard in question. Identification must also include determination of the risk of long-term disability associated with the condition.
   • Supervisor initiative—The involvement of the supervisor in spotting potential problems, and catching them early—before they become

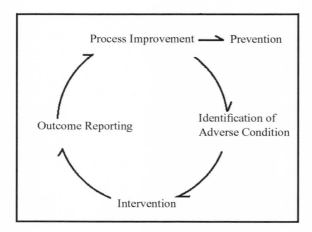

Fig. 9.1. Dynamics of a disability management and prevention program.

major issues—is particularly important. Often, supervisors and employees can quickly develop effective ergonomic solutions to workplace problems.

- Employer initiative—Common-sense solutions are usually preferable to those imposed by the Occupational Safety and Health Administration (OSHA). The agency itself admits that, in some cases, companies have reported *increased* musculo-skeletal disorders after OSHA inspectors mandated workplace changes that had been resisted by employers and employees alike.

2. Intervention
   - Immediate response—Long-term resolution of risk-related disability and sustained productive employment correlate with early and, at times, comprehensive intervention.
   - Evidence-based medical care—As the level of sophistication in managing work-related disability increases, employers will benefit by involving health professionals with specialized expertise in occupational medicine. Standardized, evidence-based approaches to managing a host of occupational conditions have been developed, and should be used routinely.

3. Outcome reporting
   - A mechanism for tracking the results of medical treatment and long-term outcomes should be in place. Data should be reviewed periodically with professionals in ergonomics and occupational medicine.

- After data analysis, actionable recommendations for disability prevention and more effective treatment approaches can be developed.

4. Process Improvement
   - Data management—Capturing appropriate data about the injury and its treatment and outcome is the first step in applying process improvement to disability management.
   - Job analysis—Problematic working conditions should be studied carefully. Observation of job performance, including videotaping, may be helpful. Measurements of stress factors (heat and cold, weight, push/pull force, etc.) should be made. In some cases, completion of a "Job Strain Index," or similar measurement instrument for predicting problem tasks, may be warranted. Consultation with ergonomics professionals or rehabilitation engineers may be appropriate.

5. Prevention

   The role of prevention in disability management cannot be overstated. Participants in the OSHA's Voluntary Prevention Program have been able to reduce accident and injury rates by 60% below industry norms (Chao 2001). Research indicates that for every dollar it invests in prevention, business can expect a return of four to six dollars (Layne 2001). Ultimately, prevention is the most effective method of disability management.

   Illness and injury can be prevented or minimized through a variety of means:
   - Comfort provision—e.g., padding, supports, and special lighting.
   - Job reconfiguration—e.g., task sharing, rotation, and worker repositioning.
   - Personal protective equipment—e.g., masks, braces, cushions, and vibration absorbers.
   - Assistive devices—e.g., automated tools (power nailers, power screwdrivers), lifting and carrying equipment, and robotic and remotely operated machines.
   - Compensating actions—e.g., work restrictions, more or longer breaks, exercise opportunities, and massage.
   - Training—covering issues such as hazard identification, lifting techniques, and accident and injury prevention.

- Incentives—e.g., pay and promotions tied to safe performance, and bonuses for completing injury-free periods of work.
- In all cases, preventing accidents and illness is in the best interest of both the employer and the employee. Joint cooperation can provide an additional benefit: preventing unnecessary governmental meddling in the workplace.

Chronic Injury and Ergonomics

In the closing days of his administration, President Bill Clinton signed an executive order putting into effect a host of regulations establishing "final rule" standards for the long-awaited "Ergonomics Program" of the Occupational Safety and Health Administration.[3] The purpose of these standards, according to OSHA, was "to address the significant risk of employee exposure to ergonomic risk factors in jobs in general industry workplaces." During the early days of President George W. Bush's administration, after protests from the business community that the new rules were unduly burdensome and enacted without sufficient time for employers to respond, the program was rescinded. Although it remains to be seen when and if these or similar rules will finally go into effect, the trend toward greater governmental involvement in workplace safety and ergonomic issues is clear. Regardless of the eventual political outcome, all employers should be concerned about the issues of worker safety and comfort. In the future, health issues relating to ergonomics—especially musculo-skeletal disorders (MSD) and repetitive motion injuries (RMI)—are certain to demand increasing attention from business.

MSDs and RMIs can be found in almost all industries, especially manufacturing, construction, transportation, telecommunications, food processing, waste management, and forestry. Risk factors include the following:

- poor or strained posture
- repetitive movement
- excessive or sustained loads
- contact stress (including vibration, constriction of blood flow, impact, and excessive heat or cold)

Workers' Compensation

Workers' compensation costs represent a major expense for business. Although the numbers of claims and the overall cost to business have recently declined, the value of an *average* claim is in excess of $34,000, and rising.[5] Cost drivers within the system include medical claims related to occupational conditions or injuries, compensation for wages during periods of disability, and indemnification for liability claims against the employer. Minimizing injury claims and returning injured workers quickly to the job is the goal of every employer.

The workers' compensation process has obvious relevance to matters of disability law and rights protection. Workers' compensation laws protect employees injured on the job; however, the ADA is designed to protect individuals from discrimination on the basis of disability in general. While a worker injured on the job may well receive protection under the ADA, not all employees who make workers' compensation claims are covered by this legislation. Losing, through illness or injury, the capability to perform the essential duties of a job is not a sufficient qualification for protection under the ADA.

To be covered under the ADA, an employee must meet the definition of a "qualified person with a disability." The individual must have an impairment that "substantially limits a major life activity," or have a "record of" or be "regarded as having" such an impairment. The employee must also be able to perform the essential functions of the job in question, with or without reasonable

HEALTH AND SAFETY IN THE WORKPLACE

- In 1999, the United States labor force consisted of approximately 133 million workers.

- Of these 133 million workers, approximately 121 million were covered by workers' compensation.

- Injuries and illnesses have declined from 8.4 per 100 full-time workers in 1994 to 6.1 per 100 full-time workers in 2000.

- 5.7 million injuries and illnesses in private industry were reported in 1999.

- In 1999, 3 million of the 5.7 million reported cases involved lost workdays.

- Of the 5.7 million cases reported in 1999, 5.3 million involved injuries.

- From 1993 through 1998, workers' compensation costs to employers declined by 38 percent.

Sources: Bureau of Labor Statistics and Pennsylvania Workers' Compensation Legal Center[4]

accommodation. Because of these criteria, the majority of employees who make claims for workers' compensation are not qualified for protection under the ADA. Employers must decide on a case-by-case basis whether a workers' compensation claimant is a "qualified person with a disability," and therefore entitled to such protection.

In regard to employee health and disability insurance, the issue of medical examinations is particularly important. Employers may require post-offer-of-employment medical examinations before work begins, provided such exams are required of all of those in that job classification. In addition, employers may conduct "fitness-for-duty" examinations if they are job-related—for reasons such as determining whether an individual can perform the essential functions of a job after an illness or injury, or determining what accommodations may be required. If an employer needs to determine whether an individual has the ability to continue to perform a job, it may make disability-related inquiries, including medical examinations that are job-related. Finally, employers are entitled to make such inquiries if there is a legitimate concern about an employee representing a "direct threat" to health and safety.

Return-to-Work Programs

In order to return injured workers to the job as quickly as possible, many employers have instituted return-to-work programs. Although not all employees involved will qualify for protection under the ADA, return-to-work and other disability management programs must be in accord with that legislation, and also state workers' compensation laws, the Family and Medical Leave Act of 1993, and any other applicable disability-related federal statutes.[6]

Light or modified duty is one return-to-work consideration that can be especially helpful both to people with disabilities and to employers. The ADA does not require an employer to allow a person with a disability to work permanently on a "reduced productivity" basis, but many companies provide what is known as "light duty," "modified work," or "alternate work" status for employees who are recovering from an accident or illness. In such cases, modified duty might involve changes in job responsibilities, temporary reassignment to another position, or permission to work at less than full productivity. Such provisions often make great economic sense for both employer and employee, reducing workers' compensation costs and allowing disabled workers to return to work much faster than would otherwise be possible.

Procedures in a return-to-work program should include the following:[7]

- maintaining contact with the ill or injured employee, or if appropriate, the employee's family
- visiting the employee, if possible, to demonstrate concern and initiate discussion of the return-to-work process
- determining what information about his or her absence the employee wants to be shared with co-workers, customers, clients, and other contacts
- providing the employee with any information he or she requests, especially information required to apply for health insurance or workers' compensation benefits
- providing the employee with assistance in applying for benefits
- discussing possible accommodations, adjustments, and work reintegration procedures, including light or modified duty, prior to the employee's return to work

Health and Disability Insurance Coverage and the ADA

In the provision of health care insurance, employees with disabilities must be treated exactly like all other employees similarly situated. The same is true for disability insurance. Employers must keep in mind that protections under the ADA extend not only to applicants and employees: the ADA prohibits discrimination against individuals with disabilities, people who have family members with disabilities, or people with who are associated with disabled individuals.[8] An employer may not discriminate even if it fears that by hiring, promoting, or insuring a particular individual its health insurance premiums or related costs might increase. In addition, employers are liable for any discrimination resulting from a contract with an insurance company, health maintenance organization, third-party administrator, stop-loss carrier, or other organization that administers an insurance plan on behalf of the company.

Although, in general, an employer must offer workers with disabilities equal access to health and disability coverage provided to all other employees, it may offer plans containing limitations in health care coverage. Limitations in the number of treatments and exclusions from coverage that are not "disability-based," including pre-existing conditions, are permissible under EEOC regulations. For example, an employer's health plan might limit mental health coverage to a certain number of counseling sessions per year, providing that the limitation applies to all employees similarly situated. Most insurance carriers are fully aware of applicable EEOC regulations and guidelines, but employers should review existing policies for possible discriminatory provisions.

Although, because of the increased likelihood they are economically disadvantaged, adults with disabilities are less likely to have health insurance than
other workers, they are *more* likely to be eligible for government-subsidized
coverage.[9] Employers may benefit by familiarizing themselves with all health
insurance options available to their employees who are disabled. New legislation that allows disabled employees to carry such coverage with them even after
they are employed is discussed in the section on Tax Incentives in this chapter.

Disability Management, Workers' Compensation, and Health and Disability Insurance Checklist

☐ Senior management has clearly communicated the importance of effective
disability management and of injury and illness prevention.

☐ Management and human resources staff have received appropriate training
in the ADA, disability management and prevention, workers' compensation and return-to-work programs, and health and disability insurance.

☐ Health and disability insurance plans have been reviewed for compliance
with the ADA, the Family and Medical Leave Act of 1993, and other applicable legislation.

☐ Medical examinations, if required, are obtained from all similarly situated
employees, or obtained only for appropriate business-related purposes.

☐ Process improvement programs for medical management and disability
management have been established and are audited periodically.

☐ All employees have been informed of the necessity of immediately notifying their supervisor of any accident, injury, or other disability-related matter, and clearly understand procedures in place to make such notification.

☐ All employees making workers' compensation claims are evaluated regarding whether or not they qualify for protection under the ADA.

☐ Employer has coordinated the approach to safety and claims management efforts with disability insurance carriers and health care insurance providers.

☐ Work sites have received a safety analysis/design review conducted by
safety experts and ergonomics professionals.

☐ Accident reports and workers' compensation claims are periodically reviewed according to an established schedule.

☐ Data on the results of medical treatments and long-term outcomes are maintained, and a process establishing actionable recommendations pursuant to
review of that data has been established.

☐ Procedures have been established for developing individual return-to-work solutions.

☐ Employees receiving workers' compensation are regularly evaluated for change in status.

☐ Workers' compensation premiums, previous claims, and current costs are professionally audited.

☐ All employees have received appropriate training in accident and injury prevention.

☐ Accident and injury prevention and disability-related cost containment are regularly evaluated, and effective management is rewarded.

Tax and Other Financial Incentives

Employment of people with disabilities presents an unusual win-win-win situation: the person with a disability gains a livelihood, the employer gains a qualified worker, and the government transforms a dependent individual into a taxpayer. Because governments increasingly realize that promoting the employment of people with disabilities is in their best interest, they have created some important incentives.[10]

Accessibility-Related Tax Incentives

Small Business Tax Credit
Small businesses may take an annual tax credit for making their businesses accessible. "Small businesses" are defined as those that had $1 million or less in revenue the preceding year, or had thirty or fewer full-time employees.

The credit is 50 percent of expenditures over $250, not to exceed $10,250, providing a maximum benefit of $5,000. This credit is available annually, and can be used to subsidize a wide variety of expenditures including removing architectural barriers, producing materials in alternate formats (Braille, large print, audiotape), and providing readers and sign language interpreters. New construction is not covered, and building modifications are covered only for structures in service before November 5, 1990.

Small businesses interested in claiming this credit should complete IRS Form 8826.

Architectural/ Transportation Tax Deduction

Businesses of any size may take an annual deduction of up to $15,000 a year for expenses incurred removing barriers for people with disabilities. Expenditures over $15,000 may be depreciated. Small businesses may take both this tax deduction and the Small Business Tax Credit.

Covered expenses include providing accessible parking spaces, ramps, and curb cuts; providing accessible telephones, public transportation vehicles, water fountains, and restrooms; and widening walkways to at least 48 inches. Expenses related to new construction or complete renovations are not covered, nor can a tax deduction be claimed for the normal replacement of depreciable property.

For more information, consult IRS Code Section 190.

Work Opportunity Tax Credit

The Work Opportunity Tax Credit (WOTC) rewards employers who hire members of certain targeted groups: vocational rehabilitation referrals, former AFDC recipients, veterans, ex-felons, food stamp recipients, summer youth employees, and SSI recipients. Local state employment security agencies (SESAs) provide employers with required certifications.

Employers may claim a tax credit of up to 40 percent of the first $6,000, or up to $2,400, in wages paid to certified employees during the first twelve months for each new hire. Eligible employees must work 180 days or 400 hours; summer youth must work 20 days or 120 hours. A partial credit of 25 percent for certified employees who worked at least 120, but less than 400 hours, may be claimed.

This tax credit is subject to yearly congressional renewal. Interested employers should complete and submit IRS Form 8850 (Pre-screening Notice and Certification Request for the Work Opportunity and Welfare-to-Work Tax Credits) to their local state employment security agency (SESA). Finally, they should complete IRS Form 5884 (Work Opportunity Tax Credit or WOTC).

A WOTC fact sheet may be obtained at http://www.doleta.gov/wotc.htm.

Ticket to Work and Work Incentive Improvement Act (TTWWIIA)

Financial disincentives created by public policy have long posed major barriers to employment for people with disabilities. In the past, disabled individuals' government-sponsored benefits, especially health insurance, were placed in jeopardy soon after the recipients began working, since their income quickly made them ineligible for coverage. This phenomenon has been referred to as the "earnings cliff," because newly hired workers quickly "fell off" the benefit eligibility list. Even low-wage jobs jeopardized benefits, making typical "career starting" employment impractical for many. Consequently, many qualified job candidates with disabilities concluded they were better off unemployed.

That situation has changed. On December 17, 1999, President Clinton signed into law the Work Incentive Improvement Act, commonly referred to as the "Ticket to Work." According to the Social Security Administration,[11] the TTWWIIA:

- increases beneficiary choice in obtaining rehabilitation and vocational services;
- removes barriers that require people with disabilities to choose between health care coverage and work; and
- assures that more Americans with disabilities have the opportunity to participate in the workforce and lessen their dependence on public benefits.

Specifically, the TTWWIIA permits recipients of Social Security disability benefits to maintain their Medicare health insurance for up to eight and one-half years after they return to work. The law also allows certain qualified individuals to purchase Medicaid health insurance coverage if they are above the income threshold. The UnumProvident Insurance company, the nation's largest provider of employee disability insurance, estimates that this "will help many of the 8 million people currently receiving federal health insurance benefits to re-enter the work force."[12]

Unfortunately, Ticket to Work is more like a complicated travel itinerary, with various phase-in provisions, and certain states permitted to participate before others. Some aspects—like provisions for technology and support services—appear clearly beneficial, but in its early conceptualization Ticket to Work may be too complex to appeal to many businesses. On the other hand, much of the bureaucratic burden of Ticket to Work will fall on the benefit recipients themselves, and employers may find that many of the ambiguities of the law have been clarified by the time they are approached by potential workers or their representatives within the rehabilitation system.

If the hypothesis about the Americans with Disabilities Act presented in chapter 2 is correct—that its failure to promote employment is largely due to the fact that it ignored counterproductive public policy—the Ticket to Work program may eventually prove to be a breakthrough. Before that occurs, however, the program will have to be simplified significantly.

Employers can check with the Social Security Administration for current details on the Ticket to Work program at www.ssa.gov/work.

Other Financial Incentives and Resources

> A young lady who had been unemployed for an extended period of time interviewed for a position as a receptionist/secretary. She reviewed the essential functions of the position with the employer, and said she could perform them all with one exception: because she used a wheelchair and had a problem with physical stamina, she could not deliver packages of up to ten pounds in weight within a four-block downtown radius.
>
> The state rehabilitation agency, upon being informed of this impediment to employment, immediately made available to the candidate a motorized wheelchair. The chair, which cost thousands of dollars, was beyond the capacity of the employer to provide as a reasonable accommodation. With it, all of the essential functions of the job could be performed, and employment was possible.

So motivated is the government to promote the employment of disabled individuals that it often makes extraordinary provisions to advance the cause. For example, although it is the employer's responsibility to provide "reasonable" accommodations to qualified job candidates, state rehabilitation agencies have been known to provide expensive adaptive equipment or services, such as extended on-the-job training, to enable employment that otherwise would be prohibitively costly. Some state agencies will actually subsidize the cost of new manufacturing equipment, work site expansion, or building purchase, in return for an employer's commitment to hire a specified number of disabled workers within a given period of time.

Many of these programs are unknown to most employers. The best way for an employer to identify and access such resources is by establishing a close working relationship with area rehabilitation agencies, especially the state rehabilitation agency in charge of contracting with smaller providers. These are usually listed in the telephone book under "vocational rehabilitation agencies."

Tax and Other Financial Incentives Checklist

☐ Accountants/business managers have reviewed current information on
  ○ Small Business Tax Credit, if applicable

- ○ Architectural/ Transportation Tax Credit
- ○ Work Opportunity Tax Credit
- ☐ Human resources managers have reviewed current information on
  - ○ Work Opportunity Tax Credit
  - ○ Ticket to Work and Work Incentive Improvement Act
- ☐ Employers participating in the Work Opportunity Tax Credit have
  - ○ determined likely eligibility of applicants by including the WOTC Pre-screening Notice as part of the application process
  - ○ signed (along with the employee) the Pre-screening Notice on or before the day employment is offered, and mailed it to the SESA within twenty-one days after the employee begins work
  - ○ documented WOTC eligibility (based on information received from the employee) and submitted documentation to the SESA
  - ○ received from the SESA written certification of individuals eligible for the WOTC
  - ○ filed for the WOTC tax credit
- ☐ Employer has contacted local state rehabilitation agency regarding the availability of employment candidates who qualify for the Ticket to Work and Work Incentive Improvement Act (TTWWIIA).
- ☐ Employer has assisted current qualified employees with disabilities in determining whether they qualify for benefits under the TTWWIIA.
- ☐ Employer has contacted local state rehabilitation agency regarding the availability of new, unusual, or unpublicized employment incentives.

Resources

http://www.abledata.com/
ABLEDATA is a national database of information on assistive technology and rehabilitation equipment available from domestic and international sources. ABLEDATA contains information on more than 23,000 assistive technology products.

American Diabetes Association
http://www.diabetes.org/
1701 North Beauregard St.
Alexandria, Va. 22311
(800) 342-2383 Voice
customerservice@diabetes.org

Business Leadership Network (BLN)
www.usbln.com/
1331 F St. N.W.
Washington, D.C. 20004-1107
(202) 376-6200, extension 35 Voice
(202) 376-6868 Fax
(202) 376-6205 TTY
dunlap-carol@dol.gov

Disability and Business Technical Assistance Centers (DBTACs)
http://www.adata.org/dbtac.html/
(800) 949-4232 Voice/TTY
This number will automatically route your call to the DBTAC in your region.

http://www.disabilitydirect.gov/
A website of the Office of Disability Employment Policy designed to pull together a wide variety of disability information, especially from federal government sources.

Equal Employment Opportunity Commission (EEOC)
http://www.eeoc.gov/
For technical assistance:
(800) 669-4000 Voice
(800) 669-6820 TTY
To obtain documents:
(800) 669-3362 Voice
(800) 800-3302 TTY

Internal Revenue Service
http://www.irs.gov/
(800) 829-1040 Voice
Mark Pitzer, Attorney
Office of Chief Counsel–IRS
1111 Constitution Avenue N.W.
Washington, D.C. 20224
(202) 622-3110 Voice

Job Accommodation Network (JAN) of the Office of Disability Employment Policy
http://janweb.icdi.wvu.edu/
West Virginia University
P.O. Box 6080
Morgantown, W.V. 26506-6080
(800) 526-7234 Voice/TTY

National Business & Disability Council (NBDC)
http://www.business-disability.com/
201 I.U. Willets Rd.
Albertson, N.Y. 11507
(516) 465-1515 Voice
(516) 465-3730 Fax

The National Organization on Disability (NOD)
http://www.nod.org/
910 Sixteenth St. N.W.
Suite 600
Washington, D.C. 20006
(202) 293-5960 Voice
(202) 293-5968 TTY
(202) 293-7999 Fax

ADA ON CD-ROM

The U.S. Department of Justice offers a free CD-ROM containing extensive technical information on the ADA. The CD-ROM is in a variety of formats, including WordPerfect, HTML, and text (ASCII). The CD-ROM includes:

- The new electronic version of the ADA Standards for Accessible Design;
- The ADA Guide for Small Businesses;
- Common ADA Errors and Omissions in New Construction and Alterations;
- The Americans with Disabilities Act Checklist for New Lodging Facilities;
- The ADA Guide for Small Towns;
- A series of commonly asked question and answer publications; and
- Technical Assistance Manuals for Titles II and III of the ADA.

Single copies can be ordered online at:

http://www.usdoj.gov/crt/ada/cdrequestform.htm
or by calling the Department's ADA Information Line:
(800) 514-0301 (Voice) or (800) 514-0383 (TTY).

Internet users can access the same information at: http://www.usdoj.gov/crt/ada/adahom1.htm

Office of Disability Employment Policy (ODEP)
(formerly The President's Committee on Employment of People with Disabilities)
http://www.dol.gov/odep/
1331 F St. N.W., Suite 300
Washington, D.C. 20004
(202) 376 6200 Voice
(202) 376 6205 TTY
(202) 376 6219 Fax

SOAR (for Searchable Online Accommodation Resource)
http://www.jan.wvu.edu/soar/index.html

Society for Human Resource Management
http://www.shrm.org/
1800 Duke St.
Alexandria, Va. 22314
(703) 548-3440 Voice
(703) 535-6490 Fax
shrm@shrm.org

U.S. Dept. of Justice ADA Home Page
http://www.usdoj.gov/crt/ada/adahom1.htm/
U.S. Department of Justice
950 Pennsylvania Ave. N.W.
Civil Rights Division
Disability Rights Section-NYAVE
Washington, D.C. 20530
(800) 514-0301 Voice
(800) 514-0383 TTY
(202) 307-1198 Fax

U. S. Department of Labor
http://www.dol.gov/
200 Constitution Ave. N.W.
Washington, D.C. 20210
(202) 219-6871 Voice
(866) 4-USA-DOL Voice
(877) 889-5627 TTY

U.S. Department of Labor Occupational Safety & Health Administration (OSHA)
http://www.osha.gov/
Office of Public Affairs—Room N3647
200 Constitution Ave.

Washington, D.C. 20210
(202) 693-1999 Voice
(800) 321-6742 Voice
(877) 889-5627 TTY

Workers Compensation Research Institute
http://www.wcrinet.org/
955 Massachusetts Ave.
Cambridge, Mass. 02139
(617) 661-9274 Voice
(617) 661-9284 Fax
wcri@wcrinet.org

10

A Plan for Inclusive Marketing

Part I: Accessibility Issues

Inclusive Marketing and Management Leadership

During the past two decades, several factors, including an aging of the American population, a growing awareness of disabilities, and the passage of the Americans with Disabilities Act, have combined to make businesses much more aware of the potential of the "disability market." That market includes not only people who have various physical, mental, and emotional impairments, but also their families and friends, and all of those who are aware of disability-related issues (see fig. 10.1). As a result, marketers have begun to consider the needs and preferences of consumers with disabilities, engaging in

> *"If you build it in a way that is inaccessible, they might come, but they won't be able to get in."*

what is known as "inclusive marketing." Companies that have conducted inclusive marketing carefully have found it to be an effective business strategy.

What makes the difference between an effective and an ineffective approach to the disability market? Effective inclusive marketing cannot begin to

Fig. 10.1. The disability
market

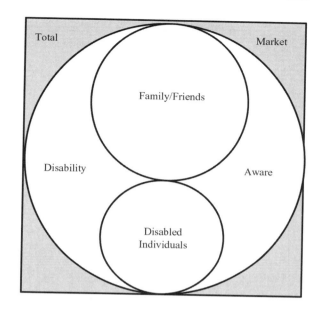

occur without the leadership of top management. Without it, there will be in-sufficient coordination of the many participants inclusive marketing requires—supervisors, human resources personnel, product designers, suppliers, contrac-tors, retail staff, building managers, marketers, and advertising agencies. A fully committed management can successfully coordinate all the necessary participants.

Getting managers interested usually is not difficult. There are several rea-sons why the practice can be very appealing (see table 10.1). Getting managers *fully* committed is another matter.

Some will be interested in inclusive marketing for strictly pragmatic rea-sons. Even if they have no relevant previous experience, many managers al-ready know that consumers with disabilities, their families, and their friends represent an enormous segment of the total market. They will be tantalized by the prospect of reaching this market. Others will realize they have legal respon-sibilities related to people who are disabled, and will respond out of a sense of obligation. A growing number will commit because they have seen inclusive marketing work before, and they recognize that it is simply good business prac-tice. They will remain committed as long as such methods are rewarded.

Many managers will have more substantial motivations. Some will act out of a sense of morality, ethics, or social responsibility. Finally, a large number

Table 10.1. Inclusive marketing: management motivation

Motivator	Advantages	Disadvantages
Profit potential	Traditional business rationale	Superficial
Compliance	Legal safety	Superficial
Previous experience	Proven benefits Persuasive	Result-dependent
Morality/ethics	Deep commitment Inspirational	None
Personal interest	Deep commitment Persuasive Inspirational	None

will want to be involved because they consider it "their" issue—because they themselves, someone in their family, or a close friend has a disability.

What if managers still are not motivated? Those who fail to utilize inclusive marketing techniques can miss enormous opportunities. Even worse, they can expose their company to legal liability under Title III of the Americans with Disabilities Act, which mandates disability-related accessibility provisions for public accommodations like offices, theaters, hotels, and retail stores.[1] ADA complaints that pertain directly to customer accessibility issues are increasingly common:[2]

- Disability advocates have filed complaints against several national department store chains, claiming their aisles are too narrow to allow access by customers in wheelchairs.
- A Hawaii shuttle service received a complaint that its services were inaccessible to consumers in wheelchairs. It made arrangements with another transportation company to provide accessible service to patrons who use wheelchairs and subsequently purchased an eleven-passenger van equipped with a wheelchair lift.
- In Massachusetts, a person with a visual impairment complained that an educational institute did not provide information about course offerings in alternative formats and did not make reasonable modifications in its procedures and practices to enable people with disabilities to take the courses. The institute agreed to make information about registration

times and course offerings available on audiotape on a telephone information service used by people with disabilities.

- A restaurant in Texas received a complaint that one of its restrooms was inaccessible. After mediation, it agreed to provide directional signage at an inaccessible restroom to indicate the location of the accessible restroom, and write a letter of apology to the plaintiff.
- Through a consent decree, the U.S. Attorney for the Western District of Tennessee settled a lawsuit in which it had intervened to enforce the barrier removal requirements of Title III against Valenti Mid-South Management, LLC, a franchisee operating a chain of fifty-four Wendy's restaurants. Under the consent decree, Valenti agreed to make a wide range of improvements to each of these restaurants to provide greater accessibility. The required barrier removal for each restaurant varies but generally includes providing new curb ramps from parking lots to sidewalks, creating more clear space at entrances to facilitate the opening of doors, reconfiguring customer service lines to allow access to wheelchair users, providing more accessible dining tables, lowering service and condiment counters, widening restroom doors, replacing toilets, adding or remounting grab bars, replacing lavatories, and lowering paper towel dispensers.

Although most such complaints are eventually settled through arbitration or mediation, they can still be expensive and time-consuming. Companies can avoid such hassles by having in place a well-designed inclusion strategy.

The previous chapters laid the basis for an effective corporate inclusion strategy. That strategy stresses that before engaging in inclusive marketing, companies should address issues related to inclusive employment. If a company has followed the plan for inclusion as it has been presented, it has already taken a comprehensive look at its employment practices, and it can now begin to approach the disability market with an inclusive marketing strategy.

Management Leadership Checklist

☐ Top management has clearly communicated the company's intent to be inclusive.

☐ Top management has initiated a review of its inclusion-related employment practices.

☐ Top management has carefully reviewed all relevant information pertaining to inclusive marketing.

☐ Top management has communicated to its marketing staff and advertising agency its specific intent to engage in inclusive marketing practices.
☐ Top management has commended and rewarded those responsible for its effective inclusive marketing programs.

Accessibility Considerations in Marketing

The first consideration of a company's inclusive marketing strategy should be accessibility—the accessibility of its products and services, retail locations, communications, and so on.[3] Products and services marketed to people who have disabilities must be usable by them. More than any other issue, accessibility is what makes inclusive marketing a unique business challenge.

The movie *Field of Dreams* is known for its catchy aphorism, *"If you build it, they will come."* In the world of disability-related marketing, that advice isn't always true. A marketer who aspires to inclusiveness must consider the following themes:

- *"If you build it in a way that is inaccessible, they might come, but they won't be able to get in."* (Retail Site Accessibility)
- *"If you build it so that they can't use it easily, they won't buy it."* (Accessible Product Design)
- *"If you can't communicate with them, they'll find someone who can."* (Accessible Communication)

Retail Site Accessibility

Issues of accessibility in retail locations are similar, but not identical, to issues encountered on the job site. (See the discussion of job location physical accessibility considerations in chapter 8.) Almost all retail locations require parking, doorways, signage, and restroom provisions—just like a job site. They will, however, have some additional features. For example, almost all retail sites have places for transactions to be made, cash to be taken, or credit purchases confirmed. They also are likely to have display areas, dressing rooms, rest spots, and other customer service features. While accessibility considerations in the workplace often involve primarily building codes and ADA standards, retail accessibility issues are more likely to be "user friendliness" issues that go beyond legal compliance.

The following are some fundamental accessibility considerations for retail locations.

- Entrances should be free of obstructions—not only fixed impediments like posts or trees, but temporary ones like repair work, snow, or leaves.
- Optimally, the entrance should offer an automatic door. If an automatic door is not feasible, the entrance door should require no more than eight pounds of force to open. Internal doors should require no more than five pounds of force.
- Lighting and sound levels should promote, rather than interfere with, accessibility. In general, bright lighting and low (or no) background sound is best. Flashing, pulsing, or strobe lighting should not be used.
- All signage (including point-of-sale displays) should feature large lettering and universal symbols.
- Aisles should be at least 36 inches wide. Aisles narrower than this will not allow a person in a wheelchair to pass with ease.
- An accessible cash register/voucher signing spot a maximum of 36 inches off the floor should be provided.
- A portion of any bar or food service counter should be 36 inches off the floor.
- If public restrooms are provided, they should meet ADA standards. Separate accessible "unisex" restrooms are helpful for some people, especially those who require the assistance of a companion.
- Resting spots—chairs, benches, or sofas—should be provided. These especially benefit elderly customers, and those with mobility impairments.
- Fitting rooms should be fully accessible, and large enough to permit someone to accompany a disabled customer.
- If merchandise is displayed so that customers can view price tags, those tags should be written in an easily viewable type size. If possible, they should be viewable from a sitting position.
- All retail locations should be equipped with teletypewriters (TTYs) for people who are deaf. Although many businesses now have TTYs, studies have shown that a very high proportion do not function properly when called. This is often because employees have no idea how to work the

machine. All customer service staff should be trained in the operation of the TTY, and it should be checked on a regular basis.

- Architects, building managers, and supervisors should evaluate issues of retail site accessibility, and their reports should be reviewed by top management. Small businesses without access to expensive professional expertise can contact the Disability and Business Technical Assistance Center (DBTAC), which can answer most basic questions or recommend other resources. A call to (800) 949-4232 will automatically be routed to the appropriate regional DBTAC.

Retail Site Accessibility Checklist

☐ Retail locations have been evaluated for accessibility.
  ○ Architects and building managers have reviewed facilities for accessibility.
  ○ Retail entrances are without obstructions.
  ○ Entrances have automatic doors, or doors meet maximum opening force requirements.
  ○ Designated parking spaces are available.
  ○ Designated parking spaces at least 96 inches wide with access aisles at least 60 inches wide to accommodate vans with wheelchair lifts are available.
  ○ Lighting and sound levels are appropriate.
  ○ Signage uses large lettering, Braille, and universal symbols.
  ○ Retail aisles are at least 36 inches wide.
  ○ Accessible cash register/voucher signing spot a maximum of 36 inches off the floor is available.
  ○ A portion of any food service or bar area is 36 inches off the floor.
  ○ Restrooms meet ADA standards.
  ○ Resting spots are provided.
  ○ Accessible fitting rooms are available.
  ○ Price tags are easily viewable from a sitting position.
  ○ A TTY is available and functioning properly.
  ○ Staff members have been trained to operate a TTY.

Accessible Product Design

Products and services used by consumers with disabilities can be divided into two categories: generic and disability-related items. Although "crossover" items are blurring this distinction with increasing frequency, this differentiation is still helpful for purposes of discussion.

Generic Product Design

Generic products, of course, include everything used by the general consumer market. These must be brought to the market in ways that make them useful to the greatest number of consumers, including those with disabilities. This point bears repeating: customers with disabilities want and need all of the goods and services demanded by everyone else. Accessibility needs of customers with disabilities are *in addition to* the typical requirements of consumers, not *instead of* them.

Universal Design

The practice of devising goods and services that appeal to the largest possible market is known as accessible, inclusive, or "universal" design. The Center for Universal Design at the University of North Carolina defines the concept as follows:

> Universal Design simply stated says that products and services should be usable by . . . as many people as possible. This is regardless of disability, language barriers, or any other obstacles to use.[4]

Universal design takes into account the needs of consumers who are disabled, but benefits many others as well. The Telecommunications Industry Association explains how this has implications for broader consumer markets:

> Accessible product design consideration by planners and designers of the needs of persons with functional limitations and disabilities results in features that make products usable by persons with functional limitations and disabilities. It also makes them convenient for everyone else. Incorporating appropriate human factors opens up the market to everyone.[5]

Some examples of this concept were given in the first chapter—homes with stepless entries, kitchen utensils with easy-to-grip handles, televisions with captioning available as well as sound. In each case, product improvements intended to benefit those with disabilities provide benefits to many others. A pizza wheel made according to principles of universal design is easier for anyone to hold, not just people with arthritis. A car with easy-to-read instrument numerals and symbols on its dashboard is not just "disability friendly," it's "user friendly." (Elderly people especially favor large numerals and symbols.) Of course, universal design, despite the name, can't meet the needs of every consumer. If a person with lower-limb paralysis wants to drive, for example, his or her car will have to be equipped with hand controls. But a thoughtful design expands the potential market to its optimum, which is in the best interests of both businesses and consumers.

Practical Issues in Designing Accessible Products

(The following section is from *Marketing to Consumers with Disabilities* [1993] by Joel Reedy [Chicago: Probus Publishing Company]. Reprinted with permission.)[6]

Keep It Simple

The marketing research effort should produce a wealth of information and suggestions to improve the design and use of the marketer's proposed product. Real people using (or being unable to use) the existing or proposed product are the best judges of performance; by carefully listening, the marketer will embrace many of these design suggestions:

- Improve the efficiency/effectiveness of the main product or service functions; think through possible utilization problems encountered by the four major groups of disabilities (mobility, sight, hearing, or speech impairments).

- Eliminate unnecessary, trivial, redundant and/or noncontributing secondary functions; in other words, design or manufacture the product to achieve the primary function well before (or possibly eliminate) considering any possible secondary feature.

- Maintain a commitment to function over form, in design and operation. This does not mean that ugly is preferred, but that function is the top priority.

- Reduce the number of steps required to carry out the usage function; be aware of growing resentment among the *whole* population of increasing complex product assembly or operating instructions. Remember, the product was bought to reduce problems, not create them.

- Reduce the human effort (either dexterity or strength) required to operate a product or perform a function.

- Particularly with services, automate functions and systems so they can be accessed 24 hours a day, seven days a week. And keep the operating steps simple.

- For users with sight impairments, consider including tactile uniqueness in controls differentiation.

- Keep the mindset that it's the marketer's fault if the product is difficult to use or program. Customers want only the time; they don't want an explanation of how to build a watch.

Here are some ease-of-use examples that marketers have added to existing products; these disability-friendly touches improve value to current or potential customers or clients:

- Built-in comfort and convenience benefits all your markets segments, both disabled and non-disabled. Where would we all be without
  - Cordless telephones for mobility?
  - Remote control devices for convenience—garage doors, TVs, and VCRs?
  - Automatic timers for coffeemakers, sprinklers, or alarm systems?

- Concentrate on making products easy to open and close. Eliminate small caps by incorporating the cap as an extension of the bottle or package:
  - Product dispensers like pump toothpaste or squeeze catsup, mustard, or salad dressings.
  - Snap-open and shut pouring spouts like the Tide detergent example.
  - Snap-open or screw-off lids for cans and bottles.

- Make products easier to handle or dispense:
  - Simplify access, such as water and ice through an in-the-door dispenser on refrigerators.
  - Consider dexterity problems resulting from having to grasp or turn small or smooth knobs; push or pull levers on plumbing fixtures or entry doors are helpful.
  - Recognize that range of motion restrictions affect dexterity too; hard-to-close fasteners, such as buttons or other closures in the back of clothing, can be replaced, as well as lowering light switches or using detachable controls.
  - Consider nonskid surfaces for containers, particularly if the contents are refrigerated and the container "sweats" at room temperature.
  - Investigate smaller packages for lighter weights.
  - Explore many container shapes, with or without handles, grips, or lowered centers of gravity.

- ■ Test smaller bottle necks or openings to slow down spilled contents if the container is overturned.
- If envelopes are required, reduce the strength or dexterity needed to open them. Can an envelope be designed to be opened with one hand? Think about strength and dexterity for Styrofoam packing forms; make sure the fit is snug but not "frozen" in place.
- If statements are being mailed, are the pages already collated or printed on perforated "tractor-feed" paper so recipients don't have to struggle with unfolding, stacking, or attaching several pages?
- Insist on easy-to-read, highly visible user-friendly instructions:
  - ■ Be sure to test the instructions; call together a focus group of people with various disabilities to read and follow the instructions.
  - ■ Consider initiating an 800 information line, staffed with knowledgeable people who can answer product or service questions. This is a great strategy to improve customer satisfaction and also to build customer name and address lists for future product introduction or testing.
- Weigh safety considerations as well as convenience:
  - ■ Nonbreakable bottles and containers (plastic not glass) for kitchen and bathroom use.
  - ■ Auditory or tactile warnings around potentially hazardous areas (step-downs, exterior exits, stairs).
  - ■ Improved antitampering wraps that allow the user with disabilities an adequate means to break the seal without breaking an arm.
  - ■ Inclusion of a "smart-chip" (like those music-playing greeting cards) to alert sight-impaired persons to operating instructions or of a toll-free number to call for verbal step-by-step directions for product use.

Consumer Testing

A telecommunication company hired consultants who had various types of disabilities. Their task was to study several aspects of the company, including its retail locations, its marketing, and the accessibility of its principal products—cellular telephones.

The consultants included three people who were blind or severely visually impaired, one who had spina bifida, one who had cerebral palsy, one who had experienced strokes, one who was deaf, one who had a spinal cord injury, and one person with Down syndrome. Occupations represented included social service worker, educational psychologist, editor, stockbroker, and volunteer.

The company was impressed by the observations and recommendations of the consultants. They knew, for example, that their cell phones were very difficult to use for people with visual impairments, but they were impressed to learn that two consumers who were blind had developed their own methods of making the phones useful.

The consultants also included a person whose right hand had been paralyzed by a stroke more than a decade earlier. This consultant's observations were of particular interest to the company, since it knew that many of its customers used their phones with one hand while driving, eating, or carrying a briefcase.

The company was not surprised by the consultants' observation that its advertising ignored customers with disabilities, that its marketing brochures were written in hard-to-read type, and that some of its retail locations had some significant accessibility problems. After receiving the consultants' report, it initiated a program to remedy these problems.

One of most effective ways to evaluate the success of accessible design efforts is to employ disabled consultants as product and service evaluators, or "ghost shoppers." Consultants who have disabilities provide first-hand information that can often suggest valuable modifications and improvements. Sales, customer service, and help-line personnel can also be trained to gather accessibility-related consumer information.

Disability-Related Products and Services

Specialized products and services that compensate for the practical effects of disabilities—such as text magnifiers and hearing aids—have an obvious appeal to disabled consumers. Generic products that address psychological effects can also be extremely attractive.

A young school counselor, partially paralyzed as the result of spina bifida, spent her entire savings on a shiny new sports car. The car came equipped with hand controls in lieu of accelerator and brake pedals.

"I might walk with crutches, but I drive a Corvette!" she explained.

The young lady enjoyed inviting friends to sit in the driver's seat, watching their befuddlement with the auto's unusual control system. After the guests realized they were unable to operate the car, the young lady would ask them to take the passenger seat, as she demonstrated her skill at driving.

She quickly gained a reputation as a speed demon, and joked: "I've been accused of driving with a 'lead hand.'"

Disability-related items include prosthetic devices, ambulatory aids, and medical and rehabilitation goods and services. All of these are of great importance to people with disabilities, but may be of little or no interest to others. Disability-related goods and services must be designed in ways that effectively meet the needs of intended consumers—all their needs. Disabled consumers do not simply have physical requirements; they also have preferences, antipathies, likes, and dislikes. One of these needs is to manage the societal perception of their disability. Disabled consumers may be very comfortable with their impairment, but they are unlikely to want to emphasize the fact that they have one.

To be functional, disability-related products should incorporate a few simple, but critical, design considerations. Generally, designers of disability-related products and services should consider all the issues involved with generic items. Safety and ease-of-use features (e.g., crutches with non-skid caps, ultralight walkers, rehabilitation services provided in multiple convenient locations) should be maximized.

In addition, disability-related products should be designed with "psychological accessibility" in mind. The term "psychological accessibility" refers to the characteristics of a product or service that address the social context of disabilities. Because stigma is commonly associated with impairments, psychological accessibility attempts to provide a neutralizing influence, or to counterbalance stigma with positively valued associations and images. At a minimum, products and services that are psychologically accessible avoid calling attention unnecessarily to impaired capabilities; they may also exhibit affirmative attributes not usually associated with disabilities.

In order to promote psychological accessibility in disability-related products and services, designers should do the following:

- Minimize features that call attention to the consumer's disability (e.g., miniaturized hearing aids, hidden shoe lifts, blood glucose monitoring equipment in purse-sized kits, rehabilitation services delivered in commercial settings).
- Incorporate characteristics of ordinary equivalents (e.g., bandages and prosthetic devices available in various skin tones, wheelchairs that look like bicycles, slings that come in fashionable colors).
- Offer product and service alternatives associated with positively valued images (e.g., prosthetic devices made of elegant leather, services delivered in "exclusive" locations, products with fashion designer affiliations).
- Consider psychological accessibility in product placement—the final marketing component. Disability-imaged placements need not be the exclusive, or even the primary, marketing venues. (E.g., a flashing alarm

clock might have greater appeal to some people with hearing impairments if featured in a *Sharper Image* catalog, rather than in a medical products flyer or a website specially intended for deaf consumers.)

When properly done, provisions for psychological accessibility can help make disability-related products and services strongly appealing to consumers with accessibility requirements, and may even promote the "curb-cut" and "electronic curb-cut" effects—marketing crossover phenomena that can blur the distinction between disability-related and generic products.

Products offered by Hammacher Schlemmer, for example, are marketed in a way that carefully respects the way consumers perceive their own capabilities and limitations. The items are presented in a way that makes them appear of obvious value for consumers with disabilities, while carefully preserving their appeal for those who do not consider themselves disabled, but might "prefer" to experience better hearing and sight.

Product Design Checklist

☐ Design staff have received training in principles of universal design.

☐ Prospective products and services incorporate features of universal design.

Fig. 10.2. These products are among disability-related items featured in Hammacher Schlemmer catalogs ([800] 543-3366) and at the company's website at www.hammacherschlemmer.com. *(Photos courtesy of Hammacher Schlemmer)*

□ Current products and services have been evaluated for accessibility and ease of use.

□ Suppliers and contractors have reviewed products for accessibility and ease of use.

□ Individuals with disabilities are involved in product design, service testing, and evaluation.

□ Customer service, help-line, and other staff collect accessibility-related consumer information.

□ Disability-related products
   ○ maximize safety and ease-of-use features
   ○ minimize features that call attention to the consumer's disability
   ○ incorporate aspects of typical equivalents
   ○ are offered in alternatives associated with positively valued images
   ○ are available in placements that maximize psychological accessibility

Accessible Communication

Companies use an enormous array of media to reach consumers, including print, radio, and television ads; audio recordings; promotional videos; Internet sites; and customer service. In all of these venues, businesses have an opportunity to reach out to individuals with accessibility requirements. Too many simply take the easy route—they operate in standard, traditional ways, rather than utilizing the best possible options. Like accessible products, accessible communication is designed to have a maximum impact with the largest number of potential customers. To communicate inclusively, companies must reach the nation's largest minority in ways accessible to them.

Following are steps that businesses can take to maximize the inclusiveness of their marketing communication in print, audio, and video media, the Internet, and customer service.

Accessible Written Marketing Materials and Alternatives

Written marketing materials can present communication barriers to customers with visual, perceptual, or cognitive disabilities. Several strategies can minimize such problems.

• In general, written marketing pieces should be in type no smaller than 14 point. Copy should be written in simple, nontechnical language.

- Whenever possible, layouts should employ high-contrast formats.
- While some companies may want to invest the time and resources to develop marketing materials in Braille, others may wish to do so only upon request.
- Photographs, illustrations, video, and audio messages can often be used instead of, or in addition to, written materials. Some examples:
  - Some financial service firms, automobile companies, and retailers provide audiocassette recordings, VHS tapes, or CD-ROMs with their written marketing materials.
  - Restaurants that want to serve customers with visual impairments can record their menu on a small cassette recorder and make it available upon request. This is usually less expensive and easier to update than Braille.
  - Restroom faucets, towel dispensers, and hand driers often feature illustrated operating instructions
  - Marketing displays can incorporate "talking signs" that allow customers to generate a pre-recorded message into earphones or a hand-held receiver just by aiming an electronic device and pushing a button. The message might describe a product or commercial exhibit, or simply indicate "exit."
- Simply changing the size of the type font used can generate large-type copies of documents stored in computers and word processors.
- Photocopy machines can enlarge documents in standard type.
- Written marketing materials made available in electronic file formats (on disc, by email, or downloaded from a website) allow visually impaired computer users to increase the size of print and illustrations, or use their "text reader" to hear the message. (Most computer manufacturers and software developers now routinely include multiple accessibility features. Microsoft estimates that the total number of consumers with disabilities who could benefit from accessible personal computer design is 30 million.)[7]

McDonald's is one company that uses every opportunity to promote its inclusiveness. One of many examples that could be cited is the design of their standard beverage lids. Each beverage cover is embossed with the "McDonald's" name along with information about the beverage itself (the lids of cold beverages indicate the type of soft drink in the container, coffee lids indicate whether regular or decaffeinated), but the information is also expressed in Braille. The extra dots on the lids cost the company nothing, but they make the information accessible to customers who are blind, and communicate a subtle "we are inclusive" message to all customers who are disability "savvy."

Accessible Audio Marketing Materials and Alternatives

Marketing by audio communication can be ineffective in reaching consumers with hearing impairments and some forms of learning disabilities. Simple adjustments can make audio messages more accessible, or substitute preferable formats:

- Many hearing-impaired consumers provide their own accommodations: hearing aids, audio equipment with variable volume and audio clarifying technology (telephones, computers, radios, etc.), and televisions equipped with captioning capabilities.
- Low-cost audio assistive devices (headphones and earjacks) can be made available for group presentations, seminars, conventions, and other events. Some devices connect directly into existing sound systems, while others amplify and clarify natural sound.
- Companies can use toll-free numbers or local telephone lines to provide product and service information through recordings. Consumers can use their own equipment to amplify or clarify the sound. They can also repeat messages without embarrassment. Movie theaters and places of worship routinely offer such recordings, and other businesses, such as electronics manufacturers, restaurants, and software developers, are following suit.
- Sign language interpreters can facilitate communication with customers who are deaf. Interpreters can serve individual clients, or groups of deaf individuals.
- Transcribers can provide "real-time captioning" of live presentations, their transcriptions projected on screens behind or near speakers.
- Voice recognition technology can provide fairly accurate automatic reception and transcription of speech. Many consumers with disabilities are already using voice recognition systems, and improved technology and declining costs will soon make this communication alternative commonplace.

Accessible Video Marketing Materials and Alternatives

Video marketing materials obviously can be inaccessible to consumers with visual impairments, but they can also be problematic for hearing-impaired and deaf viewers, since much of the information they contain is delivered orally. Alternatives and enhancements are often easily provided:

- Television spots and marketing videos should be produced with closed captioning as a matter of course, and open-captioned versions should also be made available. Closed captioning provides a written script only on a special track, to be seen only when a television is operating in "captioning mode"; open-captioned versions provide the written script for all to see. Most video production houses can provide captioning, and the service adds only modestly to the cost of production.
- "Audio described" versions of marketing videos can be made available to consumers with visual impairments. Audio description explains what is being seen on the screen, generally inserting descriptions during breaks in dialogue or narration. When provided by someone with the appropriate training, audio description can be unobtrusive.
- Videos, speeches, or stage productions being presented to large audiences can feature an "audio description" track broadcast by a closed-loop FM radio or infrared signal to visually impaired audience members equipped with receivers.
- Sign language interpreters can be shown "split-screen" style in live or recorded video presentations.
- Large, multiple, and individual video screens can meet the needs of many customers who have mild and moderate visual impairments.
- With the increased use of DVD (digital video device) technology, which can provide multiple presentation options, audio description and captioning are likely to be increasingly available.

Accessible Internet Communication and Alternatives

In the past, the World Wide Web has been difficult for people who are blind or visually impaired to access. Much of the Internet is visually based—like most computer programs, for that matter—and those who cannot see have been at a great disadvantage. In addition, physical disabilities that can impair computer operation, such as cerebral palsy and paraplegia, have kept some people from going online.

That situation is changing rapidly. Many Internet accessibility options have been created during the past decade, and for many people with disabilities, the Internet now presents an incomparable opportunity to utilize skills unaffected by their disability. Consider the following:

- Many commercial websites are now available in universal design formats that can be used by visually impaired computer users who have "text readers." Text readers are simply voice synthesizing computer chips that "read" what is on the screen, going from top to bottom, left to right, or following the user's command. Universal design web formats can "hide" text below pictures or icons, where it is decoded by the text reader but does not inconvenience those who are using the site visually.
- Other websites make available alternate "text only" versions that eliminate graphics completely—perfect for people who use text readers, but boring for everyone else. A carefully developed universal design website generally eliminates any need for a text-only version.
- Most computers come equipped with many accessibility options that make Internet browsing easier for many—everything from adjustable keyboard repeat rates to single-key logon. Computers can also be equipped with alternative input devices, everything from head-pointing attachments to voice recognition technology, which can enable the participation of people with severe physical and sensory disabilities.
- Many Internet resources are now available to businesses and web designers to help them design or remodel sites to maximize accessibility. One website, known as "Bobby," allows Internet users to electronically "test" a website to determine the extent to which it is accessible. (See the resources listed at the end of this chapter.)

All of these accessibility improvements help explain why, despite some disadvantages, consumers with disabilities have a near-average rate of computer ownership, and tend to spend twice as much time online as their nondisabled counterparts. The Internet is now a compelling medium for marketing to disabled consumers.

Accessibility in Customer Service

Customers with disabilities can require assistance in purchasing goods and services. More and more businesses are providing their customer service staff with training in how to serve customers who have various types of disabilities.

Experience has shown that such training develops the staff's ability to attend to the individual needs of *all* customers, not just those with disabilities. Usually, the employee with the greatest skill in serving customers with disabilities will be the best customer service employee, period.

The Office of Disability Employment Policy (formerly the President's Committee on Employment of People with Disabilities) recommends the following practices for serving customers with disabilities:[8]

Key to Quality Customer Service

The key to providing quality services to customers with disabilities is to remember that all customers are individuals. Persons with disabilities come in all shapes and sizes with diverse personalities, abilities, interests, needs, and preferences—just like every other customer. Below are some basic tips for interacting with customers who have disabilities. However, in most cases, the best way to learn how to accommodate customers with disabilities is to ask them directly.

Etiquette considered appropriate when interacting with customers with disabilities is based primarily on respect and courtesy. Listen and learn from what the customer tells you regarding his or her needs. Remember, customers with disabilities will continue to patronize businesses that welcome them, are helpful, are accessible, and provide quality products and/or services at competitive market prices.

Serving Customers with Cognitive Disabilities

- Be prepared to provide an explanation more than once.
- Offer assistance with and extra time for completion of forms, understanding written instructions, writing checks, and decision-making; wait for the customer to accept the offer of assistance; do not "over-assist" or be patronizing.
- If a customer has difficulty reading or writing, she or he may prefer to take forms home to complete.
- Be patient, flexible, and supportive; take time to understand the customer and make sure the customer understands you.
- Consider moving to a quiet or private location, if in a public area with many distractions.

Serving Customers with Mobility Impairments

- Put yourself at the wheelchair user's eye level. If possible, sit next to the customer when having a conversation.

- Do not lean on a wheelchair or any other assistive device.
- Do not assume the customer wants to be pushed—ask first.
- Provide a clipboard as a writing surface if counters or reception desks are too high; come around to the customer side of the desk/counter during your interaction.
- Offer assistance if the customer appears to be having difficulty opening the doors.
- Make sure there is a clear path of travel.
- If a person uses crutches, a walker, or some other assistive equipment, offer assistance with coats, bags, or other belongings.
- Offer a chair if the customer will be standing for a long period of time.
- If you telephone the customer, allow the phone to ring longer than usual to allow extra time for her or him to reach the telephone.

Serving Customers Who Are Blind or Visually Impaired

- Speak to the customer when you approach her or him.
- State clearly who you are; speak in a normal tone of voice.
- Never touch or distract a service dog without first asking the owner.
- Tell the customer when you are leaving; never leave a person who is blind talking to an empty space.
- Do not attempt to lead the customer without first asking; allow the customer to hold your arm and control her or his own movements.
- Be descriptive when giving directions; give the customer verbal information that is obvious to persons who can see. For example, if you are walking and approaching steps, mention how many and the distance to them.
- If you are offering a seat, gently place the customer's hand on the back or arm of the chair and allow her or him to sit down.
- When dealing with money transactions, tell the customer the denominations when you count the money he or she is receiving from you.
- Make sure the customer has picked up all of her or his possessions before leaving.
- Ask if the customer needs assistance signing forms. Offer to guide her or his hand to the appropriate space for signature.
- Offer assistance if the customer appears to be having difficulty locating a specific service area.

Serving Customers Who Are Deaf or Hard of Hearing

- Gain the customer's attention before starting a conversation (i.e., tap him or her gently on the shoulder or arm).
- Identify who you are (i.e., show the customer your name badge).
- Look directly at the customer, face the light, speak clearly, in a normal tone of voice, and keep your hands away from your face; use short, simple sentences.
- Ask the customer if it would be helpful to communicate by writing or by using a computer terminal.
- If the customer uses a sign language interpreter, speak directly to the customer, not the interpreter.
- If you telephone a customer who is hard of hearing, let the phone ring longer than usual; speak clearly and be prepared to repeat the reason for the call and who you are.
- If you telephone a customer who is deaf, use your state telecommunications relay service. The number is listed in the front of the telephone directory. Consideration should also be given to purchasing a TTY.
- Discuss matters that are personal (e.g., credit qualifications) in a private room to avoid staring or eavesdropping by other customers.

Serving Customers with Speech Impairments

- If you do not understand something, do not pretend you do; ask the customer to repeat what he or she said, and then repeat it.
- Be patient; take as much time as necessary.
- Try to ask questions that require only short answers or a nod of the head.
- Concentrate on what the customer is saying; concentrate on listening and communicating.
- Avoid barriers like glass partitions and distractions such as noisy, public places.
- Do not speak for the customer or attempt to finish her or his sentences.
- If you are having difficulty understanding the customer, consider writing as an alternative means of communicating, but first ask the customer if this is acceptable.
- If no solution to the communication problem can be worked out between you and the customer, ask if there is someone who could interpret on the customer's behalf.
- Discuss matters that are personal (e.g., financial matters) in a private room to avoid staring or eavesdropping by other customers.

Remember

- Provide access to facilities and services.
- Relax.
- Listen to the customer.
- Maintain eye contact without staring.
- Make the customer feel comfortable.
- Treat the customer with dignity, respect, and courtesy.
- Offer assistance, but do not insist.
- Ask the customer to tell you the best way to help.
- Deal with unfamiliar situations in a calm, professional manner.

The information above is available from the Office of Disability Employment Policy at http://www.dol.gov/dol/odep/public/media/reports/ek98/provide.htm.

Communication and Customer Service Checklist

☐ Marketing information has been evaluated for inclusiveness and accessibility.
  ○ Advertising, catalogs, promotional items, and related material have been reviewed for inclusiveness and accessibility.
  ○ Advertising, catalogs, promotional items, and related material are available in multiple formats.
  ○ All video materials created and used by the company is available with captioning.
  ○ Corporate website has been evaluated for accessibility.
☐ Retail staff has been trained to serve customers with disabilities.

Resources

Apple Computer—People with Special Needs
http://www.apple.com/disability/
specialneeds@apple.com

Architectural and Transportation Barriers Compliance Board (Access Board)
http://www.access-board.gov/
1111 18th St. N.W.
Suite 501
Washington, D.C. 20036
(800) 872-2253 Voice

(800) 993-2622 TTY
(202) 272-5448 (Electronic Bulletin Board)
Telecommunications Act Accessibility Guidelines:
http://www.access-board.gov/telecomm/html/telfinal.htm/
Transportation Guidelines:
http://www.access-board.gov/transit/html/vguide.htm/

Business Leadership Network (BLN)
www.usbln.com/
1331 F St. N.W.
Washington, D.C. 20004-1107
(202) 376-6200, extension 35 Voice
(202) 376-6868 Fax
(202) 376-6205 TTY
dunlap-carol@dol.gov

The California Governor's Committee for Employment of Disabled Persons
(Producers of the Windmills Training Program)
http://www.edd.ca.gov/gcedpind.htm/
P.O. Box 826880
Sacramento, Calif. 94280-0001
(916) 654-8055 Voice
(916) 654-9820 TTY
(916) 654-9821 Fax

Center for Applied Special Technology
"Bobby" website accessibility test
http://bobby.cast.org/

The Center for Universal Design
http://www.design.ncsu.edu/cud/
School of Design
North Carolina State University
Box 8613
Raleigh, N.C. 27695-8613
(919) 515-3082 Voice and TTY
(800) 647-6777 Info. requests
(919) 515-3023 Fax
cud@ncsu.edu

Disability and Business Technical Assistance Centers (DBTACs)
http://www.adata.org/dbtac.html/
(800) 949-4232 Voice/TTY
This number will automatically route your call to the DBTAC in your region.

W. C. Duke Associates, Inc.
(Producer of the Opening Doors customer service training program)
http://www.wcduke.com/
8049 Ormesby La.
Woodford, Va. 22580
(804) 633-6752 Voice
cz@wcduke.com

Human-Computer Interaction Accessibility Webibliography
http://www.hcibib.org/accessibility/

The Inclusion Network
http://www.inclusion.org/
312 Walnut Street, Suite 3600
Cincinnati, Ohio 45202
(513) 345-1330 Voice
(513) 345-1336 TTY
include@one.net

Microsoft Accessibility Site
http://www.microsoft.com/enable/

National Braille Press
(Braille publications and transcription)
http://www.nbp.org/
88 St. Stephen St.
Boston, Mass. 02115
(888) 965-8965 Voice
(617) 437-0456 Fax

National Business & Disability Council (NBDC)
http://www.business-disability.com/
201 I.U. Willets Rd.
Albertson, N.Y. 11507
(516) 465-1515 Voice
(516) 465-3730 Fax

National Center for Accessible Media
http://ncam.wgbh.org/
125 Western Ave.
Boston, Mass. 02134
(617) 300-3400 Voice
(617) 300-2489 TTY
(617) 300-1035 Fax
ncam@wgbh.org

National Library Service for the Blind and Physically Handicapped
http://www.loc.gov/nls/
Library of Congress
Washington, D.C. 20542
(202) 707-5100 Voice
(202) 707-0744 TTY
(202) 707-0712 Fax
nls@loc.gov

The National Organization on Disability (NOD)
http://www.nod.org/
910 Sixteenth St. N.W.
Suite 600
Washington, D.C. 20006
(202) 293-5960 Voice
(202) 293-5968 TTY
(202) 293-7999 Fax

ADA ON CD-ROM

The U.S. Department of Justice offers a free CD-ROM containing extensive technical information on the ADA. The CD-ROM is in a variety of formats, including WordPerfect, HTML, and text (ASCII). The CD-ROM includes:

- The new electronic version of the ADA Standards for Accessible Design;
- The ADA Guide for Small Businesses;
- Common ADA Errors and Omissions in New Construction and Alterations;
- The Americans with Disabilities Act Checklist for New Lodging Facilities;
- The ADA Guide for Small Towns;
- A series of commonly asked question and answer publications; and
- Technical Assistance Manuals for Titles II and III of the ADA.

Single copies can be ordered online at:

http://www.usdoj.gov/crt/ada/cdrequestform.htm
or by calling the Department's ADA Information Line:
(800) 514-0301 (Voice) or (800) 514-0383 (TTY).

Internet users can access the same information at: http://www.usdoj.gov/crt/ada/adahom1.htm

Office of Disability Employment Policy (ODEP)
(formerly The President's Committee on Employment of People with Disabilities)
http://www.dol.gov/odep/
1331 F St. N.W., Suite 300
Washington, D.C. 20004
(202) 376 6200 Voice
(202) 376 6205 TTY
(202) 376 6219 Fax

Registry of Interpreters for the Deaf
http://www.rid.org/
8630 Fenton St., Suite 324
Silver Spring, Md. 20910
(301) 608-0050 Voice/TTY
(301) 608-0508 Fax

Reedy, Joel. 1993. *Marketing to Consumers with Disabilities.* **Chicago: Probus.**

Terry, E., ed. 1997. *Pocket Guide to the ADA: Americans with Disabilities Act Guidelines for Buildings and Facilities.* **Rev. ed. New York: John Wiley and Sons.**

Universal Designers and Consultants, Inc.
http://universaldesign.com/
6 Grant Ave.
Takoma Park, Md. 20912-4324
(301) 270-2470 Voice and TTY
(301) 270-8199 Fax
UDandC@UniversalDesign.com

World Wide Web Consortium's Web Accessibility Initiative
http://www.w3.org/WAI/
MIT/LCS Room NE43-355
200 Technology Square
Cambridge, Mass. 02139
(617) 253-2613 Voice

11

A Plan for Inclusive Marketing

Part II: Message, Media, and Image Issues

Inclusive Use of Media

During the past few years, more and more companies have conducted marketing efforts that take into account the needs and preferences of people with disabilities—a practice known as "inclusive advertising." One characteristic of this practice is that it usually incorporates images of disabled people themselves, in violation of the long-accepted Madison Avenue dogma that models

---

"We deeply understand the issue of disability, and we want to include you the way you want to be included."

---

must be physically perfect. The introduction of images of disabled individuals into pictorial advertising coincides with their integration into neighborhoods, schools, the workplace, and society in general. In many ways, it also parallels the progress of the racial civil rights movement of the 1960s and '70s, when black models first began to appear in advertising targeted at general audiences.

In 1984, Levi Strauss became the first advertiser to feature a person with a disability in a television commercial. The ad showed a man in a wheelchair "popping a wheelie" (Kaufman 1999). McDonald's followed in 1986 with its first inclusive commercial, one that highlighted one of its disabled employees (Realwork.com). The next year DuPont aired a television ad featuring a Vietnam veteran named Bill Demby, shown playing basketball while using his two prosthetic legs (Shapiro 1993, 35). As trailblazers, these companies had no way of knowing how the public would respond to their commercials. They need not have worried. All three ads drew an enormously positive response, and gained each company an important place in disability history. After these breakthroughs, the inclusion of disabled individuals in pictorial advertising slowly became more common.

Approaches to Inclusive Marketing

There are five different ways in which corporations can implement strategies of inclusive marketing. Each has its own characteristics and advantages.

> **FIVE APPROACHES TO INCLUSIVE MARKETING**
>
> • Disability-Focused General
> • Disability-Focused Narrowcast
> • Disability-Focused Cause-Related
> • Disability-Highlighted
> • Disability-Integrated

Disability-Focused General Marketing

This approach utilizes generic media to promote disability-related products or services. Disability-focused general marketing is conducted for profit, not for purposes of philanthropy or social responsibility.

In the past, disability-focused marketing was almost always undertaken in "narrowcasting" venues, such as direct mailings and the publications of non-profit organizations that served disabled consumers. Recently, however, changing demographics and more relaxed attitudes toward impairments have allowed advertisers to use typical venues like commercial television, radio, and popular magazines. Some examples:

- National television and magazine ads feature actor Wilfred Brimley promoting medical supplies for people with diabetes.
- A national cancer treatment program airs thirty-second spots on network television. The ads feature the testimonial of a former cancer patient, now in remission, who attests to the quality of care he received in the program.
- In many local markets, psychiatric treatment centers and drug rehabilitation programs use newspaper, radio, television, and magazine media to promote their services.

Disability-Focused Narrowcasting

Out of the sight of many consumers, companies that provide products and services to individuals with disabilities have long engaged in "narrowcasting" to them. Narrowcasting—the opposite of broadcasting—directs messages to carefully selected subgroups in ways most likely to reach them and influence their purchasing decisions. Disabled consumers tend to pay close attention to media messages directed to them particularly, both because of the relevance of the material and the "insider" association of the marketing vehicle. This approach, like disability-focused general marketing, differs from the other three in that there is no aspect of "philanthropic economics" involved. The marketer is promoting goods and services directly to people who are disabled for the purpose of making a profit.

Over time, many companies that provide disability-related products and services have developed considerable expertise in reaching their markets. From their experiences, certain procedures have become standard. To have a maximum effect, a disability narrowcasting marketing campaign should include the following components:

1. Determining the demographics of the target population—Statistics on the incidence of disability, and other factors such as income levels, educational attainment, and population distribution, are available through the U.S. Bureau of the Census. Figures are available on a national, state, or county-by-county basis.

2. Understanding the particular communication and media preferences of the target population—Some preferences will be a matter of common sense, such as those dictated by the needs of consumers with sensory impairments. Generalizations can be deceiving, however. For example,

among consumers with hearing impairments, not only is there a distinction between people who are deaf and those who have some hearing; there can be a distinction between deaf people who communicate by sign language and those who communicate using lip reading. Messages that reach one group might fail to reach another. Likewise, some service organizations might appeal only to younger consumers, those with less education, militant advocates, and so on.

3. Determining the most cost-effective narrowcasting vehicle—Companies have a wide variety of options: direct mailing (using selected lists provided by mailing list providers), print advertising in disability-related publications, advertising through Internet portals that are disability focused, distribution through disability-related product retailers, and advertising on, or subsidizing, a handful of disability-focused radio and television shows. (See the list of narrowcasting vehicles that follows.)

Despite the abundance of disability-related products and services, very little research has been done on the general purchasing habits and media preferences of disabled consumers. However, some distinct characteristics of consumers with disabilities, based on related data, can be assumed:

- Disabled consumers tend to be economically disadvantaged relative to the rest of society.
- Although less likely to be employed, they are more likely to be eligible for government-subsidized benefits and service programs.
- Average income tends to decline as the severity of disability increases. As an income determinant, severity of disability is more significant than type of disability.
- Disabled consumers are more likely than typical consumers to influence family buying decisions.
- Although the educational attainment of people with disabilities is improving, it still tends to lag behind that of typical consumers.
- People with disabilities are sensitive to disability-related marketing messages and images.
- They tend to be in frequent contact with other individuals who have disabilities, especially through service providers and disability-related publications.
- Individuals with sensory impairments have strong preferences for user-friendly media.

Just as there has been little research into the market behaviors of disabled consumers in general, little has been conducted on disability subgroups. One exception, a study done by John J. Burnett and Pallab Paul at the Daniels College of Business, University of Denver (1996), focused on consumers with mobility impairments. It found that:

- Mobility-disabled consumers are particularly sensitive to products that "make their lives easier."
- They use direct marketing services such as toll-free numbers, catalogues, home shopping cable channels, etc.
- They express a preference for broadcast media over print.
- They prefer broadcasts that "fill time," such as prime-time and late-night movies.
- They prefer country and western and religious (gospel) radio formats.
- They tend to be limited readers of newspapers, perhaps because of their limited physical abilities.

With the growth of the population of disabled individuals in the United States, and the increase in their economic influence, similar studies of other subgroups are likely to occur.

Narrowcasting Vehicles

For corporations that want to reach concentrations of people with disabilities directly, there are a number of options. Listed below are some of the best known.

Periodicals

Ability Magazine
California-based lifestyle magazine.
(949) 854-8700 Voice
www.abilitymagazine.com.

Abilities Magazine
Canadian disability lifestyle magazine.
(416) 923-1885 Voice
www.enablelink.org

Accent on Living Magazine
Lifestyle magazine by and about people who have a disability. Focus is on people with mobility impairments.
(800) 787-8444 Voice

Disabled Outdoors Magazine
Sports and recreation oriented quarterly.
(312) 284-2206 Voice

Exceptional Parent
Cross-disability focus on family and parenting issues.
(800) E-PARENT Voice
www.eparent.com

Modern Maturity
Magazine distributed to members of the American Association of Retired Persons.
http://www.modernmaturity.org/

New Mobility Magazine
Nationally distributed monthly targeted at consumers with physical disabilities.
(888) 760-7655 Voice
www.newmobility.com

The Ragged Edge
Views public issues from a disability-rights perspective; politics, culture, technology, society, issues that affect us all.
www.raggededgemagazine.com

Reach Out Magazine
Features personal ads helping disabled people meet one another. Also a full-feature magazine.
www.reachoutmag.com

Sports 'n Spokes
Bi-monthly that focuses on competitive wheelchair sports.
(602) 242-6862 Voice

Internet Portals

www.wemedia.com
Offers multiple products, resources, and services.

www.halftheplanet.org
Similar to Wemedia.com.

www.ican.com/
Portal containing news, opinion, shopping, financial and relationship disability-related information.

Radio Program

On a Roll
Nationally syndicated talk radio program on life and disability.
Host: Greg Smith
(937) 767-1838 voice
http://www.ican.com/

Product Vendors

The vendors listed below retail items of special interest to elderly consumers and people with disabilities.

www.goldviolin.com
Products for older adults and people with disabilities.
(877) 648-8465

www.youcantoocan.com
Special products and apparel for people with special needs.
(888) 663-9396

Disability-Focused Cause-Related Marketing

In the lexicon of Madison Avenue, "cause-related marketing" is advertising that positions a company and its products or services in juxtaposition with an appealing social issue—anything from environmental conservation to disease research. Cause-related marketing has recently grown in popularity because it is known to be a powerful strategy: three out of four adults say they would be likely to switch to a brand associated with a good cause, and in the 1997 holiday season 56 percent of Americans said they patronized retailers associated with a cause (Realwork.com).

But a cause-related marketing approach does not guarantee the public's goodwill. Campaigns that are poorly conceived can backfire:

- When, in an apparent attempt to protest the death penalty, fashion manufacturer Benneton featured convicted death row inmates in its national magazine advertising, the immediate public outcry forced the company to cancel its campaign.
- A *Super Bowl 2000* television spot featured actor Christopher Reeve, who has quadriplegia, in a fantasy sequence showing him rising from his chair and walking across a stage to present an award. The ad, for the Nuveen investment management company, aroused the ire of disability advocates,

Fig. 11.1. NCR used this advertise-ment to promote the company's commit-ment to inclusive employment. *(Photo courtesy of NCR)*

who accused it of promoting unrealistic expectations for people with spi-nal cord injuries. Columnist Charles Krauthammer, who incurred a spinal cord injury at the age of twenty-two, called the ad "disgracefully mislead-ing" (2000). Lost in the controversy was the ad's intended message, and much of the goodwill that Nuveen had hoped to generate.

• In 1997, General Motor's Saturn ran an ad that featured a supposedly deaf customer conveying a "sign" for the car. The actor, an interpreter who was not deaf, was exposed by a deaf reporter. Saturn quickly pulled the ad, but the incident nonetheless earned a scathing cover story in *Deaf Life* magazine (Kaufman 1999; Suggs 1997).

Problematic disability-related marketing efforts show the importance of taking great care in the design and execution of media messages. Experienced marketers have learned that good intentions are not enough; they must devote the time, energy, and resources required to understand disability-related marketing thoroughly.

Because people with disabilities constitute society's largest minority, and disability issues are a matter of interest and concern to a large portion of the population, the subject is a natural for a cause-related marketing approach. In most such ads, heavy emphasis is placed on a particular disability or nonprofit organization that serves people who are impaired. Typically, people with disabilities are *not* portrayed in the context of promoting the typical products or services of the company conducting the marketing. Rather, they are shown *because* they have a disability and because the advertiser wishes to focus on a disability-related topic, such as research, treatment, or programming, or to provide information about the condition.

For example, when a cereal manufacturer features children and young adults with disabilities on the box of its product in order to promote the Special Olympics, it is directly associating the company with the cause, although the Special Olympics is not directly related to cereal consumption or to the manufacturer.

Occasionally, companies focus on disabilities in their advertising without actually showing disabled individuals. Some marketers, for example, feature on their product packaging the pink ribbon symbol associated with breast cancer research, along with information related to making donations in support of the charity. They do not, however, depict an individual who actually has, or has recovered from, the disease.

Examples of a disability-focused cause-related marketing approach are innumerable, with companies supporting everything from AIDS awareness to local rehabilitation centers. As with cause-related marketing in general, the primary reason for the popularity of this approach with marketers is that the consumer is known to respond to it quite favorably. In its own polling, the Atlanta Paralympics found that consumers were 20 percent to 30 percent more disposed to patronize companies associated with its cause, and other marketing studies have reached similar conclusions.[1]

Carefully designed disability-related campaigns rarely produce a negative response from the public, and at times they have even been used to solve public relations problems. When the United Way suffered a devastating cascade of bad publicity related to financial mismanagement and impropriety in its national headquarters, the nonprofit successfully countered with a series of television ads that featured disabled people who had benefited from their services (Williams 1999, 31).

In addition to the social benefits and marketing impact that result from disability-focused cause-related marketing, there is another compelling reason to consider this approach. Affiliations developed through this type of marketing can often provide employers with direct access to disabled individuals who may be willing to work for them, and assist them in designing and evaluating their inclusive marketing campaigns.

Disability-Highlighted Marketing

In recent years more and more companies have featured disabilities thematically in their advertising, typically by focusing on a disabled customer or employee. Such campaigns are less intense than disability-focused messages. They do not discuss impairments or disability issues directly or highlight nonprofit services, but the disability message is clearly there.

A television ad for Best Western motels depicts a blind customer ecstatically listening to the wind blowing through the Grand Canyon. The message is about all of the delights of travel. The piece subtly makes a point about the capabilities and interests of people who have visual disabilities, but it also implies that the motel chain is sensitive to disability issues—a very important consideration in the hospitality industry. In a similar way, a commercial for Charles Schwab highlights a blind investor being served by the investment firm. The ad is about Schwab's ability to meet the unique needs of its customers—not just about blindness. It does not mention that the company's founder and CEO has a serious learning disability.

Similarly, a Merrill Lynch television commercial features a customer who, although not deaf, is fluent in sign language. The man is shown coaching and signing to members of a basketball team who are hearing impaired, while talking about his experience as a hearing person in the deaf community, and making reference to the positive relationship he enjoys with his stockbroker. The commercial conveys interesting information about communication in the deaf community, and the message that the company "speaks the same language" as its customers is implied rather than stated.

McDonald's has frequently highlighted disabilities in its national ads by featuring both employees and customers with a wide range of impairments. Its commercials are often innovative and trend setting. One thirty-second TV spot that premiered in 1999 (fig. 11.2) features a little girl reading "her first book," and then going with her mother to McDonald's to celebrate the achievement. Only toward the end of the commercial does the viewer realize that the child has

Fig. 11.2. A still image from a McDonald's television ad featuring a young customer reading "her first book" in Braille. *(Photo courtesy of McDonald's Corporation)*

read her book in Braille, just as she has the restaurant's menu. Not a word is said about blindness or the company's inclusiveness. Yet, by highlighting one customer who happens to be blind, McDonald's delivers an effective message about both.

The "her first book" ad generated an enormously favorable response from the public. It was also lauded by disability advocates. Said Carl Augusto, president of the American Foundation for the Blind: "We commend McDonald's for its commitment to make eating at McDonald's restaurants fun and convenient for all its customers, including the nearly 10 million visually impaired Americans. I know that accessibility drives greater independence and encourages people who are blind or visually impaired to enjoy everyday life to the fullest" (McDonald's 1999).

In a press release at the time the commercials aired, McDonald's stressed that the commercial was part of a longstanding corporate commitment to inclusion:

> Through the years, McDonald's commercials have featured real people in real situations including a McDonald's crew person with Down's [*sic*] syndrome and hearing impaired customers. Twenty years ago, McDonald's was the first quick-service restaurant to offer Braille menus at its restaurants nationwide. Today, with assistance from the American Foundation for the Blind (AFB), McDonald's continues to be the only quick-service restaurant to offer them nationally. The company also offers picture menus to assist customers who have speaking or reading difficulties.

The disability-highlighted approach presents a subtler message about disability than more focused ads, but the results can be just as powerful. The Atlanta Paralympics study, referred to above, found that 54 percent of all households are more attentive to advertisements that feature individuals with disabilities, and more likely to patronize inclusive businesses.

A less direct approach, one that simply highlights individuals with disabilities rather than focusing on the issue, has the advantage of depicting people in the roles of customer or employee, rather than as service recipients. This approach appeals to disabled people (and their families and friends) by avoiding damaging stereotypes, and portraying them in positive ways.

Disability-Integrated Marketing

An even more subtle approach to the issue can be termed "disability-integrated advertising." Advertisements using this approach feature individuals with disabilities, but in a way that calls no "special" attention to them. They are simply included, frequently along with several or many others. Here are several examples:

- Magazine apparel ads for Dillard's, Target, Nordstrom, Sears, and many other retailers frequently feature one model with a disability among several others. Such models frequently are shown in wheelchairs or scooters, or wearing leg braces. Individuals with Down syndrome, especially children, are also featured frequently.
- A television ad for Ford vans features several obviously satisfied customers using its products. One customer happens to be sitting in a wheelchair. He is shown serenely fly casting, his wheelchair positioned in the middle of a mountain stream, a lift-equipped Ford van gleaming in the background.
- A RE/MAX realty ad features a family touring one of its listings. The "lady of the house" happens to be in a wheelchair, but no mention of her disability is made, nor is any disproportionate attention paid to her.
- A thirty-second television spot that touts the many activities available to passengers on a Royal Caribbean cruise features a quick glimpse of a wheelchair athlete racing around a ship's exercise track.

To those unfamiliar with the human dynamics of disability, this "understated" approach to advertising might seem self-defeating. Why incorporate people with disabilities in an ad if you don't intend to call attention to them? Why downplay your message to the point where it might be missed? Doesn't this diminish the potential benefits of inclusive marketing?

In fact it doesn't, and it may amplify them. Perhaps more than anything

Fig. 11.3. Nordstrom frequently features models with disabilities in its catalogs and on its website. *(Photo courtesy of Nordstrom)*

Kaelin XT **62a.** 'Peach-skin' microfiber warm-ups, in black/pale lime/teal, navy/light blue/yellow or periwinkle/navy/yellow polyester, with cotton/polyester jersey lining, xs-xl. Also in petites s-xl. 129.00. Norsport **62b.** French terry hooded gym jacket; 62.00. **62c.** French terry drawstring pants; 48.00. Both, in periwinkle, white, light amethyst, light petunia or light heather grey cotton. **62d.** Cotton turtleneck in white, ivory, black or red; 19.00. All, xs-xl, imported. Exclusively ours. **Women's Active.**

EXCLUSIVE: three color combinations only available at Nordstrom

nordstrom.com

62

else, people with disabilities struggle to be seen as normal—just like everybody else, in the things that really matter. This is a top priority for many, if not most. A company that understands this, and respects it, is far ahead of those that do not.

Companies that practice disability-integrated marketing are indeed sending a subtle message, and one very different from the traditional disability-related approach. But it is a message that reaches the disability market in a powerful way, and the message says: We deeply understand the issue of disability, and we want to include you the way you want to be included. The very ordinariness of this approach makes it so powerful.

In *No Pity*, Joseph Shapiro relates the impact of what is undoubtedly the first disability-integrated ad, a Target store national magazine advertising piece that showed a model with an obvious disability among many other people:

A partial list of companies that have employed people with disabilities in their television and print advertising:[2]

AT&T	The Gap	Nordstrom
Bank of America	Gatorade	Nuveen
Bell Atlantic	General Mills	Pacific Bell
Best Western	General Motors	Pepsi
Boeing	Giorgio Armani	RE/MAX
Budweiser	Hallmark	Royal Caribbean
Calvin Klein	IBM	Sears
Campbell's	JC Penney	Snap.com
Charles Schwab	Kmart	Sony
Chevron	Levi Strauss	Starbucks
Chrysler	Marriott	Target
Coca-Cola	Merrill Lynch	Toyota
Dillard's	Microsoft	Toys "R" Us
Disney	Motorola	UnumProvident
DuPont	Nabisco	VISA
Ford	NationsBank	WalMart
	Nike	Xerox

The Minneapolis-based Target department store chain put its first model with mental retardation, a young girl with Down syndrome, in a Sunday newspaper advertising insert in 1990. "That ad hit the doorsteps at six a.m. Sunday and a half hour later my phone was ringing," recalls George Hite, the company's vice-president for marketing. "It was the mother of a girl with Down syndrome thanking me for having a kid with Down syndrome in our ad. 'It's so important to my daughter's self-image,' she said." That ad, one small picture among dozens in the circular, generated over two thousand letters of thanks to stunned Target executives. (1993, 16)

One of the most impressive aspects of inclusive advertising is that it continues to generate a positive response from consumers. Outstanding efforts can still elicit enormous goodwill, as evidenced by the public's reaction to McDonald's "her first book" television ad in 1999, thirteen years after the company broadcast its first inclusive television commercial. In fact, that same year Snap.com ran a television ad featuring a boy using the Internet to learn to sign to his deaf friend. The company was also quickly deluged with thousands of positive responses (Williams 1999, 29).

As the list above indicates, the number of companies now using inclusive marketing has grown so much that individual examples probably no longer surprise viewers, although they can still impress them. One indication of the penetration of inclusive advertising into the popular culture is that a recent movie poked fun at it, calling it "wheelchair chic."

Message and Media Checklist

☐ Top management has communicated to its marketing department/advertising agency its commitment to participate in inclusive marketing that incorporates one or more of the following approaches:
  ○ disability-focused general
  ○ disability-focused narrowcast
  ○ disability-focused cause-related
  ○ disability-highlighted
  ○ disability-integrated
☐ Marketing strategy incorporates one or more of the following venues:
  ○ disability-related publications
  ○ disability-related broadcast and cable media
  ○ disability-related Internet portals
  ○ disability-related retailers
  ○ disability-related service organizations and activities
  ○ inclusive-generic media vehicles
☐ Advertising department/agency has received training in cause-related marketing and issues related to inclusive marketing.
☐ Advertising department/agency has allocated resources required to design an inclusive marketing campaign.
☐ Advertising department/agency has recruited disabled models or contacted modeling agencies that feature individuals with disabilities.

Image Issues

Company Images

As the examples cited indicate, people with disabilities can be depicted in many ways. Some call great attention to them or their condition; others seem to barely notice the disability. Marketing creativity has provided a wide variety of approaches, and within the five major marketing approaches to disability are infinite possibilities. The best examples, however, not only employ effective approaches to their messages, they avoid all the pitfalls and errors that could easily befall advertisers who do not fully understand the topic. A business that embarks on inclusive marketing for superficial reasons, or before it understands the issue of disability, is at least demonstrating some interest in the topic. That can be a start, but it can also be a precarious strategy.

Without an understanding of, and commitment to, disabled people and the issues they care about, a company can quickly find that its attempts at inclusive advertising are ineffective or even counterproductive. Businesses that lack an overall inclusion strategy can unwittingly employ stereotypical images, reflect popular misinformation about disabled people, or use outmoded or even offensive terminology—all of this alienating the very people they are attempting to attract, and causing great embarrassment to the company. In addition, marketers who have no intention of using inclusive marketing techniques, but wander unwittingly into disability-related consumer sensitivities, can also get into serious trouble. Marketing mistakes of this sort, as we shall see, are by no means rare.

A company can also suffer embarrassment if its disability-related marketing messages lead to questions it would rather not answer about its record of employing people who are disabled. A company that attempts to project an inclusive, "disability-friendly" image may be challenged to demonstrate that it "walks the walk" while it "talks the talk," and can suffer embarrassment when its record on employment proves to be unsatisfactory. That is why, as we have emphasized, employment must be the initial focus of any inclusion initiative. Initiating disability-related marketing before attending to employment issues is like eating dessert before the main course—tempting, but inappropriate.

Conversely, a company with a good record of employing workers who are disabled, or of making an effective effort to improve its performance, will be more credible to employees and consumers alike, and will derive the maximum benefit from its inclusive marketing efforts.

Disability Images

Before examining some prominent marketing mistakes, it might be helpful to review a few of the fundamental errors that can be made in the presentation of disability images. The fourth chapter of this book discussed the most common stereotypes associated with people who have disabilities. Those stereotypes depicted them as sick, subhuman, pitiful, ridiculous, inspirational, perpetual children, menaces, being punished for assumed transgressions, or having "phantom" disabilities.

Marketing messages and depictions of people with disabilities should obviously avoid all of these insulting and damaging images. Unfortunately, this is not always the case. Although some stereotypes are now rarely seen, even among some supposedly "sophisticated" marketers, appeals to the public's sense of pity, portrayals of adults as childish, and depictions of people with disabilities as being ill, burdensome, and laughable are all too common.

What Not to Do, Part I: Nike Stumbles

Nike is the world's leading manufacturer of athletic apparel, a position the company has reached largely because of its skillful marketing, which has positioned the company as fashionable and reliable, the choice of many celebrity athlete endorsers. When it comes to addressing the issue of disability, however, few companies have blundered so badly. The story of how Nike erred, how the public reacted, and how the company was forced to respond, clearly demonstrates how serious and complex disability-related marketing can become—even for those who never intend to engage in it.

In the December 2000 issue of *Backpacker Magazine,* Nike placed a two-page ad for its *Air Dri-Goat* trail footwear. The ad said in part:

> Right now you're probably asking yourself, 'How can a trail running shoe with an outer sole designed like a goat's hoof help me avoid compressing my spinal cord into a Slinky® on the side of some unsuspecting conifer, thereby rendering me a drooling, misshapen non-extreme trail-running husk of my former self, forced to roam the earth in a motorized wheelchair with my name embossed on one of those cute little license plates you get at carnivals or state fairs, fastened to the back?'

Response to the ad was immediate. Almost as soon as the magazine came off the presses, disabled individuals, advocates, and their friends deluged the company and the magazine with complaints. Paralympic athlete Ann Cody wrote in a highly publicized email to the company: "I have made sure that everyone in my personal network is aware of the prejudice and stereotyping Nike has demonstrated toward people with disabilities through this ad" (Bondi 2000). Others asked the company how a message so offensive to people with physical disabilities could ever have been foisted upon the public. How could Nike's marketing staff have approved such copy? How could its advertising agency have developed the concept in the first place? How could its management have allowed the ad to run? And how could *Backpacker Magazine* have agreed to run the ad? Wasn't there a single responsible person along the way who had the sense to recognize that the ad was outrageously offensive?

Realizing that the ad was indefensible, Nike was swift to apologize. It rushed to post a statement on its website, saying in part:

> Purely and simply, we made a mistake.
>
> The ad should never have been approved, much less written, and we are examining our internal approval system to make sure such a mistake does not happen again. We offer a sincere apology to anyone who was offended by that ad and we have immediately pulled it from all publications that have not already gone to print.
>
> We are also submitting apologetic letters to the editor to these same magazines. We are discussing both internally and with external advocacy groups some positive additional measures we can take to attempt to right this wrong.

The company went on to stress that the ad was an anomaly in what it regarded as its otherwise distinguished record of inclusion:

> [The ad is] also a contradiction of Nike's strong record on employing people with different abilities, which has included athletes as diverse as Casey Martin, Ric Munoz and others in our advertising. (Nike also outfitted the 2000 Paralympic Team and provided uniforms to the US and Kenyan Paralympic Teams.)[3]

Nike's apology failed to satisfy some critics. Writer Nicole Bondi noted that "in its apology for the ad, Nike refers to a former company president who 'suffered a spinal cord injury and is confined to a wheelchair'—language many in the disability community find offensive" (2000). Bondi added that other advocates were calling for additional preventive measures, including sensitivity training for Nike's employees and contractors, including—presumably—its advertising agency.

What Not to Do, Part II

A Midwestern small appliance manufacturer retained a consultant to conduct a thorough review of their disability-related practices. When he was only a few days into his research, the company's advertising agency came out with three thirty-second radio commercials for their new product. The agency called the ads the "No Brainer" series, its theme being that buying the company's product was a very easy decision—a "no brainer."

The following is from a transcript of one of the "No Brainer" radio spots:

> Say hello to Tammy, the world's simplest adult woman.
> Tammy has names for the buttons on her blouse;
> Tammy gets lost in her own home.
> Today we're going to ask her a few questions. Let's begin.
> Tammy, I want you to tell me who this is. That's right, just look in the mirror and tell me who you see. (Silence)
> No, no! Don't be startled! O.K. Let's try an easier one.
> What do you want for Christmas, Tammy?
> Ah! It appears we've gotten through! Tammy is pointing to (advertiser's product). They're only $49.
> Which just happens to be the exact value that the scientific community has placed on Tammy's brain . . .

This ad was the first of the series, and the others in the "No Brainer" campaign were equally offensive. Within minutes of the first ad's running, the company began to get angry phone calls from offended consumers.

Later that same day, the consultant got an urgent phone call from a company executive asking if he could attend a meeting with the marketing staff the following morning. The consultant agreed, and the executive said she would send him an audiotape of the commercials by courier within the hour. She asked him to review the spots before the meeting.

Early the next morning the consultant met with two very anxious marketers—the individual responsible for approving the "No Brainer" campaign and her supervisor. While he was in the process of detailing to them all of the reasons the ads should be pulled immediately, the company's receptionist interrupted the meeting to say, "There's another angry call. What should I say?" The supervisor replied, "Please tell them that we're meeting about the ad right now."

Less than ten minutes later the receptionist interrupted the meeting again. "A lady says she has a daughter who is severely disabled, and she's very disappointed in us. What can I tell her?"

The supervisor stared blankly at the transcript she had been reviewing. "Tell her we're very sorry, and that we're taking all of the ads off the air today."

What Not *to Do, Part III*

The Anheuser-Busch Company is well known for its clever television and radio ads for Budweiser beer. In the past, they have featured their own Clydesdale horse teams, talking reptiles, and Gen Xers asking "Whazzup?" In the summer of 2001 the company introduced a new radio ad aimed at promoting the company's "Bud Ice" product. The ad was known as the "Tycoon" spot.

The Tycoon ad featured the testimony of a young gold digger:

> Last year, I married oil tycoon Steven Buck Simpson. He was 93; I was 22. And it was true love, hmm, or so I led him to believe until the wedding. After that I fired his lawyer and cardiologist. I . . . alienated him from his children . . . I deflated the tires on his wheelchair, soaked his dentures in turpentine, and hid his oxygen . . . I replaced his blood pressure medication with Red Hots, fed him high fat, high cholesterol foods. And . . . I liquidated 100% of his Swiss bank account.

What does all of that have to do with beer? An announcer made the connection: *"Ooh, ooh, man that's cold! But not as cold as Bud Ice!"*

Although Anheuser-Busch did not intentionally target this ad to either elderly or disabled people, they managed to reach them nonetheless. Almost immediately, the company was deluged with complaints, both from offended consumers and watchdog organizations like the American Association of Retired Persons. As protests grew, the company issued a statement of apology: "It's never our intention to offend anyone with our advertising. Anheuser-Busch has discontinued use of this ad and has no plans to use it in the future" (Benson 2001).

What Not *to Do, Part IV*

Comedian Jerry Lewis has been a spokesperson and leading fundraiser for the Muscular Dystrophy Association USA for decades. He is perhaps best known for an annual national Labor Day telethon that raises millions of dollars for research into the disease.

Whatever his personal commitment to eradicating the disease and helping people who have it, Lewis has long been criticized for raising money by tugging on the heartstrings of potential donors. Says disability advocate Gary Presley:

"The real pity is the man has a huge audience for his telethon, and he refuses to change his 19th century attitude about people with disabilities" (2001).

In May of 2001, "pity" became the subject during an interview with Lewis on *CBS News Sunday Morning*. The comedian was asked about objections of disability activists that his approach to fundraising exploited the "pity" stereotype of people with MD. He responded: "I'm telling people about a child in trouble. If it's pity we'll get money. I'm just giving you the facts. You don't want to be pitied because you're a cripple in a wheelchair? Stay in your house."

As might be expected, there was an immediate outcry from people with disabilities and disability advocates. Lewis eventually apologized for his remarks. Even after his apology, advocates continued to call on the Muscular Dystrophy Association to end its long relationship with the comedian.

Images in Successful Inclusive Marketing Strategies

Marketing strategies that successfully appeal to disabled consumers and their friends do not happen by chance; they must be crafted carefully. The first consideration is to recognize and steer clear of all stereotypes and myths about disabilities. Inclusive marketers should:

- Avoid depicting people with disabilities as dependent on others, or images that stress their incapability.
- Avoid depicting disabled people in large numbers, generally numbers greater than typically found in society. Clusters of disabled people imply segregation—an extremely negative association.
- Avoid depictions of multiple people with differing types of disabilities. This implies that disabilities are all very much the same, or that disabled people "like to be with their own kind."
- Avoid images that imply that adults with disabilities are childish. This can involve treating various disabilities as strictly juvenile matters, or surrounding disabled adults with childish images such as toys, games, and novelties.
- Avoid depicting individuals with disabilities with animals other than service companions. This sometimes hints at a "subhuman" status, or social rejection: "Well, at least their *cat* likes to be with them."
- Avoid all images associated with circuses, sideshows, and carnivals. These include barkers, magicians, acrobats, and, of course, performing animals. Such images hearken back to the dark days when disabled people were exhibited in "freak" shows.

- Avoid disability clichés, even if well intended, such as children in wheelchairs receiving oversized checks from corporate executives, people of short stature portraying Santa's elves, visually impaired adults with a "natural talent" for music, and people who are mentally retarded, but have a "heart of gold."
- Avoid ambiguous attempts at humor that could be interpreted as laughing "at" rather than "with" disabled people.

Images in Successful Inclusive Marketing Messages

Avoid	Emphasize
Dependency	Social integration
Incapability	Competencies
Clusters/Segregation	Wealth, position, authority
Different disabilities depicted together	Close relationships
in groups	Inclusive interaction
Childish images	
Animals	
Carnival items and activities	
Disability clichés	
Ambiguous humor	

Avoiding counterproductive images is critical in designing an inclusive marketing message, but advertisers can create truly compelling ads by also injecting positive concepts that contradict negative preconceptions.[4] The very best ads will not only avoid disability myths, stereotypes, and prejudices; they will speak to disabled consumers and their friends in ways that are most appealing to them.

The following are some suggestions for marketers who wish to depict people with disabilities in positive and appealing ways:

- Consider using images of people with disabilities in socially integrated groups—images that show them mixing easily with nondisabled individuals.
- Consider images of disabled people that indicate valued competencies, such as athleticism, public speaking, mastery of a foreign language, artistic ability, and so on.

- Consider images of disabled people that imply wealth, position, and authority.
- Consider images of nondisabled individuals interacting warmly in close personal relationships with people who have disabilities.
- Consider images of individuals without disabilities modeling inclusive behaviors—using sign language, acting as a sighted guide, listening carefully to someone speaking slowly, and so on.

It is unlikely that any marketing message could contain all or even most of these concepts; however, the most effective examples of inclusive marketing are likely to reflect at least one of them.

Advertising as Employment

Although concerns about images and market impact are certainly warranted, marketers must remember that advertising is also a matter of employment. Companies and advertising agencies employ models and actors to work in the commercials and pictorials they produce. If a company or its contractor refuses to hire a disabled person who can perform the essential functions of a modeling or acting job, with or without a reasonable accommodation, that company or contractor is in violation of the Americans with Disabilities Act.

A company that hires an advertising agency to produce its marketing materials puts a bit of distance between itself and the hiring process, but that distance might not be enough to escape liability for employment discrimination. Such a strategy *might* have legal merit (it has not yet been litigated extensively),[5] but in the public mind, at least, there is no distinction between a company and the advertising agency it uses. No consumer looks at an inclusive commercial and credits the advertising agency that made it. Conversely, the public holds a company responsible for the messages that market its product. They may also ultimately hold an advertising agency to account, but the client will be looked to first. For these reasons, companies that respect the law, value the public's goodwill, and wish to be inclusive marketers should clearly communicate their commitment to all those involved in their marketing, including their advertising agency.

Many agencies are now accustomed to serving clients who specify a preference for inclusive advertising, and they have experience in designing ads that use models with disabilities. For others—those who might be new to the concept—the resources listed below can assist in providing disabled models.

Modeling Resources

The Shot Model Management
100 Park Avenue, 16th Floor
New York, N.Y. 10017
(212) 941-7095 Voice
(212) 880-6499 Fax
The Shot Model Management is an agency that specializes in commercial and fashion models with disabilities.

http://www.ntcp.org/
Non-Traditional Casting Project, Inc.
1560 Broadway, Suite 1600
New York, N.Y. 10036
(212) 730-4750 Voice
(212) 730-4820 Fax
(212) 730-4913 TTY
info@ntcp.org
The Non-Traditional Casting Project (NTCP) is a nonprofit organization established to address and seek solutions to the problems of racism and exclusion in theater, film, and television.

Image Checklist

☐ Disability images avoid negative stereotypes.

☐ Images emphasize positive attributes of people with disabilities.

☐ Images are accessible and available in multiple formats.

☐ Individuals with disabilities participate in design, implementation, and evaluation of the marketing products.

☐ Evaluation/customer satisfaction survey of people with special needs is performed.

Resources

American Marketing Association
http://www.marketingpower.com/
311 S. Wacker Dr.
Suite 5800
Chicago, Ill. 60606
(800) AMA-1150 Voice

(312) 542-9000 Voice
(312) 542-9001 Fax
info@ama.org

Business Leadership Network (BLN)
www.usbln.com/
1331 F St. N.W.
Washington, D.C. 20004-1107
(202) 376-6200, extension 35 Voice
(202) 376-6868 Fax
(202) 376-6205 TTY
dunlap-carol@dol.gov

Disability and Business Technical Assistance Centers (DBTACs)
http://www.adata.org/dbtac.html/
(800) 949-4232 Voice/TTY
This number will automatically route your call to the DBTAC in your region.

Disability Statistics Center
http://www.dsc.ucsf.edu/
3333 California St., Suite 340
Campus Mail Box 0646
San Francisco, Calif. 94118
(415) 502-5210 Voice
(415) 502-5205 TTY
(415) 502-5208 Fax

National Business & Disability Council (NBDC)
http://www.business-disability.com/
201 I.U. Willets Rd.
Albertson, N.Y. 11507
(516) 465-1515 Voice
(516) 465-3730 Fax

The National Organization on Disability (NOD)
http://www.nod.org/
910 Sixteenth St. N.W.
Suite 600
Washington, D.C. 20006
(202) 293-5960 Voice
(202) 293-5968 TTY
(202) 293-7999 Fax

Office of Disability Employment Policy (ODEP)
(formerly The President's Committee on Employment of People with Disabilities)
http://www.dol.gov/odep/
1331 F St. N.W., Suite 300
Washington, D.C. 20004
(202) 376-6200 Voice
(202) 376-6205 TTY
(202) 376-6219 Fax

Reedy, Joel. 1993. *Marketing to Consumers with Disabilities.* **Chicago: Probus.**

The Solutions Marketing Group
http://www.disability-marketing.com/
2334 S. Rolfe St.
Arlington, Va. 22202
(703) 920-0225 Voice
(703) 920-0262 Fax
info@disability-marketing.com

Telecommunications Industry Association
(Authors of *Extend Their Reach: Marketing to Customers with Disabilities: Interpreting the Numbers.* An analysis of statistics on the disability market, with applicability outside of the telecommunications industry.)
http://www.tiaonline.org/access/etr_brochure.html/

U.S. Census Bureau
http://www.census.gov/
Washington, D.C. 20233
(301) 457-4608 Voice

Inclusive Employment Checklist

1. Management Commitment

☐ Management has carefully examined its legal and ethical obligations pertaining to people with disabilities, and the potential benefits of becoming an inclusive corporation.

☐ Management has clearly and convincingly communicated to employees a commitment to inclusive employment beyond mere legal compliance.

☐ Management has provided the necessary resources and established goals for implementation.

☐ Management has begun to implement practical steps to reinforce this commitment, such as tying progress in inclusion to compensation and promotion.

☐ If appropriate, the company's commitment has been communicated to affiliates, customers, contractors, suppliers, and the public.

2. Legal Review

☐ Management has reviewed the requirements of Title I of the ADA, and any other pertinent legislation.

☐ Legal counsel has reviewed policies and procedures for compliance.

☐ Management has reviewed the company's policies and procedures for compliance.

☐ Management has evaluated the status of physical facilities for compliance, and has sought professional review where appropriate.

☐ Management has reviewed disability-related insurance coverage with carriers.

☐ Management has reviewed the company's record of accommodation requests, disability-related complaints, injuries and illnesses, and so on.
☐ Policies, procedures, and experience are reviewed on a regular basis.

3. Accessibility

Application, Testing, and Evaluation Location

Physical

☐ Architects/property managers have reviewed all facilities for ADA compliance.
☐ Accessible and appropriately designated parking spaces are available close to entrance.
☐ At least one lift-equipped van (oversized) space is available.
☐ Accessible pathway from parking to entrance is available.
☐ External ramps are appropriately graded (slope no greater than 1:12) and have handrails if appropriate.
☐ All access doors are at least 36 inches wide.
☐ Doors are automatic or easily opened.
☐ Doors have easy-to-grasp handles.
☐ Elevators have control panels lower than 54 inches from floor.
☐ Restrooms are accessible.
  ○ Automatic or easily opened door is available.
  ○ Door opens easily for both entrance and egress.
  ○ At least one oversized stall is available.
  ○ Oversized stall is equipped with handrails.
  ○ Commode is raised.
  ○ Accessible sink is available.
  ○ Accessible towel dispenser is available.
☐ Public telephone is accessible (installed at lower level).
☐ Accessible water fountain or dispenser is available.
☐ Pathways to all facilities are clear and accessible.
☐ Interview/testing room is accessible.
☐ Appropriate room lighting is provided.
☐ Background noise is eliminated or minimized.
☐ Appropriate desk/testing station lighting is provided.
☐ Physical accessibility features have been evaluated by consumers.

Communication

- [ ] Human resources staff has received training in ADA requirements, particularly in regard to interviewing and hiring procedures.
- [ ] Recruitment materials indicate that reasonable accommodations are available, and suggest applicants notify human resources office of any needs.
- [ ] Driving directions indicate location of accessible parking.
- [ ] Signage clearly indicates location of accessible parking.
- [ ] Raised symbols/Braille signage is provided on elevator.
- [ ] All facility signage is appropriate and accessible to individuals with visual and cognitive disabilities.
    - ○ Large lettering is used.
    - ○ Graphics and symbols are used.
- [ ] TTD or similar device is available.
- [ ] Sign language interpreter is available if requested.
- [ ] Reading service is available if requested.
- [ ] Written, large-type, audio, or Braille instructions are available.
- [ ] Application and testing materials are written in clear and uncomplicated language.
- [ ] Large-type, audio, or Braille application and testing materials are available.
- [ ] Computer testing procedures have large-print capabilities.
- [ ] Assistance in completing application or testing materials is available if requested.
- [ ] Flexible test timing is available.
- [ ] Notepads and writing instruments are available.
- [ ] Emergency procedures consider needs of people with disabilities.
    - ○ Emergency warning system includes both audio and visual alarms.
    - ○ Evacuation procedures are established.
    - ○ Emergency notification procedures are established.
    - ○ At least one evacuation chair is provided if required.

The Job Site or Potential Job Site

Physical

- [ ] Architects/property managers have reviewed all facilities for ADA compliance.
- [ ] Accessible and appropriately designated parking spaces are available close to entrance.
- [ ] At least one lift-equipped van (oversized) parking space is available.
- [ ] Accessible pathway from parking to entrance is available.
- [ ] External ramps are appropriately graded (slope no greater than 1:12) and have handrails if appropriate.

☐ All access doors are at least 36 inches wide.
☐ Doors are automatic or easily opened.
☐ Doors have easy-to-grasp handles.
☐ Elevators have control panels lower than 54 inches from floor.
☐ Restrooms are accessible.
  ○ Automatic or easily opened door is available.
  ○ Door opens easily for entrance and egress.
  ○ At least one oversized stall is available.
  ○ Oversized stall is equipped with handrails.
  ○ Commode is raised.
  ○ Accessible sink is available.
  ○ Accessible towel dispenser is available.
☐ Public telephone is accessible (installed at lower level).
☐ Accessible water fountain or dispenser is available.
☐ Pathways to all facilities are clear and accessible.
☐ Work areas are accessible.
☐ Pathways to and around work areas are clear and accessible.
☐ All equipment used in job performance is appropriate and accessible.
☐ All off-site training and work are conducted in accessible facilities.
☐ Appropriate room and lighting are provided.
☐ Appropriate work station lighting is provided.
☐ Background noise is eliminated or minimized.
☐ Physical accessibility features have been evaluated by consumers.
☐ Emergency procedures consider needs of people with disabilities.
  ○ Emergency warning system includes both audio and visual alarms.
  ○ Evacuation procedures are established.
  ○ Emergency notification procedures are established.
  ○ At least one evacuation chair is provided if required.

Communication

☐ Signage clearly indicates location of accessible parking.
☐ Raised symbols/Braille signage is provided on elevator.
☐ All facility signage is appropriate and accessible to individuals with visual and cognitive disabilities.
  ○ Large lettering is used.
  ○ Graphics and symbols are used.
☐ TTD or similar device is available.
☐ Sign language interpreter is available if requested.
☐ Reading service is available if requested.
☐ Written, large-type, audio, or Braille instructions are available.

☐ Internet use is accessible.
- ○ Company Internet site is accessible.
- ○ Internet access accommodations are available.

☐ Emergency warning system includes both audio and visual alarms.

Benefits and Privileges

Physical

☐ All employee benefits and privileges are equally provided to people with disabilities.

☐ All training, meeting, convention, and official socializing sites are accessible.

☐ Physical sites associated with job benefits and privileges are accessible.

Communication

☐ Information pertaining to employee benefits, corporate activities, and related events is available in appropriate formats.

☐ Reasonable accommodations are available if requested (e.g., readers, audio description, large-type materials, transportation).

☐ Videos and audio-visual materials are available with captioning.

4. Recruiting

☐ Corporation has clearly communicated intent to hire qualified workers with disabilities
- ○ within the corporation
- ○ to appropriate disability-related vocational agencies
- ○ to affiliates, suppliers, contractors
- ○ to the public

☐ Detailed job descriptions have been developed for all positions.

☐ Human resources staff has received appropriate training in recruiting qualified workers with disabilities.

☐ Human resources staff has established working relationships with appropriate state vocational rehabilitation agency and other referral sources.

☐ Procedures for narrowcasting employment openings to appropriate state vocational rehabilitation agency and other referral sources have been established.

☐ Current disabled employees are involved in, or consulted concerning, recruitment procedures.

5. Interviewing and Pre-employment Procedures

☐ Human resources personnel and all employees involved in employment interviewing have received training in ADA-related regulations and procedures.

☐ Human resources personnel and all employees involved in employment interviewing are familiar with accommodations that can be provided during the interview process.

☐ Confidentiality policy and procedures have been established.

☐ Standard interviewing forms and procedures have been developed for use with all applicants.

☐ Interviewing procedures, applications, and questionnaires do not include disability-related questions.

☐ Physical examinations, if required, are required of all candidates in a job category, and are performed only after a conditional offer of employment has been made.

☐ Medical information is maintained confidentially, in a file separate from personnel file.

☐ Rehabilitation professionals or other noncustomary personnel (e.g., sign language interpreter) are not involved in interview unless requested by applicant.

☐ Interviewer notes are kept for all job applicants.

☐ Interviewer notes specify whether applicant initiated discussion of disability or requested an accommodation, and subsequent actions taken.

6. Training Employees about Disabilities

☐ The employer has identified training needs as part of a complete inclusive employment strategy.

☐ Training personnel have received special instruction in inclusive employment, or qualified training consultants have been identified.

☐ Management has communicated the specific goals of training.

☐ Specific training modules have been identified and developed to deal with fundamental inclusion-related issues.

☐ Senior management personnel have received comprehensive training in inclusive employment practices.

☐ Supervisors have received comprehensive training in inclusive employment practices.

☐ Employees have received comprehensive training in inclusive employment practices.

☐ All training is conducted in accessible locations.

☐ Training formats and procedures are appropriate to needs of all employees.

☐ Employees with disabilities are involved in training, if they so desire.

7. Accommodating Employees

Management Preparations

☐ Management has developed appropriate procedures for requesting, identifying, developing, providing, and evaluating accommodations.

☐ Procedures for appeals and revisions have been developed and approved.

☐ Procedures for maintaining confidentiality throughout the accommodations process have been developed and implemented.

☐ Accommodation policies and procedures have been communicated to all employees.

☐ Human resources personnel have received training in regulations and best practices relating to accommodating employees with disabilities.

☐ Job descriptions have been written to indicate the essential functions of each position.

Procedure for Specific Requests

☐ Essential functions of the position have been reviewed.

☐ Employee has been determined to be qualified to perform essential functions of the position with or without a reasonable accommodation.

☐ Relevant functional limitation/s of employee has/have been identified.

☐ Employee has been consulted about needs and preferences.

☐ Rehabilitation personnel have been consulted, if necessary.

☐ Potential accommodations have been identified.

☐ Potential accommodations have been evaluated for effectiveness and cost.

☐ Employee has participated in evaluation of potential accommodations.

☐ Selected accommodation/s has/have been monitored and evaluated for effectiveness and user friendliness.

☐ Accommodation/s has/have been modified, if necessary.

☐ Monitoring/evaluation of accommodation/s is ongoing, if appropriate.

8. Supervising and Supporting Employees

☐ Management has clearly communicated priorities and goals.

☐ Management has established procedures to cover equitably the costs associated with inclusive employment.

☐ Supervisors have received training in disabilities, accommodations, support strategies, the ADA, and other issues relating to inclusive employment.

☐ Effective supervision and support of employees with disabilities is valued, promoted, and rewarded.

☐ Supervisors have been given all related information, including

   ○ specific information about the accommodation needs of employees they supervise

   ○ information pertaining to the disabilities of employees they supervise

   ○ contact information for counselors, rehabilitation personnel, interpreters, or other professional resources they might need

☐ Assistance of rehabilitation personnel or other professional resources is available, if necessary.

☐ Mentoring relationships are encouraged.

☐ Workgroup supports are encouraged.

☐ Supervisors and co-workers promote workplace enculturation, networking, and socialization.

☐ Employees have been given clear instructions and goals.

☐ Employee performance feedback is frequent and constructively communicated.

☐ Employees with disabilities know how to obtain necessary assistance and support.

☐ Employee training is appropriate, accessible, and ongoing.

9. Disability Management, Workers' Compensation, and Health and Disability Insurance

☐ Senior management has clearly communicated the importance of effective disability management and of injury and illness prevention.

☐ Management and human resources staff have received appropriate training in the ADA, disability management and prevention, workers' compensation and return-to-work programs, and health and disability insurance.

☐ Health and disability insurance plans have been reviewed for compliance with the ADA, the Family and Medical Leave Act of 1993, and other applicable legislation.

☐ Medical examinations, if required, are obtained from all similarly situated employees, or obtained only for appropriate business-related purposes.

☐ Process improvement programs for medical management and disability management have been established and are audited periodically.

☐ All employees have been informed of the necessity of immediately notifying their supervisor of any accident, injury, or other disability-related matter, and clearly understand procedures in place to make such notification.

☐ All employees making workers' compensation claims are evaluated regarding whether or not they qualify for protection under the ADA.

☐ Employer has coordinated the approach to safety and claims management efforts with disability insurance carriers and health care insurance providers.

☐ Work sites have received a safety analysis/design review conducted by safety experts and ergonomics professionals.

☐ Accident reports and workers' compensation claims are periodically reviewed according to an established schedule.

☐ Data on the results of medical treatments and long-term outcomes are maintained, and a process establishing actionable recommendations pursuant to review of that data has been established.

☐ Procedures have been established for developing individual return-to-work solutions.

☐ Employees receiving workers' compensation are regularly evaluated for change in status.

☐ Workers' compensation premiums, previous claims, and current costs are professionally audited.

☐ All employees have received appropriate training in accident and injury prevention.

☐ Accident and injury prevention and disability-related cost containment are regularly evaluated, and effective management is rewarded.

10. Tax and Other Financial Incentives

☐ Accountants/business managers have reviewed current information on
  ○ Small Business Tax Credit, if applicable
  ○ Architectural/Transportation Tax Credit
  ○ Work Opportunity Tax Credit
☐ Human resources managers have reviewed current information on
  ○ Work Opportunity Tax Credit
  ○ Ticket to Work and Work Incentive Improvement Act (TTWWIIA)
☐ Employers participating in the Work Opportunity Tax Credit have
  ○ determined likely eligibility of applicants by including the WOTC Pre-screening Notice as part of the application process
  ○ signed (along with the employee) the Pre-screening Notice on or before the day employment is offered, and mailed it to the SESA within twenty-one days after the employee begins work

○ documented WOTC eligibility (based on information received from the employee) and submitted documentation to the SESA

○ received from the SESA written certification of individuals eligible for the WOTC

○ filed for the WOTC tax credit

○ Employer has contacted local state rehabilitation agency regarding the availability of employment candidates who qualify for the TTWWIIA.

○ Employer has assisted current qualified employees with disabilities in determining whether they qualify for benefits under the TTWWIIA.

○ Employer has contacted local state rehabilitation agency regarding the availability of new, unusual, or unpublicized employment incentives.

(Adapted from the regulations of the Equal Employment Opportunity Commission, "Workplace Accommodation Process" of the Office of Disability Employment Policy at http://www.dol.gov/odep/pubs/ek97/process.htm and "Ready, Willing, and Available," at http://www.dol.gov/odep/pubs/rwa00/toc.htm)

Inclusive Marketing Checklist

1. Management Leadership

☐ Top management has clearly communicated the company's intent to be inclusive.

☐ Top management has initiated a review of its inclusion-related employment practices.

☐ Top management has carefully reviewed all relevant information pertaining to inclusive marketing.

☐ Top management has communicated to its marketing staff and advertising agency its specific intent to engage in inclusive marketing practices.

☐ Top management has commended and rewarded those responsible for its effective inclusive marketing programs.

2. Accessibility Considerations in Marketing

Retail Site

☐ Retail locations have been evaluated for accessibility:
   ○ Architects and building managers have reviewed facilities for accessibility.
   ○ Retail entrances are without obstructions.
   ○ Entrances have automatic doors, or doors meet maximum opening force requirements.
   ○ Designated parking spaces are available.
   ○ Designated parking spaces at least 96 inches wide with access aisles at least 60 inches wide to accommodate vans with wheelchair lifts are available.

○ Lighting and sound levels are appropriate.
○ Signage uses large lettering, Braille, and universal symbols.
○ Retail aisles are at least 36 inches wide.
○ Accessible cash register/voucher signing spot a maximum of 36 inches off the floor is available.
○ A portion of any food service or bar area is 36 inches off the floor.
○ Restrooms meet ADA standards.
○ Resting spots are provided.
○ Accessible fitting rooms are available.
○ Price tags are easily viewable from a sitting position.
○ A TTY is available and functioning properly.
○ Staff members have been trained to operate a TTY.

Product Design

☐ Design staff have received training in principles of universal design.
☐ Prospective products and services incorporate features of universal design.
☐ Current products and services have been evaluated for accessibility and ease of use.
☐ Suppliers and contractors have reviewed products for accessibility and ease of use.
☐ Individuals with disabilities are involved in product design, service testing, and evaluation.
☐ Customer service, help-line, and other staff collect accessibility-related consumer information.
☐ Disability-related products
  ○ maximize safety and ease-of-use features
  ○ minimize features that call attention to the consumer's disability
  ○ incorporate aspects of typical equivalents
  ○ are offered in alternatives associated with positively valued images
  ○ are available in placements that maximize psychological accessibility

Communication and Customer Service

☐ Marketing information has been evaluated for inclusiveness and accessibility.
  ○ Advertising, catalogs, promotional items, and related material have been reviewed for inclusiveness and accessibility.
  ○ Advertising, catalogs, promotional items, and related material are available in multiple formats.
  ○ All video materials created and used by the company is available with captioning.
  ○ Corporate web site has been evaluated for accessibility.

☐ Retail staff has been trained to serve customers with disabilities.

3. Message and Media Checklist

☐ Top management has communicated to its marketing department/advertising agency its commitment to participate in inclusive marketing that incorporates one or more of the following approaches:
  ○ disability-focused general
  ○ disability-focused narrowcast
  ○ disability-focused cause-related
  ○ disability-highlighted
  ○ disability-integrated
☐ Marketing strategy incorporates one or more of the following venues:
  ○ disability-related publications
  ○ disability-related broadcast and cable media
  ○ disability-related Internet portals
  ○ disability-related retailers
  ○ disability-related service organizations and activities
  ○ inclusive generic media vehicles
☐ Advertising department/agency has received training in cause-related marketing and issues related to inclusive marketing.
☐ Advertising department/agency has allocated resources required to design an inclusive marketing campaign.
☐ Advertising department/agency has recruited disabled models or contacted modeling agencies that feature individuals with disabilities.

4. Image Issues

☐ Disability images avoid negative stereotypes.
☐ Images emphasize positive attributes of people with disabilities.
☐ Images are accessible and available in multiple formats.
☐ Individuals with disabilities participate in design, implementation, and evaluation of the marketing products.
☐ Evaluation/customer satisfaction survey of people with special needs is performed.

Resources

(Websites and email addresses in this list were current at the time of publication.)

http://www.abledata.com/
ABLEDATA is a national database of information on assistive technology and rehabilitation equipment available from domestic and international sources. ABLEDATA contains information on more than 23,000 assistive technology products.

American Diabetes Association
http://www.diabetes.org/
1701 North Beauregard St.
Alexandria, Va. 22311
(800) 342-2383 Voice
customerservice@diabetes.org

American Friends Service Committee Affirmative Action Office
(Producers of the *Guide to Etiquette and Behavior for Relating to Persons with Disabilities*)
http://www.afsc.org/etiquette.htm/
1501 Cherry St.
Philadelphia, Pa. 19102
(215) 241-7000 Voice
(215) 241-7275 Fax

The American Institute for Managing Diversity
http://www.aimd.org/
50 Hurt Plaza, Suite 1150
Atlanta, Ga. 30303
(404) 302-9226 Voice

American Marketing Association
http://www.marketingpower.com/
311 S. Wacker Dr.
Suite 5800
Chicago, Ill. 60606
(800) AMA-1150 Voice
(312) 542-9000 Voice
(312) 542-9001 Fax
info@ama.org

Americans with Disabilities Act Document Center
http://www.jan.wvu.edu/links/adalinks.htm
 (See also Job Accommodation Network [JAN].)

Apple Computer—People with Special Needs
http://www.apple.com/disability/
specialneeds@apple.com

Architectural and Transportation Barriers Compliance Board (Access Board)
http://www.access-board.gov/
1111 18th St. N.W.
Suite 501
Washington, D.C. 20036
(800) 872-2253 Voice
(800) 993-2622 TTY
(202) 272-5448 (Electronic Bulletin Board)
Telecommunications Act Accessibility Guidelines:
http://www.access-board.gov/telecomm/html/telefinal.htm/
Transportation Guidelines:
http://www.access-board.gov/transit/html/fguide.htm/

Business Leadership Network (BLN)
www.usbln.com/
1331 F St. N.W.
Washington, D.C. 20004-1107
(202) 376-6200, extension 35 Voice
(202) 376-6868 Fax
(202) 376-6205 TTY
dunlap-carol@dol.gov

The California Governor's Committee for Employment of Disabled Persons
(Producers of the Windmills Training Program)
http://www.edd.ca.gov/gcedpind.htm/
P.O. Box 826880

Sacramento, Calif. 94280-0001
(916) 654-8055 Voice
(916) 654-9820 TTY
(916) 654-9821 Fax

Center for Applied Special Technology
"Bobby" website accessibility test
http://bobby.cast.org/

The Center for Universal Design
http://www.design.ncsu.edu/cud/
School of Design
North Carolina State University
Box 8613
Raleigh, N.C. 27695-8613
(919) 515-3082 Voice and TTY
(800) 647-6777 Info. requests
(919) 515-3023 Fax
cud@ncsu.edu

Center on Education and Work
http://www.cew.wisc.edu/
1025 W. Johnson St.
Rm. 964
Madison, Wisc. 53706-1796
(800) 466-0399 Voice
cewmail@education.wisc.edu

Disabled American Veterans
http://www.dav.org/
P.O. Box 14130
Cincinnati, Ohio 45250-0301
(859) 441-7300 Voice

Disability and Business Technical Assistance Centers (DBTACs)
http://www.adata.org/dbtac.html/
(800) 949-4232 Voice/TTY
This number will automatically route your call to the DBTAC in your region.

http://www.disabilitydirect.gov/
A website of the Office of Disability Employment Policy designed to pull together a wide variety of disability information, especially from federal government sources.

Disability Social History Project
http://www.disabilityhistory.org/

255 3rd St., #202
Oakland, Calif. 94607
sdias@disabilityhistory.org

Disability Statistics Center
http://www.dsc.ucsf.edu/
3333 California St., Suite 340
Campus Mail Box 0646
San Francisco, Calif. 94118
(415) 502-5210 Voice
(415) 502-5205 TTY
(415) 502-5208 Fax

W. C. Duke Associates, Inc.
(Producer of the Opening Doors customer service training program)
http://www.wcduke.com/
8049 Ormesby La.
Woodford, Va. 22580
(804) 633-6752 Voice
cz@wcduke.com

Equal Employment Opportunity Commission (EEOC)
http://www.eeoc.gov/
For technical assistance:
(800) 669-4000 Voice
(800) 669-6820 TTY
To obtain documents:
(800) 669-3362 Voice
(800) 800-3302 TTY

Federal Emergency Management Agency (FEMA)
(Producers of "Disaster Preparedness for People with Disabilities")
http://www.fema.gov/
500 C St. S.W.
Washington, D.C. 20472
(202) 566-1600 Voice
(Also see "Emergency Evacuation Procedures for Employees with Disabilities" at
http://www.jan.wvu.edu/media/emergency.html/)

Human-Computer Interaction
Accessibility Webibliography
http://www.hcibib.org/accessibility/

The Inclusion Network
http://www.inclusion.org/

312 Walnut Street, Suite 3600
Cincinnati, Ohio 45202
(513) 345-1330 Voice
(513) 345-1336 TTY
include@one.net

Internal Revenue Service
http://www.irs.gov/
(800) 829-1040 Voice
Mark Pitzer, Attorney
Office of Chief Counsel–IRS
1111 Constitution Avenue N.W.
Washington, D.C. 20224
(202) 622-3110 Voice

Job Accommodation Network (JAN) of the Office of Disability Employment Policy (ODEP), U.S. Department of Labor
http://www.jan.wvu.edu/
West Virginia University
P.O. Box 6080
Morgantown, W.V. 26506-6080
(800) 526-7234 Voice/TTY

Memphis Center for Independent Living
(Developers of the *Disability Etiquette Guide*)
http://www.mcil.org/
163 North Angelus
Memphis, Tenn. 38104
(901) 726-6404 Voice/TTY
(901) 726-6521 Fax

Microsoft Accessibility Site
http://www.microsoft.com/enable/

National Braille Press
(Braille publications and transcription)
http://www.nbp.org/
88 St. Stephen St.
Boston, Mass. 02115
(888) 965-8965 Voice
(617) 437-0456 Fax

National Business & Disability Council (NBDC)
http://www.business-disability.com/
201 I.U. Willets Rd.

Albertson, N.Y. 11507
(516) 465-1515 Voice
(516) 465-3730 Fax

National Center for Accessible Media
http://ncam.wgbh.org/
125 Western Ave.
Boston, Mass. 02134
(617) 300-3400 Voice
(617) 300-2489 TTY
(617) 300-1035 Fax
ncam@wgbh.org

National Institute on Disability and Rehabilitation Research
http://www.ed.gov/offices/OSERS/NIDRR/
400 Maryland Ave. S.W.
Washington, D.C. 20202-2572
(202) 205-8134 Voice
(202) 205-4475 TTY

National Library Service for the Blind and Physically Handicapped
http://www.loc.gov/nls/
Library of Congress
Washington, D.C. 20542
(202) 707-5100 Voice
(202) 707-0744 TTY
(202) 707-0712 Fax
nls@loc.gov

The National Organization on Disability (NOD)
http://www.nod.org/
910 Sixteenth St. N.W.
Suite 600
Washington, D.C. 20006
(202) 293-5960 Voice
(202) 293-5968 TTY
(202) 293-7999 Fax

Office of Disability Employment Policy (ODEP)
(formerly The President's Committee on Employment of People with Disabilities)
http://www.dol.gov/odep/
1331 F St. N.W., Suite 300
Washington, D.C. 20004
(202) 376-6200 Voice

(202) 376-6205 TTY
(202) 376-6219 Fax

Program Development Associates (PDA)
http://www.pdassoc.com/
P.O. Box 2038
Syracuse, N.Y. 13220-2038
(800) 543-2119 Voice
(315) 452-0643 Fax
info@pdassoc.com

Reedy, Joel. 1993. *Marketing to Consumers with Disabilities.* **Chicago: Probus.**

Registry of Interpreters for the Deaf
http://www.rid.org/
8630 Fenton St., Suite 324
Silver Spring, Md. 20910
(301) 608-0050 Voice/TTY
(301) 608-0508 Fax

The City of San Antonio, Texas, Planning Department
Disability Access
(Developers of the *Disability Etiquette Handbook*)
http://www.sanantonio.gov/planning/disability_access.asp/
P.O. Box 839966
San Antonio, Tex. 78283-3966
(210) 207-7873 Voice
(210) 207-7957 TTY
(210) 207-7897 Fax

Society for Human Resource Management
http://www.shrm.org/
1800 Duke St.
Alexandria, Va. 22314
(703) 548-3440 Voice
(703) 535-6490 Fax
shrm@shrm.org

The Solutions Marketing Group
http://www.disability-marketing.com/
2334 S. Rolfe St.
Arlington, Va. 22202
(703) 920-0225 Voice
(703) 920-0262 Fax
info@disability-marketing.com

Telecommunications Industry Association
(Authors of *Extend Their Reach: Marketing to Customers with Disabilities: Interpreting the Numbers,* an analysis of statistics on the disability market, with applicability outside the telecommunications industry.)
http://www.tiaonline.org/access/etr_brochure.html/

Terry, E., ed. 1997. *Pocket Guide to the ADA: Americans with Disabilities Act Guidelines for Buildings and Facilities.* **Rev. ed. New York: John Wiley and Sons.**

U.S. Census Bureau
http://www.census.gov/
Washington, D.C. 20233
(301) 457-4608 Voice

U.S. Dept. of Justice ADA Home Page
http://www.usdoj.gov/crt/ada/adahom1.htm/
U.S. Department of Justice
950 Pennsylvania Ave. N.W.

ADA ON CD-ROM

The U.S. Department of Justice offers a free CD-ROM containing extensive technical information on the ADA. The CD-ROM is in a variety of formats, including WordPerfect, HTML, and text (ASCII). The CD-ROM includes:

- The new electronic version of the ADA Standards for Accessible Design;
- The ADA Guide for Small Businesses;
- Common ADA Errors and Omissions in New Construction and Alterations;
- The Americans with Disabilities Act Checklist for New Lodging Facilities;
- The ADA Guide for Small Towns;
- A series of commonly asked question and answer publications; and
- Technical Assistance Manuals for Titles II and III of the ADA.

Single copies can be ordered online at:

http://www.usdoj.gov/crt/ada/cdrequestform.htm
or by calling the Department's ADA Information Line:
(800) 514-0301 (Voice) or (800) 514-0383 (TTY).

Internet users can access the same information at: http://www.usdoj.gov/crt/ada/adahom1.htm

Civil Rights Division
Disability Rights Section-NYAVE
Washington, D.C. 20530
(800) 514-0301 Voice
(800) 514-0383 TTY
(202) 307-1198 Fax

U. S. Department of Labor
http://www.dol.gov/
200 Constitution Ave. N.W.
Washington, D.C. 20210
(202) 219-6871 Voice
(866) 4-USA-DOL Voice
(877) 889-5627 TTY

U.S. Department of Labor, Occupational Safety & Health Administration (OSHA)
http://www.osha.gov/
Office of Public Affairs Room N3647
200 Constitution Ave. N.W.
Washington, D.C. 20210
(202) 693-1999 Voice
(800) 321-6742 Voice
(877) 889-5627 TTY

Universal Designers and Consultants, Inc.
http://universaldesign.com/
6 Grant Ave.
Takoma Park, Md. 20912-4324
(301) 270-2470 Voice and TTY
(301) 270-8199 Fax
UdandC@UniversalDesign.com

VSA Arts
http://www.vsarts.org/
1300 Connecticut Ave. N.W., Suite 700
Washington, D.C. 20036
(800) 933-8721 Voice
(202) 737-0645 TTY
(202) 737-0725 Fax
info@vsarts.org

Workers Compensation Research Institute
http://www.wcrinet.org/

955 Massachusetts Ave.
Cambridge, Mass. 02139
(617) 661-9274 Voice
(617) 661-9284 Fax
wcri@wcrinet.org

World Association of Persons with Disabilities
http://www.wapd.org/

World Wide Web Consortium's Web Accessibility Initiative
http://www.w3.org/WAI/
MIT/LCS Room NE43-355
200 Technology Square
Cambridge, Mass. 02139
(617) 253-2613 Voice

Notes

(Unless otherwise noted, websites listed in the notes were accessible at the time of publication.)

Chapter 1: A Trillion-Dollar Market

1. The Harris Survey noted: "Although a large gap clearly persists between the percentage of people with disabilities who have low household incomes and the proportion of people without disabilities with low household incomes, $15,000 in 1998 dollars is, admittedly, not the same as $15,000 in 1986 dollars, as a result of inflation. However, by using the consumer Price Index (source: Bureau of Labor Statistics) to convert 1986 dollars to 1998 dollars ($15,000 in 1986 dollars is equivalent to approximately $23,000 in 1998 dollars), and interpolating (since income data is collected in terms of ranges, not actual values) a gap of twenty-four percentage points can be shown to currently exist between those with and those without disabilities."

2. Hammacher Schlemmer items shown are available at http://www.hammacher-schlemmer.com and at (800) 543-3366.

3. *Standard Periodical Directory* 2000 (New York: Oxbridge Communications).

4. Mark R. Donovan, personal correspondence, October 18, 2000.

Chapter 2: Understanding the Americans with Disabilities Act

1. Americans with Disabilities Act of 1990 (Pub. L. 101-336) (ADA), as amended.

2. A Supreme Court decision in February 2001 exempted state and local governments from punitive damages for ADA violations involving their own employees. The

case was primarily decided as a states rights issue, and many state and local govern-ments had already adopted their own ADA-related employment regulations.

3. The Telecommunications Act of 1996 later augmented Title IV of the ADA.

4. From the Social Security Administration at http://www.ssa.gov/work/ResourcesToolkit/legisregfact.html.

5. From http://www.overlawyered.com/archives/99july1.html.

6. At http://overlawyered.com/archives/99sept2.html.

7. There's something about disability-related regulations that brings out creativ-ity, and not just in Americans. In Britain, a lapdancing club applied to the local council for a variance that would allow blind patrons to touch its dancers. Mr. Kenneth McGrath, director of the Pussycats Club, said of two patrons who are blind: "Both men said they very much enjoyed the dances and sensed highly the proximity of the dancers and, in particular, enjoyed the scent of their perfume. Given their disability, they felt controlled touching ought to be permitted for registered blind persons only and with the dancer's consent" (Sapstead 2000).

8. "ADA Is Not Disabled," *Cincinnati Enquirer* editorial, January 19, 2002, B10.

9. National Center for Policy Analysis (1997), "Under the ADA." At http://www.ncpa.org/pd/law/april97b.html.

10. "Worker Denied Promotion Sues," *Detroit News,* Employment Briefs, March 19, 2000.

Chapter 3: Diversity, Disability, and Inclusion

1. At http://www.shrm.org/diversity/.

2. Ibid.

3. This is less true, however, in regard to accessibility-related litigation. There is increasing class action litigation, for example, involving charges of inaccessible retail locations.

4. *Wall Street Journal,* May 4, 1993, 1; quoted in Hayles and Russell (1997, 5).

5. This definition is based on one originally developed by the Inclusion Network in Cincinnati. For that organization's current definition of inclusion, see http://www.inclusion.org/aboutus/what_is.html.

6. NOD/Harris Survey Program on Participation and Attitudes at http://nod.org/.

7. The phrase "valued activity" is used because communities have activities that are not generally valued, such as imprisonment and drug trafficking.

Chapter 4: Disability Stereotypes and Myths

1. For an excellent bibliography of children's books that accurately and helpfully treat disability related issues, see N. Turner and M. Traxler (2000), *Children's Literature for the Primary Inclusive Classroom* (Albany, N.Y.: Delmar).

2. Shapiro 1993, 31. See also E. Bower, ed. (1980), *The Handicapped in Literature: A Psychological Perspective* (Denver, Colo.: Love).

3. See, e.g., Deaver's *A Maiden's Grave* and *The Bone Collector.*

4. Prof. Wolf Wolfensberger, professor emeritus at Syracuse University, has written and lectured extensively on disability stereotypes and role perceptions. See, e.g., Wolfensberger (1998), *A Brief Introduction to Social Role Valorization,* 3rd (rev.) ed. (Syracuse, N.Y.: Training Institute for Human Service Planning, Leadership & Change Agentry [Syracuse University]; S. Thomas and W. Wolfensberger (1982), "The Importance of Social Imagery in Interpreting Societally Devalued People to the Public," *Rehabilitation Literature,* 356–58; Wolfensberger (1975), *The Origin and Nature of Our Institutional Models* (Syracuse, N.Y.: Human Policy Press).

5. "ABC Needs an Education," November 17, 2000, at http://www.Diversityworld.com and Associated Press, "'Politically Incorrect' Host Apologizes," January 18, 2001, at http://icanonline.net/news/fullpage/572.html.

6. Partial responsibility for this stereotype must be assumed by disability advocates themselves who have designated the familiar wheelchair outline an international symbol for *all* disabilities.

7. For a summary of studies analyzing the productivity of employees with disabilities, see Career Network (2000), "Myths about Employing People with Disabilities" at www.kisser.net.au/careernetworks/default2.htm.

8. Originally at http://www.dupont.com/corp/people/disabled/disabl2.html. Accessed on April 19, 2000.

9. Ibid. I also consulted U.S. Department of Labor (2000), "Myths and Facts about People with Disabilities," originally at www.doleta.gov/access/dimyths.htm. Accessed on April 13, 2000.

Chapter 5: Language and Etiquette Strategies

1. For the origins of the terms *knucklehead, ding-a-ling,* and *dingbat* I am indebted to Dr. Wolf Wolfensberger, professor emeritus at Syracuse University.

2. See, e.g., B. Rimland (1993), "Beware the Advozealots: Mindless Good Intentions Injure the Handicapped," *Autism Research Review International* 7, no. 4: 1–3; and C. Vaughan (1999), "People-First Language: An Unholy Crusade," National Federation of the Blind, at http://www.blind.net/bpg00006.htm

3. See, e.g., The California Governor's Committee for Employment of Disabled Persons (Windmills); American Friends Service Committee Affirmative Action Office, *Guide to Etiquette and Behavior for Relating to Persons with Disabilities;* The City of San Antonio, Texas, Planning Department and the Disability Advisory Committee, *Disability Etiquette Handbook;* and Memphis Center for Independent Living, *Disability Etiquette;* all listed in the Resource section.

Chapter 6: Disability and Innovation

1. T. West (1999), "The Abilities of Those with Reading Disabilities." At http://ldonline.org/ld_indepth/abilities/thomas_west.html; West is quoting Nicholas Negroponte, author of "Being Digital."

2. At http://www.wisconsinmedicalsociety.org/savant/kimpeek.cfm

3. "Recognition for my work with the deaf has always been more pleasing to me than recognition for my work with the telephone." A. G. Bell, in *The Telephone* [video] (2000), *The American Experience,* WGBH, Boston.

4. For an excellent overview of the historical connection between disability and invention, see S. Jacobs (1999), "Fueling the Creation of New Electronic Curbcuts," at http://www.tiaonline.org/access/news.cfm?ID=37.

Chapter 7: Profiles of Four Business Leaders

1. Reported by the *Seattle Times* (1993), in Hiltzik (1999, 3).

2. McCaw at his induction into the Academy of Achievement in 1997, quoted in Taptich (2001).

3. "McCaw's Generous Gift Is All about Teamwork," *Seattle Times* editorial, October 16, 1997.

4. Moe Norman (profile) at http://www.moenorman.com/

5. T. Grandin, "An Inside View of Autism." At http://www.autism.org/temple/inside.html.

6. *Spectrum.* Feature interview: Temple Grandin at http://autism-spectrum.com/archive/grandin.htm.

7. T. Grandin, "Autistic Emotions." At http://www.autism-society.org/.

8. Grandin 1995, cover.

9. Grandin, "Autistic Emotions," 1.

10. Ibid., 3.

11. U.S. Bureau of the Census, referenced in S. Robitaille (2002), "Bringing the Blind into the Workplace," *BusinessWeek Online,* January 23, 2002, at http://www.businessweek.com/bwdaily/dnflash/jan2002/nf20020123_3614.htm.

12. National Federation of the Blind, "Job Opportunities for the Blind: Changing What It Means to Be Blind through Employment." At http://nfb.org/jobpaths.htm.

13. American Foundation for the Blind, "Quick Facts and Figures on Blindness and Low Vision." At http://afb.org/.

Chapter 8: A Plan for Inclusive Employment, Part I

1. National Organization on Disability/Louis Harris & Associates Survey of Americans with Disabilities, July 23, 1998.

2. Equal Opportunity Employment Commission at http://www.eeoc.gov/facts/ada17.html.

3. See "ADA: Feds Issue Guidelines for Legally Interviewing Disabled" at http://www.smartbiz.com/sbs/arts/swp23.htm.

Chapter 9: A Plan for Inclusive Employment, Part II

1. Adapted from the regulations of the U.S. Equal Employment Opportunity Commission, and from "Workplace Accommodation Process" and "Ready, Willing and Available," publications of the Department of Labor Office of Disability Employment Policy (ODEP) at http://www.dol.gov/odep/.

2. For a detailed discussion of the experience of supervisors who participated in focus groups, see J. Butterworth and M. Pitt-Catsouphes (1996), "Workplace Experiences with the Employment of Individuals with Disabilities: Recommendations for Policy and Practice," Center on Promoting Employment (RRTC), Institute for Community Inclusion at http://www.gotowork.org/906385499.html. For a detailed discussion of supervisory issues relating to various disabilities, consult the publications of National Materials Development Project on the ADA Employment Provisions (NIDRR Grant No. H133D10155) to Cornell University, ILR Program on Employment and Disability (1993).

3. For more information, see Ergonomics Program; Final Rule. - 65:68261-68870, Occupational Safety and Health Administration.

4. At http://stats.bls.gov/opub/ted/1999/apr/wk4/art03.htm and http://www.workerscompensationresourcecenter.com/facts/index.html.

5. For more detailed information see Office of Disability Employment Policy, "Workers' Compensation: Developing Company Policies" at http://www.dol.gov/odep/.

6. Office of Disability Employment Policy, "Facilitating Return-to-Work for Ill or Injured Employees." At http://www.dol.gov/odep/.

7. For a more detailed discussion, see Office of Disability Employment Policy, "Facilitating Return-to-Work for Ill or Injured Employees," at http://www.dol.gov/odep/.

8. For more detailed information, see Office of Disability Employment Policy, "Insurance and Benefits," at http://www.dol.gov/odep/.

9. See M. P. LaPlante, D. P. Rice, and J. K. Cyril (1994), "Health Insurance Coverage of People with Disabilities in the U.S.," Abstract 7 at http://dsc.ucsf.edu/.

10. Information in this section is derived from several federal government sources, including IRS Publication 907, "Tax Highlights for Persons with Disabilities"; and Department of Labor Office of Disability Employment Policy, "Tax Incentives for Business" and "Ticket to Work and Work Incentive Improvement Act" at http://www.dol.gov/odep/.

11. From http://www.ssa.gov/work/ResourcesToolkit/legisregfact.html.

12. From http://www.unum.com/workbill/disability_bill.htm.

Chapter 10: A Plan for Inclusive Marketing, Part I

1. Theoretically, marketers who discriminate against people with disabilities in their advertising-related employment can be charged with violations of Title I of the ADA. However, few, if any, charges have been filed in this area.

2. Source: U.S. Department of Justice at http://www.usdoj.gov/crt/ada/adahom1.htm.

3. The same principle applies to organizations other than companies, such as educational and religious groups. One church created a campaign to develop accessible restrooms using the slogan "If they can't go, they won't come." Another used a more biblical approach: "Let my people *go!*"

4. The Center for Universal Design at http://www.design.ncsu.edu/cud.

5. Telecommunications Industry Association, "Extend Their Reach: Marketing to Customers with Disabilities: Interpreting the Numbers," 1, at http://www.tiaonline.org/access/etr_brochure.html.

6. Joel Reedy is a Marketing Instructor at the University of South Florida. The author extends his thanks to Professor Reedy for permission to quote this excellent treatment of accessible product design.

7. M. Fellman (1999), "Selling IT Goods to Disabled End Users," *Marketing News* 33, no. 6, March 15, American Marketing Association at http://www.ama.org/pubs/article.asp?id=433.

8. Office of Disability Employment Policy, "Providing Quality Services to Customers with Disabilities." At http://www.dol.gov/dol/odep/public/media/reports/ek98/provide.htm.

Chapter 11: A Plan for Inclusive Marketing, Part II

1. The Solutions Marketing Group at http://disability-marketing.com/benefits/market-profile.php3.

2. Compiled from Shapiro (1993); Williams (1999); Farmer (2000), "New Models and New Roles." Originally at www.womenswire.com; and BBC News Online (1999), "Health: Campaign to Get Disabled in Adverts," May 24, at http://news.bbc.co.uk.

3. Nike's Apology for the Air Dri-Goat Ad, at http://www.nike.com/nikebiz.

4. This approach is based upon the philosophy of "Social Role Valorization" developed by Dr. Wolf Wolfensberger, professor emeritus at Syracuse University. I am indebted to him for his development of this crucial and revolutionary approach to devaluation.

5. One exception can be found in "Settlement Agreement under the Americans with Disabilities Act between the United States of America and Sears, Roebuck and Co. and Coordinated Corporate Programs, Inc." at http://www.usdoj.gov/crt/foia/f19.txt.

Works Cited

(Unless otherwise noted, websites listed were accessible at the time of publication.)

Acemoglu, D., and J. Angrist. 1998. "Consequences of Employment Protection? The Case of the Americans with Disabilities Act." National Bureau of Economic Research. NBER Working Paper no. W6670. Issued in July.

"ADA: Feds Issue Guidelines for Legally Interviewing Disabled." At http://www.smartbiz.com/sbs/arts/swp23.htm

Agee, J. 1995. "Affliction Fables—Forest Gump and the 'New Disability.'" *Interaction,* National Council on Intellectual Disability (Australia) 9, no. 2. At www.rehab-international.org

American Association on Mental Retardation. 1988. "Policy on Terminology." AAMR Board of Directors, July 24, 1988.

———. 1994. "Editorial Policy." *Mental Retardation* 32:87.

American Foundation for the Blind. "Quick Facts and Figures on Blindness and Low Vision." At http://afb.org/

Americans with Disabilities Act of 1990 (Pub. L. 101-336) (ADA), as amended.

Anderson, W. 1997. *The Confidence Course.* New York: Harper Perennial.

Armbrister, T. 1998. "A Good Law Gone Bad." *Reader's Digest,* May, 145–55.

Arts and Entertainment Network. 1998. *Mystery of Genius: Masters and Madmen.* John Motherell, Producer.

Baskerville, B. 2001. "Va. 'Regretful' for Eugenics Sterilization Program." Salon.com, February 15. At http://salon.com/mwt/wire/2001/02/15/sterilization/

BBC News Online. 1999. "Campaign to Get Disabled in Adverts." May 24. At http://bbc.co.uk/

Benson, B. 2001. *Bill Benson's Weekly Washington Aging Report,* nos. 120 (July 13) and 121 (July 23). At http://www.uphs.upenn.edu/aging/

Blair, J. 2000. "Online Deliveries Lighten the Burden for the Disabled." *New York Times,* September 5, A28.

Blume, H. 1997. "Temple Grandin: Wiring." *Boston Book Review,* March. At http://amug.org/~a203/temple_blume.html

Bondi, N. 2000. "Nike Apologizes, Pulls Controversial Magazine Ad." Ican.com, October 24. At http://www.ican.com

Bower, E., ed. 1980. *The Handicapped in Literature: A Psychological Perspective.* Denver, Colo.: Love.

Burnett, J., and P. Paul. 1996. "Reliable Data Needed to Target Mobility-Disabled Consumers." American Marketing Association, *Marketing News* 30, no 24, November 18. At http://www.ama.org/pubs/article.asp?id=3652

Butterworth, J., and M. Pitt-Catsouphes. 1996. "Workplace Experiences with the Employment of Individuals with Disabilities: Recommendations for Policy and Practice." Center on Promoting Employment (RRTC), Institute for Community Inclusion at http://www.gotowork.org/906385499.html

Career Network. 2000. "Myths about Employing People with Disabilities." At www.kisser.net.au/careernetworks/default2.htm

Cassidy, Marcia. 1998. Inclusion Network, meeting of the Community Committee, November.

Chao, E. 2001. Prepared remarks to the Voluntary Protection Program Participants Association, August 27. At http://www.osha-slc.gov

Cincinnati Enquirer. 2002. "ADA Is Not Disabled." Editorial, January 19, B10.

Clegg, R. 2000. "Disabling Our Prisons." *Weekly Standard,* March 27, 17.

Coelho, A., chairman, President's Committee on Employment of Persons with Disabilities. 1997. Colorado Business Leadership Network Corporate Leadership Luncheon, Denver, April 10.

———. 1999. "Think Ability: Educational Kit 1999."

Corr, O. 2000. *Money from Thin Air.* New York: Crown.

Coyle, M. 1999. "ADA: Clarified or Ruined?" *National Law Journal,* July 5.

Crowley, B. 2000. "Erasing Barriers." *The Wall Street Journal Interactive Edition* at http://interactive.wsj.com/archive/retrieve.cgi?id=SB974933873450082145.djm

Darwin, C. 1859. *On the Origin of Species.* In R. Hutchins, ed. 1952. Great Books of the Western World, vol. 49. Chicago: William Benton.

Day, J. 1996. *Population Projections of the United States by Age, Sex, Race and Hispanic Origin: 1995–2050.* Washington, D.C.: U.S. Dept. of Commerce, Economics and Statistics Administration, Bureau of the Census.

Deaf Life magazine. June 1997. At www.deaflife.com/back_issue/listing/108.html

Deaver, J. 2000. *The Empty Chair.* New York: Pocket Star Books.

Detroit News. 2000. "Worker Denied Promotion Sues." Employment Briefs, March 19.

Dietsch, D. 2001. "Universal Design Is No Barrier to Style." *Washington Post*, February 22, H01.

Digh, P. 1998. "America's Largest Untapped Market: Who They Are, the Potential They Represent." *Fortune,* March, special section.

Disability Rights Advocates. 1999. *Forgotten Crimes: The Holocaust and People with Disabilities.* Oakland, Calif.: Disability Rights Advocates.

Eckberg, J. 2000. "New Chances to Show Abilities." *Cincinnati Enquirer,* February 11, D10-8.

Edelson, S. 1996. Center for the Study of Autism. Interview with Dr. Temple Grandin. At http://www.autism.org/interview/temp_int.html

Edgerton, R. 1967. *The Cloak of Competence.* Berkeley and Los Angeles: University of California Press.

Elstrom, P. 1998. "Craig McCaw: The Prophet of Telecom." *Business Week,* September 28, 84–87.

Elvin, J. 2000. "ADA's Good Intentions Have Unintended Consequences." At http://database.townhall.com/insight/printit.cfm

Farmer, A. 2000. "New Models and New Roles." At www.womenswire.com

Feder, B. 2000. "Can Craig McCaw Keep His Satellites from Crashing?" *New York Times,* June 4, BU 6.

Fellman, M. 1999. "Selling IT Goods to Disabled End Users." *Marketing News* 33, no 6. American Marketing Association at http://www.ama.org/pubs/article.asp?id=433

Fletcher, J. 1972. "Indicators of Humanhood: A Tentative Profile of Man." *Hastings Center Report* 2 (November): 1.

Frost, D. 1998. "The Fun Factor: Marketing Recreation to the Disabled." *American Demographics* 20, no. 2:54–58. At www.demographics.com

Gates, W. 1997. "Helping People with Disabilities Helps Everybody." *Microsoft Newsletter*, August 13.

Glover, K. 1999. "The Language of Disability Rights." IntellectualCapital.com, May 27.

Goodwill Industries of America, Inc. 1992. "People with Disabilities Terminology Guide." Publication #5032.10.

Graham, K. 1997. *Personal History.* New York: Vintage Books.

Grandin, T. "Autistic Emotions." At http://www.autism-society.org/

———. "An Inside View of Autism." At http://www.autism.org/temple/inside.html

———. 1995. *Thinking in Pictures.* New York: Doubleday.

Gregg, B. 2001. "Master Mind." *Cincinnati Magazine,* March.

Hardy, Q. 2000. "Craig's Higher Calling." *Forbes,* June 12, 76.

Hartman, T., and M. Fry. 1999. "Niche Marketing." *The Disability Messenger,* a publication of the President's Committee on Employment of People with Disabilities. At www.dol.gov/odep

Hayles, R., and A. Russell. 1997. *The Diversity Directive: Why Some Initiatives Fail & What to Do about It.* Chicago: Irwin Professional Publishing.

Heilemann, J. 2001. "Reinventing the Wheel." *Time,* December 10, 81.

Hiltzik, M. 2000. "McCaw Relaunching Satellite Hopes." *Los Angeles Times,* February 1, C1.

Jacobs, S. 1999. "Fueling the Creation of New Electronic Curbcuts." At http://www.tiaonline.org/access/news.cfm?ID=37

Job Accommodation Network (JAN). 2000. "Discover the Facts about Job Accommodations." At http://www.jan.wvu.edu/media/JANFacts.html

Kaufman, L. 1999. "Companies Boost Number of Deaf Actors Appearing in Commercials." *Los Angeles Times,* December 3, C1.

Kendrick, D. 2001. "Airline Passengers Tell of Struggles." *Cincinnati Enquirer*, July 29, E12.

Krauthammer, C. 2000. "Restoration, Reality and Christopher Reeve." *Time*, February 14.

Kupfer, A. 1996. "Craig McCaw Sees an Internet in the Sky." *Fortune*, May 27, cover.

Kushner, H. 1989. *When Bad Things Happen to Good People.* New York: Schocken Books.

LaPlante, M. P., and D. Carlson. 1996. "Disability in the United States: Prevalence and Causes, 1992." Table D—Conditions with the Highest Prevalence, All Causes of Limitation, 1992. Disability Statistics Center at http://dsc.ucsf.edu

LaPlante, M. P., D. P. Rice, and J. K. Cyril. 1994. "Health Insurance Coverage of People with Disabilities in the U.S." Abstract 7. At http://www.dsc.ucsf.edu

Layne, R. 2001. "Safety Works When People Work Together." South Carolina Occupational Safety Council 64th Annual Conference, April 27. At http://www.osha-slc.gov/

Leaming, H. 1977. "The Ben Ishmael Tribe: A Fugitive Nation of the Old Northwest." In *The Ethnic Frontier,* ed. M. Holli and P. Jones. Grand Rapids, Mich.: William B. Ernmans.

Lehr, S., and S. Taylor. 1986. *Roots and Wings: A Manual about Self-Advocacy.* Boston: Technical Assistance for Parent Programs.

Leo, J. 1998. "Disability Claims Threaten Professional Standards." At http://www.uexpress.com/ups/.../column/jl/text/1998/09/jl9809277828.html

Lifescape.com. 2000. "Lifescape Chat with Temple Grandin, Ph.D.: Thinking in Pictures and Other Experiences with Autism." April 17. At http://lifescape.com/features/tgrandintrans1.asp

Lubove, S. 1997. "Damned If You Do, Damned If You Don't." *Forbes,* December 15. At http://forbes.com/forbes/97/1215/6013122a.htm

Manchester, W. 1983. *The Last Lion.* New York: Dell.

Marin, Rick. 2000. "Behind the 'M' and the 'W.'" *New York Times,* August 2.

Marsh, A. 1998. "A Kinder, Gentler Abattoir." *Forbes,* July 6. At http://www.forbes.com/forbes/98/0706/6201086a.htm

McCrabb, R. 2000. "Disorder Doesn't Impede Success." *Middletown (Ohio) Journal,* September 5, at http://www.viewsource.com/news1_080100_middletown.html

McDonald's. 1999. Press release, November 12: "Blind Child Reads Her 'First Book' in New McDonald's Commercial." At National Federation of the Blind, http://www.nfbnet.org/weblist/nfb-db/msg00032.html

McNeil, J. 1997. *Americans with Disabilities, 1994–95.* Washington, D.C.: U.S. Dept. of Commerce, Economics and Statistics Administration, Bureau of the Census. U.S. Bureau of the Census, in Stoddard, S., L. Jans, J. Ripple, and L. Kraus. 1998. *Chartbook on Work and Disability in the United States.* An InfoUse Report. Washington, D.C.: U.S. National Institute on Disability and Rehabilitation Research.

Microsoft Corporation. 2000. "Curb Cuts and Carbon Paper." At http://microsoft.com/
———. 2002. "Celebrating Our Differences. Att http://microsoft.com/diversity

Miller, N. 1983. *F.D.R.* New York: Meridian.

Nash, M. 2002. "The Secrets of Autism." *Time,* May 6.

National Center for Policy Analysis. 1997. "Under the ADA." At http://www.ncpa.org/pd/law/april97b.html

National Council on Disability. 1999. "National Disability Policy: A Progress Report." November 1, 1997–October 31, 1998.

National Easter Seal Society. 1980. *Portraying Persons with Disabilities in Print* (pamphlet). Chicago.

National Federation of the Blind. "Job Opportunities for the Blind: Changing What It Means to Be Blind through Employment." At http://nfb.org/jobpaths.htm

National Institute on Disability and Rehabilitation Research. 1996. *Chartbook on Disability in the United States.*

National Organization on Disability. 2000. "N.O.D./Harris Survey Measures the Gaps, Implications." News/Press Releases, June 25. At http://nod.org
———. "Survey Program on Participation and Attitudes." At http://nod.org/

National Organization on Disability/Louis Harris & Associates. 1998. Survey of Americans with Disabilities. July 23.

Nike's Apology for the Air Dri-Goat Ad, at http://www.nike.com/nikebiz

Office of Disability Employment Policy. "Facilitating Return-to-Work for Ill or Injured Employees." At http://www.dol.gov/odep/
———. "Insurance and Benefits." At http://www.dol.gov/odep/
———. "Ready, Willing and Available: A Business Guide to Improving Your Workforce by Hiring People with Disabilities." At http://www.dol.gov/odep/pubs/rwa00/toc.htm
———. "Tax Incentives for Business." At http://www.dol.gov/odep/

———. "Ticket to Work and Work Incentive Improvement Act." At http://www.dol.gov/odep/

———. "Workers' Compensation: Developing Company Policies." At http://www.dol.gov/odep/

Olson, W. 1997. "Life, Liberty, and the Pursuit of a Good Beer: How the ADA Has Turned Alcoholism into a Right." *Washington Monthly*, September. At http://www.walterolson.com/articles/washmdrink.html

———. 1999. "Under the ADA We May All Be Disabled." *Wall Street Journal,* May 17.

O'Quinn, R. 1991. "The Americans with Disabilities Act: Time for Amendments." *Policy Analysis* no. 158, August 9. At http://www.cato.org/pubs/pas/pa-158.html

Prager, J. 1999. "People with Disabilities Are Next Consumer Niche." *Wall Street Journal,* December 15, B1.

Prasad, P., and A. Mills. 1997. "From Showcase to Shadow: Understanding the Dilemmas of Managing Workplace Diversity." In *Managing the Organizational Melting Pot,* ed. P. Prasad, A. Mills, M. Elmes, and A. Prasad. Thousand Oaks, Calif.: Sage Publications.

Presley, G. 2000. "Joe Hollywood." At http://disabilities.about.com/health/disabilities/library/weekly/aa061500a.htm

———. 2001. "Jerry Lewis: Pity the Victim of Foot-in-Mouth Disease." At www.about.com

Reckard, E. 2000. "U.S. Economic Boom Leaves Disabled Behind." *Los Angeles Times*, in *The Cincinnati Enquirer*, November 19, A5.

Reedy, J. *Marketing to Consumers with Disabilities*. 1993. Chicago: Probus.

Rimland, B. 1993. "Beware the Advozealots: Mindless Good Intentions Injure the Handicapped." *Autism Research Review International* 7, no. 4:1–3.

Roberts, K. 1995. "Managing Disability-Based Diversity." In *Managing Diversity*, ed. E. Kosssek and S. Lobel (1996). Oxford: Blackwell.

Robitaille, S. 2002. "Bringing the Blind into the Workplace." *BusinessWeek Online,* January 23. At http://www.businessweek.com/bwdaily/dnflash/jan2002/nf20020123_3614.htm

Robson, M. 1998. "A Call for Greater Travel Agent Involvement." Canadian Transportation Agency newsletter *Moving Ahead,* special issue. At www.cta-otc.gc.ca/

Sacks, O. 1995. *An Anthropologist on Mars.* New York: Alfred A. Knopf.

Sapstead, D. 2000. "Blind Customers Want to Touch Club Lapdancers." *London Telegraph,* September 26. At http://telegraph.co.uk/et?ac+003460773832016&rtmo

Schneider, J. 1998/99. "A Triple Play." *Careers & the disABLED,* Winter.

Schubert, A. "Disabled Children in Nepal." From http://www.anishaschubert.de/disability.html

Seattle Times. 1997. "McCaw's Generous Gift Is All about Teamwork." Editorial, October 16.

Shapiro, J. 1993. *No Pity.* New York: Times Books.

Sowell, T. 1998. "Race, Culture and Equality." *Forbes,* October 5, 144–49.

Spectrum. Feature interview: Temple Grandin at http://autism-spectrum.com/archive/grandin.htm

Standard Periodical Directory. 2000. New York: Oxbridge Communications.

Stoddard, S., L. Jans, J. Ripple, and L. Kraus. 1998. *Chartbook on Work and Disability in the United States.* An InfoUse Report. Washington, D.C.: U.S. National Institute on Disability and Rehabilitation Research.

Storr, A. 1988. *Churchill's Black Dog, Kafka's Mice, and Other Phenomena of the Human Mind.* New York: Grove Press.

"The Story of Moe Norman." At http://www.moenorman.com

Suggs, T. 1997. "Faking It." *DeafLife* 9, no. 12 (June).

Taptich, B. 2001. "The Enigmatic Craig McCaw" at http://thealarmclock.com/magazine/magContent/mccaw.htm

"Tax Incentives for Business" at http://www.dol.gov/dol/odep/public/archives/pubs/ek97/tax.htm

Taylor, H. 2000. The Harris Poll. #7, June 7. "How the Internet Is Improving the Lives of Americans with Disabilities." At http://harrisinteractive.com/harris_poll/index.asp?PID=93

Telecommunications Industry of America. "Extend Their Reach: Marketing to Customers with Disabilities: Interpreting the Numbers." At http://www.tiaonline.org/access/etr_brochure.html

Thomas, R. Jr. 1991. *Beyond Race and Gender.* New York: Amacom.

———. 1996. *Redefining Diversity.* New York: Amacom.

Thomas, S., and W. Wolfensberger. 1982. "The Importance of Social Imagery in Interpreting Societally Devalued People to the Public." *Rehabilitation Literature* 43, nos. 11–12:356–58.

"Ticket to Work and Work Incentive Improvement Act." At http://www.dol.gov/dol/odep/public/archives/pubs/ek00/ticket.htm

Training magazine. 1999. "Industry Report 1999." October.

Turner, N., and M. Traxler. 2000. *Children's Literature for the Primary Inclusive Classroom.* Albany, N.Y.: Delmar.

U.S. Census Bureau. 1994. "Americans with Disabilities Statistical Brief." At http://www.census.gov/hhes/www/disable/

———. 1997. "Disabilities Affect One-Fifth of All Americans." *Census Brief.* U.S. Government Printing Office, December.

U.S. Department of Labor. 2000. "Myths and Facts about People with Disabilities." Originally at www.doleta.gov/access/dimyths.htm (accessed April 13, 2000).

U.S. Equal Employment Opportunity Commission. 1999a. Americans with Disabilities Act of 1990 (ADA) Charges. FY 1992–FY 1999.

————. 1999b. Charge Statistics. FY 1992 through FY 1999.

————. "Workplace Accommodation Process" of the Office of Disability Employment Policy at http://www.dol.gov/dol/odep/

Vaughan, C. 1999. "People-First Language: An Unholy Crusade." National Federation
of the Blind at http://www.blind.net/bpg00006.htm

Very Special Arts. "Interesting Facts about Disability." At http://www.vsarts.org/text/
programs/ed/disabfacts.html

Walker, L. 2001. "They're Breaking the Sound Barrier." *Parade Magazine,* May 13, 5.

Walsh, E. 2002. "High Court Narrows Disabilities Act's Scope." *Washington Post,*
January 8, A01.

Walsh, M. 1991, orig. ed. 1756. *Butler's Lives of the Saints.* San Francisco: Harper
Collins.

West, T. 1998. "The Abilities of Those with Reading Disabilities." At http://
www.ldresources.com/articles/west.html

White, M., and J. Gribbin. 1995. *Darwin: A Life in Science.* New York: Dutton.

Wilke, H. 1984. *Using Everything, Everything, Everything, You've Got.* Chicago: The
National Easter Seal Society.

————. 1999. *Angels on My Shoulders and Muses at My Side.* Nashville: Abingdon
Press.

Williams, J. 1999. "How the ADA Has Changed America." *BusinessWeek Online,* July
27.

Williams, J. M. 1999. "And Here's the Pitch: Madison Avenue Discovers the 'Invisible
Consumer.'" *We,* July-August, 31.

Wolfe, K. 1998. "Handicapped by a Law That Helps." *Washington Post,* July 26, C01.

Wolfensberger, W. 1975. *The Origin and Nature of Our Institutional Models.* Syracuse, N.Y.: Human Policy Press.

————. 1998. *A Brief Introduction to Social Role Valorization.* 3rd ed. Syracuse,
N.Y.: Training Institute for Human Service Planning, Leadership & Change
Agentry (Syracuse University).

Index

Page references in italics indicate illustrations.